MW00353171

The Warrior Lawyer

Powerful Strategies
for Winning Legal
Battles

David Barnhizer

Bridge Street Books
Irvington-on-Hudson, NY

Bridge Street Books is a division of Transnational Publishers, Inc.

Library of Congress Cataloging-in-Publication Data

Barnhizer, David, 1944–
    The warrior lawyer : powerful strategies for winning legal battles
/ by David Barnhizer.
        p.   cm.
    ISBN 1–57105–050–7
    1. Practice of law.   2. Strategy (Philosophy)   3. Attorney and
client—United States.   4. Sun Tzu. 6th cent. B.C. Sun Tzu ping fa.
5. Miyamoto, Musashi, 1584-1645. Gorin no sho. I. Title.
K120.B37 1997
347'.0504—dc21   96–54272
                                                                  CIP

Copyright © 1997 by David Barnhizer

All rights reserved. No part of this publication may be reproduced in any
form or by any electronic means including information storage and retrieval
systems without permission in writing from the publisher.

Manufactured in the United States of America

Contents

PART III
AN EXERCISE IN STRATEGIC DIAGNOSIS:
LOUIS CLARK v. MEGA CORPORATION

PART IV
THE PATHS OF LEGAL STRATEGY:
NEGOTIATION AND MEDIATION, TRIAL AND
ARBITRATION

Preface

This book represents a distillation of knowledge and experience acquired over decades and synthesized into a coherent strategic system. As lawyer, law teacher, activist, scholar, and person, I was irresistibly drawn toward attempting to create a framework of awareness to guide action and choice. This is what I sought to do in *The Warrior Lawyer*, predicating the system on strategic insights offered by Sun Tzu and Musashi. Their two classic works, *The Art of War* and *The Book of Five Rings*, are used for several reasons. First, the philosophies of Eastern systems have long intrigued me as part of my personal and professional journey. To me they have become part of a more complete approach to understanding the world when interpreted along with the insights contained within the Western prism of knowledge and value. But the alternative approaches of the East also tend to be derived from the insights of people who have spent time seeking to penetrate and elaborate concepts and fundamental realities that have not been of interest to mainstream Western thought systems. The alternatives offer a different lens through which we can begin asking questions of the kind involved in this book, and they also force us to work with an unfamiliar vocabulary which has the important side-effect of allowing a person to stand outside his or her comfortable world of language and ideas and begin to see the world in a somewhat altered light.

The system of thought and action presented in this book is far beyond a beginning, but neither is it finished. Not only is this tapestry one that I am still weaving from my own experience and thought, but each reader will connect in a personal way with the ideas represented here and—intentionally or not—begin taking a unique individual path. Once an individual enters into the strategic dialogue, it doesn't stop. The reflective voice that lies within each of us can't be silenced and begins asking irritating questions about direction, goals, techniques, mistakes, points of leverage and vulnerability, resources, our opponent's desires and capabilities, and so forth. For those in a profession where they are often responsible for others' fates, this is an essential part of our responsibility. We must learn to constantly "teach ourselves" and become better at what we do. I hope this book makes a contribution to that mission of helping people become their own teachers.

A debt is owed to many people who contributed in some way to this book. My wife, Sue, worked tirelessly on editorial suggestions that improved the text greatly. Others who contributed directly by making critical comments and suggestions include: my brother Barry Barnhizer, my daughter-in-law Christa Barnhizer, son Daniel Barnhizer, Arthur Landever, John Applegate, J.P. "Sandy" Ogilvy, Richard Neumann, Gregory Walta, Veronica Dougherty, and Peter Joy. A very large number of law students struggled through various drafts and helped show me what made sense and what didn't. I thank them all for their insights and comments. I also thank my agent Esther Gueft and Heike Fenton of Transnational/Bridge Street Books for understanding what this book is about; and Susan Casel for her many editorial suggestions that helped polish the final manuscript. I am enormously appreciative of the work of April Mixon, Yolanda Salviejo, and Joan Shirokey, each of whom spent uncounted hours attempting to read and process my scribbled and sometimes indecipherable changes to the seemingly endless series of drafts through which this book evolved.

No lawyer's life is created without special contributions from teachers, judges, special individuals, and other lawyers—each of whom in some way helps create a role model of professionalism and integrity that guides tough judgments in difficult moments. For me those people include: Alan T. Compton, Joe Cannon, Greg Walta, Larry Gaddis, Judge John Gallagher, Judge Jack Day, Gerry Messerman, Gordon Friedman, Steve Leleiko, Victor Rubino, Norman Redlich, William Greenhalgh, John Kramer, Ernie Tullis, Judge Robert Keeton, Anthony Amsterdam, Robert McKay, William Pincus, Gary Bellow, Alan Schwarz, Thomas Stoel, Earl Finbar Murphy, James Douglas, Don Richie, Elizabeth Patterson, Judge Ann Aldrich, and Jane Picker.

This book is dedicated to my grandfather, Thomas Seth Jones, who was the finest man I ever knew; to my mother, Blanche Barnhizer, who is a model of grace and quiet strength for our family; and to my wife, who somehow has been able to put up with me through often trying times.

David Barnhizer

Part I
Introduction to Strategy

One
The Nature and Power of Strategy

"Any man who wants to master the essence of my strategy must research diligently, training morning and evening. Thus can he polish his skill, become free from self, and realize extraordinary ability. He will come to possess miraculous power. This is the practical result of strategy."
Miyamoto Musashi, *The Book of Five Rings.*

Why Study Strategy?

In *The Book of Five Rings,* Musashi emphasizes how a master in any discipline seems to achieve the desired goal effortlessly, with a measured rhythm and pace. One of my goals in this book is to communicate what is involved in a lawyer achieving professional excellence. Acquiring skill, strategic awareness, and judgment requires a combination of experience, intuition, ability, and discipline. Very early in my career, a client told me such a detailed story about police harassment during a traffic stop and how they had stolen money from him that I believed him. In fairness to myself, he really was believable. But the inescapable fact is that I was naive and overly subjective. I wanted to believe him about the alleged police misconduct because in the late 1960s I was a new and zealous civil rights lawyer. Like many fiery young people I thought I knew almost everything, while the truth was that I knew very little. I was the perfect foil for this client. He was a member of a beleaguered minority. The police were representatives of the oppressors. He was automatically right. They were inevitably wrong. We went to the prosecutor, my client told him a sufficiently credible story that, to the prosecutor's credit, he agreed to investigate. We arranged for my client to be examined by a polygraph examiner from another jurisdiction, watching silently through a one-way mirror. After one and a half hours of detailed questions with the polygraph needle making endless scratchings on the paper, the polygraph expert said, "You aren't telling the truth, are you?" My client hesitated, then said "No." The expert asked why he had made up the story and the client answered, "Because I'm a Chicano and they didn't look at me right so I thought I could get out of it this way." Then the polygraph expert asked the question on which my career depended, which was, "And did your attorney know this?" My client told the truth and said "No," and my heart started beating again. The point, however, is not that I was fortunate that the client told the truth, but that my lack of experience about being a lawyer and the fundamental role the lawyer serves caused me to become subjectively involved as a consequence of my emotional and political naivete. This combination of subjectivity and inexperience blinded me and made me vulnerable to the illusion my client had woven. But at least I was honest—and lucky—because he ultimately told the truth.

The ironic element in this story is that the prosecutor and I asked the polygraph expert to show us where it was on the chart that my client's reaction caused him to know he was lying. He replied, "Oh, the exam was inconclusive. I couldn't tell either way. But he didn't know that, and a lot of people think that the machine can catch them up. I just thought I'd take a shot at it and see how he responded." This polygraph examiner used a strategic approach to get at the truth. He used my client's uncertainty as leverage to convince him he failed the exam. The client reacted under the extreme pressure of the situation and told the truth in spite of himself. Such calculated risks are intrinsic to much of strategy and as Musashi tells us in *The Book of Five Rings*, the careful taking of such risks is essential to being able to penetrate strategic deceptions.

My error in the above case had to do with my lack of experience, my inadequate knowledge of how humans behave, the effects of my personal political agenda, and my failure to understand the processes of strategy and diagnostic evaluation of the situations clients bring to us as lawyers. The diagnostic process is a critical part of effective strategy, but it is extremely difficult. It is easy for even experienced lawyers to misdiagnose clients' problems. A recent example is found in a situation in which a plaintiff's lawyer sued for millions of dollars, failed to settle, and then tried the case. Imagine his surprise—and that of the plaintiff—when the jury rejected his client's claim, and returned a verdict on the defendant's counterclaim totaling over $7 million. Of course, there may have been good reasons for the negotiation impasse and the obviously extreme differences of professional opinion between the competing lawyers concerning the value and most probable outcome that would occur when the case was submitted to the jury. But the magnitude of the jury's decision indicates the likelihood of a serious misdiagnosis by the plaintiff. Another example of strategic diagnosis seemingly gone awry occurred when a team of lawyers for Owens Corning was defending against three asbestos plaintiffs in a consolidated trial and did not settle. The jury not only awarded the plaintiffs over $3 million in compensatory damages, but $54.6 million in punitive damages. They also reportedly used the plaintiffs' strategy as a yardstick for their award of punitives which was the Hebrew concept that the number 18 means life ($18.2 million $\times$ 3 = $54.6). Punitive damages are intended to send a powerful message that captures the attention of the defendant. We can assume Owens Corning is now paying attention and that the company's approach to case diagnosis has undergone a dramatic shift in perspective.

One of the main reasons for studying strategy is that it improves our ability to evaluate, to diagnose, to resolve the problems, and to take advantage of opportunities our clients bring to us. The lawyers in the cases just mentioned unquestionably devoted significant time to evaluating whether to settle or try their cases, and still presumably failed to come close to estimating either the probability or scale of the actual outcome. What causes such catastrophic errors in diagnostic judgments? What is involved in making the right choices and executing them effectively? How does the lawyer learn to understand the relative weight of both sides of the case, as well as the critical elements that will persuade the ultimate decision-makers?

Seeking the answers to such questions of professional excellence—diagnosis, evaluation, planning, and performance—has long intrigued me. What, for example, sets exceptional lawyers apart from good lawyers? What skills, approaches, and talents do they have that transcend the ordinary? While other lawyers seem almost to plod along in slow-motion fragments, how do exceptional lawyers develop an economical elegance of approach that raises them to a higher professional level?

After years of trying to understand the nature of professional excellence, I found the answers to be contained in the discipline of strategy. Strategic insights are explored here by merging the experience of American law practice with the wisdom of two master strategists. The first is Sun Tzu—the single most important military strategist in Asian history, with his *The Art of War* providing guidance for over 2,500 years. The second, Miyamoto Musashi, in his 17th century work, *The Book of Five Rings,* focuses on individual contests between dueling sword-fighters. Both Sun Tzu and Musashi are strategists, committed to achieving their goals, often not by expending resources in a quest for overwhelming domination, but by preventing opponents from gaining victory or by positioning themselves in ways that make their own victory much more likely. In a very real sense, this is what American lawyers do on behalf of their clients. They seek to achieve an efficient victory or forestall an opponent and prevent or force the adversary to redefine the terms of what is an acceptable victory. That connection, common to all strategic disciplines in which the practitioners need to achieve goals, provides the driving force behind this book.

These insights also help to more clearly define the basic nature of the lawyer's role in acting on behalf of the client. The lawyer is simultaneously warrior and general. The client is the legal samurai's "warlord." Just as with a warrior and military leader, the primary obligation owed the client is to avoid conflict, and to either prevent disputes from arising, or—if this is impossible—to design and conduct a campaign that engages the opponent in ways that enhance the client's chances of victory. The metaphor of the warrior lawyer is not intended to be understood as mindless physical aggressiveness, but as a commitment to the client and to the development of the full range of skills needed to enhance the chances of achieving the client's legitimate goals. The joining of the warrior with the general reflects the dual roles of the lawyer—being able to fight successfully when required, along with mastery of the diagnostic and planning dimensions within which the conflict occurs.

It is important to emphasize at this point that one of the most important benefits of strategy and the process of becoming a strategist is learning how to avoid and resolve conflict short of needlessly destructive and costly interaction. Because many of the insights in this book are derived from Sun Tzu's *The Art of War,* it is easy to think of this text as symbolizing the glorification of fighting. This is a basic and common misunderstanding of the nature of military and martial-arts strategy and the function of the warrior. Much of Sun Tzu's system involves approaches aimed at making it less likely a conflict will escalate into unnecessary hostility. Like any master strategist, Sun Tzu recognizes that the first desire of the excellent strategist is to avoid conflict, then if there is no choice, to fight no more than necessary. But if all reasonable efforts have been made to resolve a dispute and you are forced to escalate to a full-blown state of war—military or legal—then it must be done in ways that enhance your chances of victory. The combination of Sun Tzu and Musashi offers a total strategic system that begins with the desire to avoid unnecessary conflict, but teaches the strategist how to increase the probability of victory in all strategic contexts.

The insights of these two masters provide the core of *The Warrior Lawyer* because, in seeking to understand the nature of professional excellence, the conclusion I reached is that the excellent lawyer has intuitively mastered strategy, and like Musashi and Sun Tzu, has become a strategist. This intuitive mastery is the source of the exceptional lawyer's power and skill. Understanding that fact was relatively easy once the idea of a strategic system was connected to law practice. Knowing what is involved in strategic excellence, how to learn it, and how to communicate its essence and content, takes a long time to reach maturity.

Why did I turn to Asian systems of strategic thought and philosophy rather than concentrating on Western military and political strategists such as Clausewitz, Tacitus, Liddell Hart, Frederick the Great, and Machiavelli? These more familiar military and political strategists unquestionably offer insights possessing considerable merit. There were, however, special elements to these Asian systems that supplied missing pieces that enlarged and enriched the Western perspectives. One of the more important insights involves the arational nonanalytic essence of the Eastern systems, an essence that is ultimately perceivable, but logically inexplicable. Zen and Taoist thought challenge the extreme rationalism of the Western world. We who have grown up in the intellectual world of Europe and America have long been taught that true knowledge is gained only through the power of reason and the application of the scientific method. This implicit religion of the West affects us in ways of which we are not even aware. Anything that could not be explained rationally—or studied scientifically—has been considered to lack legitimacy. Such things were sneered at as "mysticism," labeled disdainfully as metaphysics, the result of imperfect emotions, and so forth. They were either not important, or not real. While this has changed in some ways, the effects of extreme and limited rationalism are still powerful. A useful and countervailing awareness of the incompleteness of the kind of explicit

[margin note: *Western thought*]

rationalism that has dominated Western approaches to knowledge is reflected in Taoist thought. As Lao Tzu states in the *Tao Te Ching*:

> *The way that can be spoken of*
> *Is not the constant way*
> *The name that can be named*
> *Is not the constant name.*

This brief passage does not assign meaninglessness to that which cannot be adequately described through language but, quite the contrary, asserts that the deepest meaning is found in the "constant way." We can understand it, but we cannot adequately describe that constant way with the limited linguistic tools we have available for communicating with others. Another critical insight to be found in Zen and Taoist perspectives is the importance of understanding ourselves and what we do as comprising an integrated and holistic system rather than a disjointed composite of fragments. This is a particularly important understanding that can help us stand against the inexorable drive toward technique and ultraspecialization that characterizes our overall culture, as well as the practice of law. A third idea is that of the interacting and singular dynamism of *yin-yang*—light and dark, male and female, mind and heart. It is not that these ideas, ways, or paths are better than the principles according to which Western thought operates, but that they provide elements that allow a fuller understanding of what we are and how to take effective action. When I first started to pursue these concepts, it seemed clear to me that either system of perception was inadequate when standing on its own. That perspective has grown as my study intensified. When important insights from each system are pulled together a powerful synthesis emerges.

This highlights another important reason to study strategy—it is far more complex, encompassing, and subtle than the limited (and limiting) realm of techniques and tactics. Musashi captures this understanding when he warns us, *"It is difficult to realize the true Way just through sword-fencing. Know the smallest things and the biggest things, the shallowest things and the deepest things."* Musashi was expressing his concern about the far too natural human tendency to fixate on the narrow concepts of technique and to confuse mastery of specific approaches with true understanding of strategy. Musashi recognized that it is easier and less demanding to excel at a narrow task. It is almost

[handwritten margin note: Eastern thought]

inevitable that we persuade ourselves—and others—that our own mastery of task and technique is more profound than it is. Many lawyers, just like the sword-fencers of Musashi's time (who he scorns because they had become fascinated with technique and lost sight of the larger system within which true combat operates) also fail to go beyond the specific context and never gain a real understanding of the total system within which they function. Because of this, they never transcend the limitations of technique.

Musashi thinks

The intuitive legal strategist, like Musashi's master strategist, avoids being trapped within technique. Technical mastery is unquestionably important to all effective strategists because no one can excel at anything without mastering technique. A skilled martial artist, in critiquing an earlier version of this book, commented that it was like a black belt in her discipline of *Tae Kwon Do*, in which the attainment of the black belt merely means one has mastered technique and can now begin the more demanding task of learning strategy and integrating the knowledge into a unified and devastating system. Regardless of the individual discipline, the tools of the strategist include the full range of techniques, but those are understood by the strategist as comprising only one part of the total system of strategy. The legal strategist, like any strategist, not only must have the knowledge needed to use all the tools and weapons, but must be capable of placing them in a context that allows their best use at the proper time and in the right way to achieve maximum effect.

Musashi tells us that when you *"appreciate the power of nature, knowing the rhythm of any situation,"* you will be able to understand strategy. As we will see, Musashi's idea of nature is a rich one, including human nature, institutions, considerations of timing, rhythm, and leverage. Much of what Musashi means by nature is nonphysical, making our success as strategists dependent on our ability to understand the texture, elements, and direction of the piece of reality with which we are engaged on behalf of our clients, and to influence and nudge it to increase the probability of achieving a beneficial outcome. We will rarely succeed as strategists if we try to contradict or dominate the flow of the natural strategic rhythms and forces. This is what King Canute (of Danish mythology) did when he ordered the ocean tides to obey his commands. Canute's feet got wet, and the strategist who struggles against the natural flow and force of a law case or any other strategic situation instead of merging with, adapting to, and using those qualities, will fail or will needlessly exhaust crucial resources.

The strategist must become part of the rhythm and harmony of the case or other strategic situation, learn to recognize when sufficient leverage exists to make a difference, and know when the rhythms and flow of the strategic processes are too strong to allow direct confrontation.

Lawyers who accept the discipline of strategy—what Musashi calls the *Way* of the strategist—will gain a significant advantage over their opponents. Their edge will be created because strategy develops a more complete awareness of the processes, detailed content, people, goals, and fabric of a law case. As will be seen throughout this book, achieving this kind of awareness requires an expanded understanding of self, of a wide variety of systems, of human nature and motivation, and of how people actually behave.

Another reason to study strategy is to avoid being deceived. This was part of the lesson I began to learn from the experience involving the client and the polygraph expert mentioned earlier. Lawyers must understand that they are "guinea pigs" for many clients. A lawyer needs to learn to see through illusions and trust no one completely. Not long ago, I was in Honduras and was involved in developing strategy for some Latin American environmental activists committed to stopping the encroachment of large agricultural businesses into traditional public lands and coastal areas upon which artisanal fisher communities have depended for centuries. The big companies and government agencies aligned with them were concerned because these groups were coming together to develop a common strategy, and after a few days offered to meet and reach some agreement. Many of the environmentalists were ecstatic at this overture and eager to meet and end the period of rising tension, which had been highlighted by a company-sponsored "demonstration" when we first arrived. At this point, even though I had been attempting to keep a low profile, I intervened and warned them that the overtures were almost certainly part of the companies' short-term damage control strategy, which would enable them to appear reasonable and conciliatory in the press but was unlikely to represent their true strategy. This caused several people to tell me my point of view could be summed up as "*no creo nadie,*" or "I believe nothing," and while this isn't quite accurate, it is a close enough description of the attitude the strategist must have. In any event, several representatives did meet with the country's Minister of the Economy and found themselves "sandbagged" by him and a group of business cronies he had invited to the meeting without the environmentalists' knowledge.

I believe Nothing

Obviously, the essential state of wariness and professional distrust that is contained in *"no creo nadie"* can lead to cynicism. This not only applies to opponents and people with clearly adverse interests, but also includes your clients and witnesses. Your own client can be your worst enemy because a client sees a lawyer as an instrumentality—a means to an end. This was demonstrated to me by another example from early in my professional life. I filed a consumer fraud class action, bludgeoned the other side into submission, and ignored the references by opposing lawyers to my messianic zeal. "Of course I am zealous," I thought, "that is my job." Then one day as I handed a settlement check to a young married couple who had been in the plaintiff group, they made a comment I had to follow up. The wife admitted that the alleged pattern of fraud hadn't happened the way they had told me. When I asked why they had misrepresented the facts, she said they just wanted to get out of the sales contract they had signed. After talking with me in the initial interview, they knew I was so committed to pursuing the class action that if they were able to fit their case into the pattern I foolishly described to them then I would be more likely to help them. I had committed a classic error during the interview when I first told them about other clients' factual assertions. They were clever enough to adjust their own "facts" to fit the pattern of consumer fraud on which the class action was based. Once again, my zealousness and the resulting subjectivity had caused the loss of balance and perspective that is essential to clear-headed professional perception.

My professional naivete was (thankfully) a reasonably short-lived condition. This was illustrated when another client told me a patently absurd story about how drugs had come into his possession. I sat and listened with a straight face. At the end I said, "That is really stupid. How the hell do you expect me to believe it?" And he said, "Look man! I thought I'd try it out on you. If you bought into it, then maybe it'd work."

This highlights the fact that we need to understand ourselves, our limits, and how the world works. Musashi tells us *"it is difficult to know yourself if you do not know others."* When I first read this I thought it oddly stated. Then it became clear that the irony was that Musashi's simple statement stands centuries of Western philosophy on its head. We have always been taught to phrase the idea in reverse sequence. We ordinarily say something on the order of, "It is difficult to know others if you don't know yourself," or the famous Cartesian point of departure, "I think, therefore I am." As an alternative, try, "I am, therefore I think, or feel." In any event, Descartes' more familiar formulation begins with the subjective "I" and makes it the center of our awareness.

The intriguing aspect of Musashi's reversal is that it causes us to step outside our inherent subjectivity and include external data about others as a way of understanding ourselves. Think about the implications of Descartes' formula. Everything is centered on the "I" to such an extent that many have said we can only be certain of our own existence, and can't truly know whether the people, events, and conditions outside us actually exist. Or at least we can't know their true nature and character. We Westerners tend to evaluate the world from within our own subjectivity and personal frame of reference. We view ourselves, the subjective "I," as being at the center of everything and interpret the world in relation to our singular context. It borders on being subtly sociopathic. It is a consequence of our idea of rugged individualism, and of Cartesianism. The psychologist and writer Rollo May has called Cartesianism a "cancer" that has diseased the soul of Western humanity, a sickness that has needlessly isolated us from our natural community. This is perhaps an overstatement, but there is an important insight contained in May's observation. Musashi's principle sweeps past this dilemma and offers a solution because it begins with the reality of the "us" along with the "I."

The truth, for the strategist at least, is that we must step outside ourselves in order to be objective. If we know others, and observe and understand their strengths and weaknesses, we can better see and evaluate our own. This includes their perceptions of us, and how they respond to us. Musashi is telling us to look at the world, to look at others, to learn what other people do, to learn human nature from observing others, and then say, "Now, let's think about me and try to understand how I fit into this picture." It is an interesting reversal of method and perspective that is available because the Chinese and Japanese have tended to focus far less on the "I,"—the "*solitary I*"—as the center of the world, than have we Westerners.

The benefits of strategy are not only ones of mistrust and the ability to see past illusions. Lawyers who study strategy will also become more effective and efficient. Regardless of the many criticisms of the legal profession, most lawyers are not venal. They aren't trying to give clients short shrift or mediocre representation. They want to perform professionally, but too often lack some critical aspect of knowledge, experience, time, skill, or resources. A serious problem for lawyers, one with which the legal profession is unable to deal, is that clients tend to want Mercedes representation at Yugo prices. The rhetoric of the legal profession feeds into this illusion. Few clients can afford the most complete and zealous level of representation that is ideally possible in a case if unlimited resources are available. Client resources are rarely sufficient, and this creates an inevitable tension between the ideal of zealous, high-quality representation, and the reality of much of law practice. One way to help overcome or at least mitigate the practical realities of law practice is for lawyers to learn how to become more focused, efficient, and knowledgeable.

Strategy can help produce this efficiency because it enables lawyers to become better at diagnosing and evaluating cases. Improved diagnosis and evaluation methods enhance the efficiency and speed with which a lawyer determines the value, options, timing considerations, expense, and outcome probabilities of a particular case. The task is daunting. Predicting what people will do involves a process of divination that is much like casting bones or reading tea leaves. Diagnosis and case evaluation represent a large part of what clients pay for, but even if a lawyer does all the work correctly, it is still relatively easy to be wrong because of the unavoidable uncertainty created by the various decision-makers in a case, including opponents, your own clients, arbitrators, administrative officials, judges, or juries.

For the strategist, the most important part of the diagnostic process is being aware of why humans tend to decide things in the ways they do. This process includes such considerations as: What themes touch people deeply? What behavior offends people to the extent they want to punish the person or institution they decide is responsible? What kinds of behavior, statements, or evidence have the power to influence judgment—either positively or negatively? What are the costs, consequences, and rules of operation and choice to which decision-makers are subject or responsive?

Another of the most critical aspects of strategy is that it is goal-driven. The goal-driven nature of legal strategy is similar in many ways to that of chess or any other competitive contest in which the primary object is to win, or at least to avoid losing. Once stated, the goal-driven premise seems simple. But it is amazing how many lawyers and clients never focus clearly on the realistic goals of the case, and fail to seek what are most accurately referred to as pragmatic definitions of victory. This insight is offered by both Sun Tzu and

Musashi in the context of their own strategic disciplines when they speak of the purpose of strategy being that of winning. The meaning of what constitutes a victory takes on character only in the context of the specific struggle and must always take into account the skills, resources, and capabilities of the competitors. There is no ideal victory, only that which the strategist is realistically capable of achieving.

The benefit to the lawyer is that studying strategy automatically improves our ability to focus on what it is we want to accomplish in a case. Even this is not a simple task that results in an immutable goal after the initial planning has been done. Strategy requires continual definition and redefinition of what we are seeking to achieve because our early hypotheses about what is desired must almost always be reinterpreted as our understanding of what is pragmatically achievable grows. We gain this knowledge through dealing with the opponent and as we acquire and refine critical strategic information through investigation, discovery, assessment, and interaction with our opponents.

On the other hand, it is easy to set our goals too low and allow that set of relatively easily achieved goals to become a self-fulfilling prophecy in which we seek too little. Setting realistically achievable goals is not the same as setting easily achievable goals. Goal definition must include pushing the concept of what is achievable a considerable distance along its logical continuum. An effective strategist's goals must be high, but they also need to be realistic. One of the benefits of setting high—but realistic—goals is that awareness of realistically achievable high-level goals helps anchor us against the inevitable stresses produced by conflict. Being driven by an awareness of what will represent a realistic victory in a specific case also helps us to better understand how to evaluate the resources, evidence, and people necessary to attain the ends sought on behalf of the client. These considerations are explored in this book, particularly in the *Louis Clark v. Mega Corporation* case example that is introduced in Part III and is applied throughout the book in the context of negotiation and trial strategy.

The Art of War and The Book of Five Rings

Sun Tzu's *The Art of War* and Musashi's *The Book of Five Rings* offer a unique strategic language. Sun Tzu and Musashi are like puzzle boxes with multilayered expositions of strategic understanding to which the strategist can return again and again. There is no finality to the insights. As the strategist's experience grows and is integrated with strategic thought, a fresh perspective is continually generated.

These two master strategists open us to alternative ways of thought that change how we are able to look at the world, not only of law practice, but in general. The *Way* of strategy is a methodology of greater awareness and effectiveness, enabling the strategist to perceive the world sharply, extensively, and deeply. Strategic thought is, however, an unfamiliar way for most people to perceive. It is often uncomfortable and threatening. It focuses, penetrates, empowers, explains, and requires that we abandon many of the illusions behind which we prefer to hide.

The altered awareness of the strategist is derived from the richer language and concepts Sun Tzu and Musashi offer. Language provides the symbols we use to think, perceive, and even feel. Language defines not only what we think about but what we are able to think about. Our linguistic frameworks filter out unfamiliar material or reinterpret dissonant data into familiar concepts. In the process, the raw data loses much of its meaning. Understanding what Musashi calls the *Way* of the strategist is difficult because we are limited by the structure, feel, and content of our own language. To gain a conceptual vocabulary of the kind essential to strategic understanding we need to force ourselves to step outside those limits. If we are successful in doing so, we alter the way we perceive the world.

The Art of War is one of history's most widely read works on strategy. It has had significant influence on military strategy in Asia, including Japan. There is some dispute whether Sun Tzu represents a historical figure or if his work reflects a composite of various notes and sources. Most scholars believe *The Art of War* has been in existence since the sixth century B.C.E. Others point to inconsistencies that suggest a slightly later origin. Such controversies are important to historians but are irrelevant to strategists. Sun Tzu could have been an early incarnation of Elmer Fudd and it would not alter the power and insights of the work.

While Chapters Four through Seven of this book present the methodologies, principles, and techniques of Sun Tzu and Musashi, it is helpful to be aware of certain aspects of their work even at this early point. Sun Tzu's basic methodology for strategic diagnosis and planning is grounded in what he calls the *five constant factors* and the *seven considerations for victory.* Evaluating the implications of the *five constant factors* and the *seven considerations* in the context of the specific war, campaign, battle, or skirmish is the means through which the military strategist calculates what will work, how resources need to be mobilized, where and when the enemy should be confronted, what approaches will be productive or counterproductive, and what will lead to victory or defeat.

This approach to conflict resolution as a comprehensive campaign is of particular importance to lawyers because it enables the legal strategist to visualize the legal process as an interacting strategic totality in which one general maneuvers forces and resources to defeat the opposing army, to escape defeat, or to create conditions in which peace can be negotiated because the costs of conflict are too extreme. The parallels between military and legal strategy are powerful once the connection is accepted. Although Sun Tzu offers many insights into other aspects of strategy, his systemic framework and structural methodology are of the greatest significance.

Art of War Strategy

Like Sun Tzu's work, Musashi's *The Book of Five Rings* is a deceptively simple book of compelling power. Writing in seventeenth-century Japan, Musashi offers an elegant formulation of martial-arts strategy applied within a context of sword-fighting. Although *The Book of Five Rings* was written two thousand years after *The Art of War*, Sun Tzu's influence on Musashi is obvious. One important difference is that while Sun Tzu is concerned with success in military conflicts, Musashi views strategy primarily from the perspective of the individual warrior, although he comments on the applicability of his approach to larger contexts. Regardless of their distinct perspectives, the insights of each strategist are broadly applicable to many strategic venues, including law practice.

To Musashi, strategy is the total discipline adhered to by the warrior who is committed to achieving victory by overcoming other men. Musashi's discipline penetrates and becomes part of the person, requiring self-awareness, rapid perception and interpretation of events, immediate choice of action, as well as mastery of the subtle and complex skills of execution, tactics, and communication. Musashi's strategist is prepared to deal with any person or obstacle, and achieves levels of clarity and focus beyond those on which most humans function. Although he concentrates on the sword-fighter, his work has many deeper implications. Musashi offers a disciplined approach to life, a *Way* of being, a process of becoming. He presents a systematic

focus that concentrates on the individual and the internalization of *[Musashi thinks]*
strategy as part of creating the strategist.

The five "rings" to which Musashi refers are the five aspects of *[5 constant factors]*
strategy representing the Buddhist cosmos, *ground, water, fire, tradition*
(or *wind*), and *void*. Full understanding of the *Way* of strategy requires
that the strategist experience and understand life, goals, human behavior and human institutions, human nature and motivation, and
the inner workings of power. An intriguing and sometimes unsettling
side-effect is that the strategist who follows the *Way* of strategy eventually loses much of the ability to deceive self. Understanding the truth
of one's own being, including flaws, "warts," and personal limits, is
an essential part of being a strategist. A fully developed strategist sees
the world with clarity, but such clarity is not always pleasant nor
permanently achieved without constant effort. Achieving wisdom in
a harsh world is not without price. It forces us to gaze into a mirror,
providing the ability to see others with equally crystalline vision. The
awareness that we must never stop training or decide that we have
achieved wisdom once and for all is captured in this 7th-century
Zen verse:

> *Our body is the tree of perfect wisdom,*
> *And our mind is a bright mirror.*
> *At all times diligently wipe them,*
> *so that they will be free from dust.*

Without the commitment to constant openness to learning, our
"mirror-mind" becomes clouded and our "body-tree" clumsy and uncontrolled.

While describing the importance of his own approach, Musashi
nonetheless rejects the idea that a single *Way* leads to victory. This
is because he recognizes that a fixed and predictable adherence to a
particular approach blinds the strategist to other approaches. Musashi
makes this point by saying, *"I have lived without following any particular
Way. With the virtue of strategy I practice many arts and abilities—all things
with no teacher."*

All things with no teacher means that teachers—including the Japanese *sensei* of Musashi's experience—and even American law teachers,
eventually tend to be captured by the strictures of their own formal
training and disciplinary dogma. Musashi's vision of the teacher was
that *the teacher is as a needle, the disciple is as thread.* The teacher is the

student's tool and facilitator, one that makes possible what the student goes on to become and to create. Life and experience are the cloth with which each person works. Our teachers not only share their knowledge but unconsciously inculcate students with precepts that both expand their understanding, but can, at some point, limit their ability to see beyond the logical extremes of the teachers' approaches. Musashi's *Way* of strategy provides a methodology that helps cut across the restricting barriers of disciplines. This allows us not only to comprehend ourselves and our world more fully, but to act more effectively in that world. The irony, of course, is that even Musashi's insights are only his particular distillation, the fabric he sewed according to his particular design. We are each responsible for going beyond his perspectives to create our own systems.

Two
The Moral Lawyer and a Warning About Strategy

*"You may have perfect technique, as a singer or a poet, you may know
how to paint or put words together, but without . . . creative beauty
inside, your talent will have very little significance."*
J. Krishnamurti, *Think on These Things.*

Strategy as practiced by Sun Tzu and Musashi evolved in a different era and culture. Sun Tzu reportedly had two women who mocked him executed as his payment for winning the bet that elevated him to prominence with the Chinese emperor. Musashi claims to have killed more than sixty opponents in duels and has often been referred to as "a bloody old man." In Western culture, the very name Nicolo Machiavelli has become *Machiavellianism*, a pejorative signifying the willingness to do anything to achieve desired ends.

American lawyers are expected to operate according to an ethical code intended to prevent the worst abuses that can result from the confusion of legitimate ends and illegitimate means. The effectiveness of this ethical code has often been questioned, as have the frequently half-hearted efforts of the organized bar to enforce its rules, but on the surface the lawyer's code of ethics differentiates law practice from hand-to-hand combat and military struggles. Although it can also be said that Musashi followed a code of sorts, it bears little semblance to any with which we would be comfortable. He, for example, agreed to duel with another sword-fencer, with the fight to take place the next morning in the isolation of a nearby island. Instead of adhering to the terms of gentlemanly dueling that prevailed in Europe and even in parts of the early United States, Musashi came to the specified island early and hid in bushes near the shore. When his opponent arrived Musashi left his hiding place and killed the man by smashing

19

his skull with an oar. Effective? Yes. Principled as we would understand that concept? No. Yet Musashi was not cowardly, nor would he consider himself unprincipled within the terms of his own ruthless system. This example brings out one of the most fundamental differences between Musashi's system and that which a lawyer must be expected to follow. Even though I use the concept of the "warrior lawyer" to communicate the essence of the legal strategist, this does not mean that "anything goes." This is particularly important to emphasize because becoming an effective strategist gives an individual more power, which for the responsible lawyer also means there is an even greater need to be constantly aware of the dangers of going too far. Part of being an effective strategist requires achieving great self-control, which accompanies the need to set ethical and moral controls on one's conduct. Some lawyers would disagree with this premise, but although a lawyer is a "warrior" on a client's behalf, the lawyer is also a principled professional with the obligation to adhere to what are actually limited and largely self-evident ethical rules and the right to make critical moral choices about points beyond which he or she will not go on behalf of the client. The problem is created when there are fundamental conflicts between those ethical and moral limits and what the client wants.

Like many others, I became a lawyer to pursue ideals of justice, make contributions to society, and to help people. Most people who go to law school do so for positive reasons. They desire to enter a principled profession, and gain the knowledge and skills that will allow them to live lives of meaning. There are other motives, which can include status, prestige, financial well-being, and political advantage. There is nothing wrong with such desires if they don't overwhelm the ideals of a helping profession committed to concerns of justice, fairness, reform, and the rectification of abuses of power. Even after years of law practice, many lawyers would still voice such ideals in explaining their concepts of the functions and responsibilities of the legal profession. Yet there is a significant gap between the principles and the reality of law practice, the values and behaviors it engenders, and the often critical and even scornful way much of the general public looks at lawyers.

People love to engage in "lawyer-bashing," and it is sometimes well-deserved. There is no question the legal profession is under enormous critical pressure and there is no sign of the attacks letting up.

A prominent lawyer recently lamented, "There is a widespread impression that the practice of law has become primarily a money-grubbing, profit-maximizing, hustling business, rather than an admired profession." We are not necessarily the world's nicest people, but others' less-than-flattering perceptions of the nature of members of the legal profession too often fail to recognize that lawyers are advocates for their clients. We are warrior lawyers, and while I don't want to overdo it, there is absolutely no question that our first responsibility is to serve the legitimate interests and desires of our clients. If we fail to do this, there is little justification for the existence of the legal profession as we know it. Some might, and in fact, do say that is the point—the legal profession should alter its basic principles and become something else. I challenge this assertion and argue instead that the profession ought to become more committed to clients rather than less, in addition to being more highly skilled than at present. As I repeatedly emphasize in this book, while a lawyer can go too far on behalf of a client and some have done so, the far greater problem is that too many lawyers don't elevate their client into the equivalent of Musashi's warlord to whom the *samurai* warrior owed obedience and respect. Because of this failure, clients don't receive the level of commitment and quality of service they have the right to expect. The problem of the legal profession is not that lawyers are too zealous in their representation of clients, but that they are often too inept and feeble, losing cases or achieving mediocre outcomes when higher-quality representation would produce a substantially better result. The consequence is that clients have the right to be represented by the "warrior lawyer" but too often find themselves at the mercy of puffed-up pettifoggers who are serving their own interests and who haven't done their homework.

If lawyers are to be criticized by the public they ought to be censured far more often for what they fail to do rather than for what they do properly within the limits of their professional role. This is a difficult thing for the general public and media to sort out because their attention is drawn to the publicized and unpopular cases that are almost always sensationalized. While they see lawyers zealously representing unpopular clients—who have often done terrible acts—and blame the lawyers for protecting these clients from community outrage, they rarely pay attention to the invisible cases in which zealous representation fails to be provided. As to the more visible cases, one of the most important and basic tasks of the lawyer is providing representation to people who have done very bad things. The affected community demands immediate justice but in our system even such clients as these have the right to effective and aggressive representation as a precondition to the enormous power of government being used to punish them through incarceration, death, or some form of civil sanction. This requirement of proof and the balancing of private rights and government power are integral aspects of our justice system. It does mean, however, that effective lawyers often will be representing clients who have behaved in ways that reflect some of the worst aspects of being human and who then want their lawyers to aggressively represent their interests—regardless of the consequences to others. I stopped working on criminal cases after a public defender asked for my help in defending a client I felt had raped and murdered a young boy, stabbing the child more than fifty times after sodomizing him. Even though I reached my limits, I consider the representation of such people to be a critical aspect of our system of justice. Nonetheless, it is completely easy to see the tension this unresolvable dilemma produces between personal values, horror, indignation, and the desire for retribution that leads to resentment of lawyers the public feels are attempting to prevent justice. But this is what members of the legal profession are obligated to do. For the "good" lawyer there is little real choice. The instrumental nature of the practice of law causes lawyers to be blamed for being "good" (i.e., effective) professionals.

This raises a deep and troubling question about the nature and conflict involved in the intrinsic tension between being a "moral" lawyer and a "good" lawyer. What does being a good or effective lawyer do to those who practice law over an extended period of time? How much of our soul does the "law-job" require be sold, surrendered, or eroded as a necessary part of the professional task? One of the striking parallels between military and sword-fighting strategy and legal strategy is reflected in the fact that war—and duels to the death—inherently operate in a milieu of inflicting and avoiding harm. Those who spend their lives within such an environment are likely to be different from people whose lives and occupations allow them to operate within a context of greater innocence, goodness, or at least neutrality. Neither Sun Tzu's general, Musashi's duelist, or the American lawyer (at least in many aspects of the professional role) has this luxury.

Few lawyers have been willing to confront the individual effects of being a lawyer. People who would have no difficulty accepting the consequences of "nature v. nurture" in another context are somehow unable to face the extremely powerful "nurture" or cultural effects of law practice. Although there are many different aspects to law practice that are largely free of the worst of these moral dilemmas, most of what we do as lawyers involves working with situations in which our clients have been harmed, will be harmed, fear being harmed, want to harm—or at least get even in some way with other people they feel have hurt or offended them. Law practice also involves dealing with people who want to come out ahead on a bargain, make more money from a situation than the persons against whom they are negotiating, are in conflict, or seek to avoid responsibility for their past, present, or future actions.

Gaining the total knowledge and capability of the legal strategist can be much like entering a Faustian pact. A certain quality of ruthlessness is part of the strategist's life. The strategist is unquestionably capable of generating fear, respect, and also admiration. The strategist pays a price, however, for the clarity and power strategy gives. One _Lawyer_ part of the price is that it is possible to know too much. We humans _role_ rely heavily on our ability to rationalize and deceive ourselves as a means of protecting our egos against unpleasant and sometimes even destructive knowledge. Lawyers learn to protect themselves by building defenses against the emotional overload and anger their cases can generate. We erect barriers to prevent an important part of our selves from being sucked into the maelstrom of others' pain, helplessness, despair, meanness, or deceit. Of course, sometimes you give in. I have a great deal of compassion for a public defender in Utah who was removed from a death penalty appeal because he said his client might deserve the death penalty. Like him, I have looked into the eyes of people who have done terrible things to other humans and are totally without remorse for their actions. Some of them are just confused. Others give substance to evil.

When I first began practicing as a lawyer in Colorado more than 20 years ago, my cases included heavy doses of child and spousal brutality, divorce and custody, consumer fraud, racial discrimination, and police brutality. I worked on the kinds of law cases that expose the worst behaviors, tragedies, and failures of humans. As a young lawyer, there were nights when I went home and cried at the pain and hopelessness of some clients. There were other times when I wanted to smash things in frustration over a client's or opposing party's stupidity, greed, dishonesty, or viciousness. Abused children, violent spouses, dependent women who returned again and again to the men who beat them, along with deceit, theft, greed, misconduct, and official lies that were covered up—such cases take a toll on the lawyers who handle them.

Think about what a lawyer goes through who is defending someone charged with murdering two innocent human beings by brutally slashing them to death. If you were that lawyer and were told by your client that he did it but wants to take his chances at trial, how would you feel? Lawyers in such situations often cope by compartmentalizing their humanity as it applies to their subjective feelings about what the client did. As individual humans, they would presumably be outraged and horrified by what the client did. The lawyer doesn't have that luxury. The rest of the world can be horrified and outraged. The lawyer, on the other hand, is obligated to help the client escape responsibility for his actions—even if he fully admits to his counsel what he did. The nonjudgmental spirit this requires is obviously a special state of mind that will be difficult for many people to achieve. If an individual decides that he or she can't achieve this state of mind (and this is not meant sarcastically), then it is better to practice patent law or tax law or some other specialized legal field in which fundamental moral dilemmas are more infrequent. The point is that anyone who thinks there is not some price to be paid for integral involvement in such emotionally traumatic situations is avoiding the truth. The effects may be subtle, but the task does do something to us, just as it affects police officers who are required to deal regularly with violence, ignorance, and depravity.

One way a profession such as law attempts to deal with the consequences of the professional role is to adopt a set of rules or norms that produces an almost split personality between the practitioners' personal and professional selves. The ethics, propriety, or morality of action is defined in terms of the role being served. In the previous paragraph, I used such a device to praise the role of the lawyer who has a duty to provide zealous representation to unpopular clients. The rationalizations implicit in what some call "role-differentiated morality" are more common than we might think. While these rationalizations do insulate our personal moral systems to some extent, the problem is that in the practice of law many of the issues with which we are involved are so profoundly central to our deeper senses of right and wrong that there is an inevitable spillover effect between our personal and professional selves. This creates a basic contradiction. From the legal strategist's standpoint the dilemma is that in trying to win for your client you often do things that would seem dishonest—or at least deceptive—if they were done by you in a non-professional, ordinary human context. There are values involved in the business of being a lawyer that conflict with our basic human values. These "lawyerly values" allow us to lie without lying, to hurt without responsibility, and to be paid according to our ability to do these things particularly well.

In my personal life, for example, I take great pains not to lie. I might lie to protect another person from harm or embarrassment, but I will try very hard not to lie or be deceptive as a human being. As a lawyer, on the other hand—while I consider myself to be honest and attempt to function at a high level of professional integrity—I unquestionably have done things I would consider devious or deceitful if I did them in my personal life. The problem is that deception, illusion, concealment, and misdirection are inescapable aspects of being a lawyer and an unavoidable by-product of the responsibility to represent a client zealously. There is a morally dangerous quality to this behavior, not only if you do it badly, but perhaps even more so if you do it very well.

Attempts to protect the personal self from the less desirable effects of the professional role are relatively common. Such dichotomies are not limited to law practice. Many competitive games create rules within which the contest is conducted. Boxing and football glorify savage behavior that would otherwise be criminal. While an individual cannot consent to violent assaults under criminal law, by making the behavior a condition of a socially acceptable game we convert "bad" behavior into something that rewards the most aggressive and talented of the athletes by giving them all-American status or paying them millions of dollars. So it is with the competitive "game" reflected in the practice of law, although because law practice is involved with fundamental moral issues, the attempted splitting of the personal and professional being is not as equally achievable as in sports.

Just as football and boxing often injure those who participate, there are consequences to any savagely competitive game. In violent physical games the consequences can be pain, broken bones, torn ligaments and cartilage, addiction to painkillers, long-term physical problems with arthritis, paralysis, and occasionally even death. In the practice of law, the injuries are more emotional and moral, but are still very real. One consequence is that the "game" can gradually produce a moral acid that etches and corrodes the souls of many

lawyers. Some lawyers have little difficulty with this, I suppose because their competitive juices overwhelm everything else, or perhaps
because they are like the *golem* of Jewish folklore, who had no soul
to begin with.

Manipulation of other humans is an inevitable and inescapable
fact of both our personal and professional lives. But there are moral
limits to manipulation, and there are differences to what is moral and
ethical behavior dictated by the particular roles people are fulfilling.
When acting in their professional roles, for example, lawyers behave
in ways that most nonlawyers would consider reprehensible. All lawyers manipulate words, concepts, symbols, people, and institutions.
So do other people. If you practice law and don't manipulate the
conditions of the environment in which you are operating (and especially other people), you aren't a very good lawyer. You may like to
think of yourself as being a nonmanipulative human being who
doesn't take advantage of other people, but as a lawyer, that is a
disingenuous posture. We continually manipulate in our pleadings,
interviews, investigations, discovery, and negotiations. We manipulate in trial—or we ought not be there. It is impossible for an effective
advocate to avoid manipulating people, but not impossible to make
moral choices about the limits of our behavior and how far we are
personally willing to go.

In other cases this would be seen badly

A 1991 study by Johns Hopkins University concluded that lawyers
were the most emotionally depressed group among those studied.
One researcher suggested the poor emotional health of many members of the legal profession "might be the result of operating in moral
ambiguity. They might be representing positions they may not like
or believe in." The fascinating aspect of this tentatively worded conclusion is that such moral ambiguity and representation of people or
positions with which lawyers might not be in agreement merely re-
states the intrinsic essence of much of law practice. Another legal
commentator identified hypocrisy as the cause of many lawyers' un-
happiness, arguing that "seeing shades of gray may signify intellectual
maturity, but it's also somehow impoverishing."

to not go over the edge

The only way to survive the power of the onslaught of law practice
and strategy is to identify what you really care about as your central
core of integrity and to build early warning signals into your awareness. These early warning signals should begin sounding and flashing
early enough to allow you to stop short of unacceptable behaviors. If
you avoid becoming entangled in the many snares of law practice,

then you have a chance to escape the worst impacts on your being. This "bright line" and "early warning signal" approach is necessary because the corruption inherent in practice and manipulation tends to infilitrate an individual's value systems subtly and quietly, rather than through a single, obvious, face-to-face situation in which the choices of right or wrong are stark and unquestionable. Corruption and the loss of the center of your being operate in subtle shades of gray, and are often brought on through rationalizations and expectations of employers and clients for such demands as institutional loyalty and the need to "behave realistically." Similarly, the increasingly harsh economics of the private practice of law and its intensifying competitiveness are putting pressure on many lawyers. Cutting corners and borderline behavior concerning cases and client interests are among the problems that are making it even more difficult to be a principled lawyer. These, and other practices, make questionable professional behavior even more likely to occur.

The warning about both the practice of law and the use of strategy is that good lawyering—as well as bad lawyering—imposes a significant cost on the practitioner, in addition to its many benefits of status, the opportunity to handle and solve complex situations, to help people, and to test your skills against others. As you read this book, be aware of what your experiences and roles have done or are likely to do to you. It is worth it to hold on to your ideals of justice and your contribution to society. Use the power gained through strategy but set your own personal limits. Be a "warrior lawyer." Represent your client zealously but adhere to the principles of professional responsibility and your strong moral sense of right and wrong. Manipulate the plays and the players in the "game," but do not lose sight of the fact of their humanity. Strategy means knowing how to play the game in actual competition and to play it hard and with great skill. But the strategist must never forget it is a game based in reality with consequences to those who play it and to the people who are used as the pawns and game-pieces. The ultimate power of strategy must be responsibly exercised within personal and systemic limits. Forgetting this fact leads to serious difficulties.

Three
Three Strategic Examples

*"When I teach my Way, I first teach by training in techniques which
are easy for the pupil to understand, a doctrine which is easy to
understand. I gradually endeavor to explain the deep principle, points
which it is hardly possible to comprehend, according to the pupil's
progress. . . . [T]he way to understanding is through experience. . . ."*
Musashi, *The Book of Five Rings.*

Strategic Planning Is the Prediction of What People Will Do

Legal strategists, like all strategists, develop the ability to perceive the future as part of the present. The legal strategist understands that law cases contain many critical factors that are contingent, inchoate, and potential. A true strategist can examine a case—even at early points—and see its variables, contingencies, possibilities, resolvable and unresolvable dilemmas and alternatives, patterns of timing and leverage, rhythms, human factors, and outcome probabilities. The strategist then identifies the best paths and alternative approaches to be followed, visualizes intersecting patterns and structures that influence the paths, perceives the nature and probable behavior of decision-makers, the quality of opponents and witnesses, and a host of other factors. The strategist also understands the limits of his or her knowledge and capability, and knows that risk and the ability to manage risk is always involved in any strategic context.

This is made more challenging because the strategic tapestry is not a simple two-dimensional image. It is a living work in which the strategist is both an integral part of the creation and simultaneously stands outside the framework and seeks to control, recognize, anticipate, influence, and inhibit the work. Competing strategists are attempting to construct a different and often contradictory work,

29

creating a dynamic tension that is intrinsic to the very nature of legal strategy. This dynamic tension is part of the substantive material with which the legal strategist works.

An important part of this process involves preparation and planning. In addition to acquisition and testing, strategic planning is nothing more nor less than the generation of realistic hypotheses concerning conditions that are likely to unfold, goals that are desirable and realistically achievable, and legitimate contingencies that need to be taken into account. Strategic planning can help identify both opportunities and threats, and can point the way to capitalizing on the opportunities and avoiding harm from the threatening factors. Done properly, planning allows the strategist to understand probabilities, and to identify strengths, weaknesses, and resources, as well as the characteristics of decision-makers, self, and opponents. When teams of people are involved, such as in large law firms, or when the strategist is working with larger institutions, the planning process also makes it more likely that everyone is working according to the same terms and with shared goals. Sun Tzu's insights into planning, strategic excellence, and the faults common to bad strategy reveal a great deal about the most effective approaches and the most common pitfalls.

Action and planning are related, but quite distinct. Strategy in action—as opposed to strategy in planning—is like the weather we actually experience compared with the previous evening's forecast. There is often a relationship between prediction and reality, but there is no certainty the one will match the other. The forecasting variables are so enormous, and the momentum of the conditions that create our weather of such a massive and interactive character, that it is impossible to be completely certain what the weather will be until the weather actually exists. So it is with strategy.

Military strategists understand that once conflict begins comprehensive strategic plans developed over months or years are instantaneously transformed into little more than scribbles on paper. Sun Tzu tells us, *"The general who wins a battle makes many calculations [before] the battle is fought."* He also says, *"The general who loses a battle makes but few calculations beforehand."* The tension between strategic planning and strategic action is unavoidable. But when a prediction is wrong, it does not necessarily represent a failure of planning or prediction, as opposed to a reflection of the limits of planning and prediction. Law cases contain significant levels of uncertainty, regardless of how hard we strive to eliminate or control the variables. The legal strategist must be prepared for virtually all contingencies, regardless of the strategic "forecast," because the conditions of actual engagement—not the detailed projections of strategic plans—dictate the nature of strategic action. Corporate and legal strategists, as well as military and martial arts strategists, must therefore plan without becoming fixated, and must adapt to the opportunities and conditions created by the force, momentum, interaction, and compulsion of the strategic actuality. Both Sun Tzu and Musashi demonstrate that planning is essential, but their planning is driven by continual acquisition and interpretation of strategic information, as close to "real time" and the actual ground of engagement as possible.

[margin note: there is lots of uncertainty]

Predictive, preliminary planning looks at a wide variety of indicators, and seeks to estimate the realistic probability of specific consequences depending on the action taken. Operational and reactive planning relates to action, and action generates and responds to actual situations. This includes adapting to surprise, and changing or modifying approaches when necessary. Often the best you can do is hope that your prediction about the most likely outcome bears some resemblance to the reality. Occasionally our strategic forecasts explode and things get a bit messy. For example, how would you like to be the defense lawyer who offered a plaintiff $10,000 to settle a case involving breach of contract that included allegations that the defendant attempted to cover up the existence of an oral contract, only to have your offer rejected by the plaintiff, the case tried, and finally see the jury return a verdict of over $33 million against your client—including $32 million in punitive damages? Whatever happens on appeal, both sides must have been stunned by this jury's decision. The lawyer in Example 3 set out later in this chapter won $4.3 million at trial after predicting a possible $1 million jury verdict. He would have settled for $500,000 prior to trial, but was forced to try the case because his opponent offered nothing. Why did the defense lawyers in this case misread the potential outcome so badly? It can be understood why the plaintiff's attorney underestimated the dollar amount because he was working from a combination of trial probability and considerably lower prior jury verdicts in the area. No one can safely predict quantum leaps in the size of jury verdicts, and while he or she could hope it might occur, any lawyer would be a fool to predict a positive sea-change in verdict levels or count on it happening. This does not mean, however, that the aggressive lawyer shouldn't attempt to structure the

[margin note: can't predict jury awards for damages]

case for both trial and negotiation in ways designed to take the outcome to levels that exceed the current pattern or, at a minimum, to push toward the higher end of the existing pattern of real outcomes.

Musashi emphasizes that constant practice and planning are essential to mastering strategy. Reading, discussing, reflecting on what has occurred, anticipating, and taking action aimed at expanding one's conceptual awareness of strategic scenarios and principles is an important part of creating and focusing the emerging strategist. Study and reflection are vital, but they are never enough unto themselves. Neither, however, are action and experience. Ultimately, the strategist is created through the combination of understanding and internalization of critical strategic concepts, enhanced self-awareness, extensive knowledge of human nature and institutions, training, actual experience, and continual reflection and reassessment. The process never ends because the strategist is always on the path of becoming, and no one ever reaches the end of the individual journey.

[handwritten margin note: how strategist is created]

Some preliminary elements of what is involved in strategic awareness are offered here by introducing three examples. These examples deal with the moral dilemmas of the advocate, the price that can be paid for principled behavior, the flaws and successes reflected in the quality of the strategic decisions, and the need to impose limits on our strategic behavior. They also reflect both on the need for the strategist to take early action that prevents problems from turning into catastrophes, and on the consequences of treating people as fungible commodities on balance sheets.

Because strategy takes on meaning only through context and application, these fact-pattern examples are used to provide concrete points of reference. As you read the examples, put yourself in the position of the various decision-makers. These decision-makers will be opposing lawyers, clients, a jury, a judge, a corporate CEO whose personal interests may not be identical with the best interest of his corporation, and an insurance company.

Although we are at a preliminary stage of our consideration of strategy, it is important to begin the process of asking questions. That is one of the most basic ways we learn from experience—both our own and that of others. Some of the questions include:

- What kinds of decisions did the relevant decision-makers reach?

- What should they have done or taken into account that wasn't pursued or understood?

- What mistakes—legal, factual, moral, ethical, relational—can be identified?

- What did they do that was most effective?

- What really should have been the outcome in each situation and how should the disputes have been resolved?

- What were the clients' goals, and to what extent did the lawyers become entangled in the conflict and were consequently blinded to their clients' best interests?

- Did the lawyers pursue their own personal agendas or interests in ways that may have harmed their clients' best interests?

- Was there any conflict between duties owed to the client and the duty to protect the public from potentially harmful consequences?

Example 1: *The Verdict*

The Verdict is a movie about a case in which a young woman was rushed to St. Catherine Laboré Hospital when she went into labor. At the hospital she was administered an anesthetic that we ultimately find was inappropriate given the fact she had eaten only one hour earlier. During the delivery process she vomited into her mask as a result of the improper anesthetic and her breathing was cut off for a period before the doctors realized what had occurred. Oxygen was denied to her brain and she went into an irreversible coma. For the past several years, Deborah Ann Kaye has been lying in a hospital ward in a vegetative state, hooked to life-support machinery.

A suit was filed by the victim's sister to ensure Deborah could be cared for throughout the remainder of her life. The sister and her husband want to move out of state and are concerned with the future care of Deborah. The plaintiff also seeks damages for medical malpractice against the Archdiocese that operates the hospital. The Archdiocese is insured, and their lawyers are a powerful Boston law firm. The defendant doctors, hospital, and Archdiocese denied liability, claiming that the anesthetic was appropriate given the fact that the hospital admission record contained the notation that the patient had last eaten nine hours before being admitted.

The plaintiff is represented by Frank Galvin. He is an alcoholic down-and-outer, without other clients. The only reason Galvin has this case is that it was referred to him by another lawyer, Mickey Morrissey, with whom he once worked. Morrissey thought he was doing his friend Galvin a favor by giving him an easy case with substantial settlement value. Because Morrissey was fully aware of Galvin's problems, there is an unresolved ethical issue concerning his own responsibility if the case turns out badly. Personal loyalties and professional responsibilities are often confused. But Morrissey fell into the trap of friendship and failing to make the best interests of the client his *raison d'etre*.

The Verdict is not only about law and legal strategy, but also examines the limits of professional and moral behavior. Frank Galvin began his career with great hopes. He was on the fast-track with a prestigious Boston law firm, married a senior partner's daughter, and achieved the lawyer's version of the American dream. Just when he seemed to have it all, Galvin's world collapsed. He discovered a senior partner attempting to rig a jury and was about to turn him in. Before he could do that, however, the well-connected partner had Galvin arrested, claiming he had been the one who tampered with the juror. Virtually overnight, Frank Galvin was out of a job, blacklisted, and considered a pariah in the Boston legal community. He was divorced by his wife, who had no time for losers who didn't know how to play the game.

Having paid the price for his moral principles, Galvin began drinking heavily while sinking to the depths of the legal profession. By the time his involvement in this case begins, he was lying, sloppy, negligent, and hustling new clients at funeral homes by pretending he was a friend of the family's deceased. His lone client was in an irreversible coma and he didn't even know her name when Morrissey reminded him the trial was in a few weeks. When the client's sister and brother-in-law came to see him only two weeks before trial, Galvin had done little work on the case, never even visited his client, had not yet spoken with witnesses, and had not talked with the opponent.

If Frank Galvin had descended into his own version of hell, his opponent was described by Morrissey as "the Prince of F _ _ _ ing Darkness." Ed Concannon is a partner in a powerful law firm and—like Musashi and Sun Tzu—is totally committed to doing anything necessary to win. This "win at any price" approach even includes planting a spy inside Galvin's camp. In military or national security strategy, spying of this sort would be a brilliant move. The fact that

Concannon's spy seduced Galvin to achieve her mission would be little more than a necessary inconvenience for the military or national security strategist. Sun Tzu repeatedly emphasizes the importance of acquiring the best intelligence information about an opponent's inside operations, and the use of spies is a time-honored way to obtain information about an enemy's true plans. In this situation, however, Ed Concannon puts too much faith in his spy, for she ultimately keeps the final piece of critical information from him. In the end he experiences the strategist's worst nightmare, finding himself betrayed, stunned, and made clumsy by his loss of balance.

Before his ultimate failure, Concannon had everything going his way. After Galvin manages to do a miserable job during most of the trial, Concannon puts on a solid defense case. He relies heavily on the two defendant doctors' professional demeanor and high standing in the medical profession, submitting hospital admission records to show that their treatment of the now comatose plaintiff was medically appropriate. When Galvin asks how the plaintiff could have suffered brain damage in so short a time, one of the defendant doctors points to the fact she was anemic and that her brain wasn't receiving as much oxygen as would a normal individual. When the doctor points this out during cross-examination, Galvin can do little more than mumble and look stunned.

After Concannon finishes his defense, the seemingly defeated Galvin offers a surprise rebuttal witness, the former admitting nurse (Caitlin Costello Price) who had filled out the original intake sheet when the plaintiff was first admitted. He located her toward the end of the trial after breaking into another nurse's mailbox and opening her telephone bill so he could obtain a lead to the witness. Then he went to New York and tried to deceive Caitlin as to his identity, confessing only after she sees through his subterfuge. The next day, as the sophisticated Concannon and his clients look on, this sweet, young, Irish-Catholic woman testifies that one of the defendant doctors ordered her to alter the plaintiff's intake record to cover his mistake in administering the wrong medication. When she refused, the world-famous doctor had her fired and blacklisted from nursing. On cross examination, the surprised Concannon suggests she is lying and had nothing to support her claim. He asks why she would make such a claim against two doctors, whether she knew the penalty for perjury, and how she expected anyone to take her testimony seriously? At that point, Caitlin Costello Price pulls out a copy of the original intake form, one she had made before the doctor changed the "1" she had written when she processed the victim during hospital admission, to a "9." As anyone who has seen this movie knows, the jury not only returns a plaintiff's verdict, but asks if they have the authority to give more than the $600,000 in damages the complaint requests. We will return to *The Verdict* in our subsequent discussion of Sun Tzu and Musashi.

Example 2: In-House Counsel for a Large Pharmaceutical Company

Assume you are general counsel for a major pharmaceutical company. Your company has just received a letter from a single law firm threatening to file a class-action suit on behalf of people the firm alleges have suffered serious side effects from one of your company's products. The demand letter doesn't surprise you because an internal investigation you did a year ago—after receiving several complaints about possible side effects—uncovered memoranda revealing that key people in your company (not you) knew there were problems with the drug and suppressed that knowledge. You submitted this assessment to the company's chief executive officer (CEO) and were told he would "take care of it." Although concerned, you did nothing further even after you became convinced your report was being ignored.

Your analysis suggests there are likely to be enough people suffering side effects from the drug that potential liability to your company is at least several hundred million dollars, and could be several times higher. Based on the internal memoranda you have no doubt the drug causes the kinds of side effects the plaintiffs have experienced, and once the plaintiffs obtain that information they will be able to easily prove their case—plus establish the coverup. You estimate the class of claimants to number at least several thousand, and possibly tens of thousands, depending on extent of use, dosage levels, and the variable levels of sensitivity. No one has tracked any of this so there is no way anyone can be certain at this point just how bad the potential exposure and damages may be. You fear the worst after reading a report about a case in which Dow Chemical was hit with a $10 million punitive damage verdict in a single silicone-implant case when the jury reacted to evidence that the company had known about the problem for a long time and covered it up. Dow Chemical's lawyers said they were going to appeal because the jury was "inflamed" by "emotions," but somehow that doesn't give you much comfort. What do you do?

what to do

If you are corporate counsel in such a situation, you must first try to figure out the extent of your company's potential exposure. Given the uncertainty in this situation, you know that answering this will not be easy but that it involves such questions as:

- How many people are likely to have suffered reactions or side effects?

- How severe are their problems?

- At what point did key company decision-makers actually know there was a problem?

- Can the nature and extent of their knowledge be proved?

- What compromising reports and memoranda exist?

- Is there a long latency period between exposure to the product and manifestation of the reactions?

- What claims were made to the Food and Drug Administration (FDA) about the drug and any potential side effects?

- Were any FDA reports falsified?

Legal problems aren't static. What you have discovered is a time bomb. You are in the position of having to create a strategy that produces effective damage control. You know that at some point the various damning memoranda will be discovered. You personally aren't going to destroy evidence and much of the material isn't protected by the attorney-client privilege and will be discoverable. Your boss may fire you or offer you a deal if you help him get rid of the worst of the evidence, but you had several classes in ethics and aren't about to risk your license. Just to be safe you decide it might be wise to make copies of all records and keep them at home. If somebody else destroys records and it comes out and they try to blame you, there is no way you are willing to take the fall for a company coverup. There is no question something bad is going to happen if the opponents are successful in proving the side effects are being produced by your company's product. This means that the longer the action takes, the less you will be able to keep the situation from becoming increasingly serious and damaging. The question is not one of the company being able to completely escape liability and responsibility, but of how bad the situation will become. If you aren't made a scape-goat and fired, you feel you can influence and seek to mitigate some of the consequences, but you know there is no way you can prevent all harmful effects.

This is a situation in which many lawyers find themselves and the tension and confusion you feel are extremely troublesome. You want to do the "right" thing, but it's not all that clear what that means. At this point you realize that the discussions about ethical problems with which other people have had to deal don't provide clear answers for you. You feel the company is putting thousands of people at risk without their knowledge, and that the CEO is "stonewalling" you about the problem. You feel a responsibility to those people, but an even stronger one to the company and to your profession. Lawyers just don't "rat" on their clients or betray client confidences or secrets. In that way, you have always felt like a priest in a confessional. Right now, however, you decide to put those questions aside and concentrate on the legal task. One of your first concerns is identifying effective ways to reduce the ultimate impact. Knowing how to do this involves being able to answer some of the following questions:

- What are your goals?
- What are your opponent's goals?
- What do you need to know to determine the extent of the company's exposure?
- Can you keep the matter in-house?
- What are you going to advise your CEO to do, the same person who ignored your first warning?
- To whom does a general counsel owe loyalty and responsibility?
- Who makes the decisions for the corporation?
- Did the CEO take your warning to the company's board of directors, or did he just file it away?
- If the CEO failed to inform the directors and now denies knowledge of the problem until recently, what will you say?
- Did you breach your obligation to the company when you did not follow up on your report to the CEO, even though you suspected it wasn't being taken seriously?

- Were you afraid the CEO would fire you if you went over his head?

- What is the connection between your professional obligation and the development of a strategy for dealing with this situation?

Example 3: The Penalty for "Monetizing" Human Beings

Several years ago, an old friend of mine represented two workers who were maimed in an explosion of an air compressor caused by an allegedly defective pressure-release valve. The defendant was advised on several occasions of concerns about the valve but failed to remedy the problem. Because the compressor was an older model that had been in service for years, the defendant company was convinced it would not be held liable by a jury and the defendant refused to even consider settlement prior to trial. The injured workers' lawyer—an experienced personal-injury and product-liability litigator—would have taken a $500,000 settlement, and told his clients they could reasonably expect to obtain a jury award of roughly $1 million although some risk was involved and there was a chance the jury would not find liability. The jury found liability existed and, to the lawyer's surprise, returned a verdict of $4.3 million. At the time, this verdict was several times higher than any jury in that specific jurisdiction had ever given similarly situated plaintiffs.

This example clearly demonstrates that case evaluation is not a science. Numbers, probabilities, statistics, and thorough research play important roles in lawyers' evaluation and diagnosis of cases. If a lawyer doesn't have a reasonable idea of what a case is worth, it is impossible to resolve the conflict at any level of professionalism. While lawyers try to put specific, reasonable numbers on the damages and outcome probabilities to create the appearance of precision and concreteness, those numbers and outcomes are often erected on foundations of sand. The plaintiffs' lawyer in this example was skilled, experienced, ethical, and an excellent trial attorney. Presumably so were the defendant's attorneys. But the predictions and expectations of each side ended up being far different than the jury's decision.

This failure of opposing lawyers to diagnose the conflict within a compatible universe is far more common in law cases than we might think. As we will see throughout this book, a variety of factors go into diagnosis of the values and probable outcomes of disputes that reach the legal system. The chapters entitled *The Paths of Legal Strategy, The Negotiation and Mediation Paths,* and *The Trial and Arbitration Paths* offer ways to determine the value and outcome probability of a case. In this specific example, one of the key factors involved the permanent nature of the disfiguring injuries and the fact that the defendant had been warned several times of the danger and simply ignored the risks to its employees. As is common with many businesses, the defendant company chose to "monetize" the health and well-being of its employees, trading the chance of their injury or death for the present value of not spending the money to remove a known risk. This kind of behavior is an important aspect of case evaluation because it significantly enhances the level of damages that a jury is likely to award a victorious plaintiff.

As we examine the ideas of Sun Tzu and Musashi, think about how their strategic principles would apply to such a situation. Consider how the jury is likely to respond to behavior that treats other humans as objects. Recognize that as we shift from decision-makers that are lawyers and clients to those who are not under the control of either party (e.g., jurors, judges, or arbitrators), the outcome takes on a greater element of risk for both sides. But in cases in which the defendant has behaved badly the scale of the potential outcome and damage award significantly increases.

Part II
Sun Tzu and Musashi

Four
Sun Tzu's Diagnostic Method:
The Art of War

> *"What enables the wise sovereign and the good general to strike and conquer, and achieve things beyond the reach of ordinary men, is foreknowledge."*
> Sun Tzu, *The Art of War.*

This chapter deals directly with the language and concepts of strategy according to Sun Tzu. At this point in the book, perhaps more than any other, I must ask the reader to approach the material with an open mind. Some of the ideas will initially seem alien, others obvious once introduced. The important point is that we are in the process of developing a system of strategy, not a list of isolated techniques and tactics. The system of strategy offered here is a different way of thinking and perceiving. No one part stands alone because the work is an integrated totality. A critical part of the process developed through the next several chapters takes the language of two master strategists—Sun Tzu and Musashi—and introduces it into the realm of evaluating and resolving legal disputes through the application of strategic methods and insights.

Only when the reader has completed working his or her way through this book, and begins to become more comfortable with its language and concepts, can the system of strategy be fully understood. I have gone through this process myself, and repeat it with my students each time I teach the course on *The Lawyer as Strategist*. Although I tell them of the need for open-mindedness and suspended judgment, for them my protestations are only words. For the first two or three weeks of the semester they inevitably think I'm operating from within a kind of personal *Twilight Zone*. Then a light goes on, and, almost without exception, they begin to understand. By the end of the process they have internalized many of the critical aspects of strategic awareness and have acquired a powerful tool.

The Five Constant Factors and The Seven Considerations for Victory

Sun Tzu's diagnostic method is central to all effective strategic planning. It helps the strategist identify what is known, what needs to be discovered, where best to direct intelligence gathering activities, and where lie the deficiencies in one's own situation and in the opponent's circumstances. A large amount of strategy involves acquisition of strategically important information, as well as protection of the strategist's information, and even the provision of disinformation to keep opponents off balance or in pursuit of a phantom enemy. Sun Tzu's diagnostic method identifies both strengths and weaknesses along with advantages and disadvantages. It tells the strategist whether victory is possible and under what conditions. It also indicates whether it would be foolhardy or even suicidal to proceed.

The five constant factors tell you the categories of strength and weakness toward which a strategist's planning must always be directed. The five constant factors are: *moral law, heaven, earth, the commander,* and *method and discipline.* These five factors take into account the natural structure within which a conflict takes place, the considerations of time, place, terrain, and resources, as well as the characteristics of the competing leaders and their forces. The five factors (and the seven considerations) are the "ground" or foundation of Sun Tzu's strategic system. They are the means by which the strategist begins the process of identifying the critical questions that must be answered before any realistic idea of how to achieve victory or avoid defeat can be developed. By giving content to these critical categories through organizing and acquiring strategic information, the strategist develops the knowledge necessary to support strategic action. That knowledge, however, can never be sufficient without addressing the seven considerations for victory.

There is a strongly interactive relationship between the five constant factors and the seven considerations for victory. The seven considerations refine and add essential specificity to the questions that must be answered before the strategist can have a clear understanding of the kinds of action that need to be taken or avoided. Strategy is both comparative and interactive. There is no "absolute" strategic position. Strategy takes into account the strengths and weaknesses of all participants in a conflict—even neutral parties—and current and potential allies whose interests and allegiances may change as the strategic process unfolds.

If the five constant factors are the ground of Sun Tzu's diagnostic system, the seven considerations provide the specific approach through which the strategist is able to assess the existence, quality, and distribution of the five constant factors. While the five factors tell what types of things tend to determine who wins and loses, the seven considerations apply the factors to the specific situation and context. The seven considerations for victory are:

(1) Depth of principle: *"Which of the two sovereigns (clients) is imbued with the moral law?"*

(2) Leadership ability: *"Which of the two generals (lawyers) has the most ability?"*

(3) Assessment of advantages: *"With whom lie the advantages derived from heaven and earth?"*

(4) Discipline: *"On which side is discipline most rigorously enforced?"*

(5) Strength: *"Which army is the stronger?"*

(6) Training and skill: *"On which side are officers and men most highly trained?"*

(7) Control and fairness: *"In which army is there the greatest constancy both in reward and punishment?"*

A critical part of any strategic methodology goes beyond the simple listing or defining of important factors. We must understand how to answer the questions Sun Tzu's method tells us to ask. The processes of strategic recognition, assessment, perception, and evaluation represent much of what this book is about. How do we know, for example, who has the most ability, who is strongest, who is most disciplined, best-trained, or who has the most important advantages and disadvantages?

The Five Constant Factors

The Moral Law

The first constant factor is the *moral law,* but this *moral law* is not morality as we Westerners usually comprehend that concept. It is not

moral law is / Not

concerned with true right and wrong, but stands for the degree to which a people, relevant group, or even individuals support their leader's decisions, goals, and efforts. If support does not exist for a war, campaign, or pursuit of a legal dispute, a strategist's effectiveness can be undermined. There is an inevitable ebb and flow in any conflict or game. Underlying support shouldn't disintegrate when a conflict's pressures become intense, costs mount, and losses pile up. Shifts of momentum, surges in action, and the need to fall back and regroup are commonplace. But people generally (and clients specifically) are fickle. Early commitment and passion often become second-guessing and radical changes of heart. The U.S. humanitarian intervention in Somalia offers a stark example. There was significant initial support for the mission, but when U.S. soldiers began to be killed, that approval evaporated. Such shifts in the intensity of support are a natural part of strategy with which strategists must contend.

The resolve and support of a nation's people have much to do with an army's spirit, and the ability to sustain a prolonged effort. France fell to the Nazis with amazing rapidity, not only because the French defensive strategy that relied on the massive fortifications of the Maginot Line was rigid and ill-conceived, but because the will of the French people to resist a powerful enemy was weak. Now compare the French to the Vietnamese. The Vietnamese outfought the French—and later the Americans—because the Vietnamese were willing to endure much greater hardship, and had the ability to adapt to their enemies. As we will see with both Sun Tzu and Musashi, adaptability is an essential element of strategy. Vietnamese strategists developed ways to confront their technologically superior adversaries in terms designed to reduce their enemies' advantages. This spirited guerrilla resistance by a determined and relentless enemy, who fought in ways designed to keep our immensely greater military power ineffective, eventually eroded the popular support of French and American citizens during the lengthy struggle. It gradually bled away both the will to fight and the arrogance from the two Western powers. This happened because the *moral law* was considerably stronger on the side of the Vietnamese and it was sustained for a longer time.

The ideal situation is obviously one in which the strategist commands the people's unquestioning support. A spirited, unified front sends your opponent the message that you will fight as long and hard as is required to gain a victory or prevent defeat. It can also be used to send the message that the costs of conflict will be catastrophic.

Examples are easy to recognize. This type of signal was sent by the British to the Germans in the early years of World War II. It was also sent by the Japanese to the Allies near the end of the war. The projected casualties incurred by Allied forces if they launched a land invasion of Japan were estimated at two million. This factor—as well as an element of racism—led to the use of the atomic bomb by the United States. A little-considered irony is that far more Japanese lives probably would have been lost than were killed in Nagasaki and Hiroshima if there had been a land invasion of Japan by the Allies.

For the defending strategist, however, the message of a strong *moral law* is that if an enemy attacks, you will be a resolute defender who will impose heavy losses. This perception doomed Japan to the American use of the atomic bomb. If the Japanese had been seen as a less-resolute enemy that might surrender under normal military conditions—as opposed to one that was bitterly opposed to any negotiated surrender acceptable to the allies—then the attacks on the two cities might not have been seen as necessary. In this way, therefore, the projection of a strong, defensive *moral law* worked against the Japanese. For the offensive strategist, the *moral law* signals a collective will of such power that your opponents must think about whether to fight, for how long, or if they should sue for peace.

Sun Tzu tells us to beware of lengthy campaigns or extended sieges because it isn't always possible to have unequivocal support—particularly for lengthy strategic campaigns—whether military or legal. The Vietnam War, for example, most likely would have had a different outcome if the people of the United States had been unified behind our military intervention. It also might have ended differently if the Soviets, Chinese, and Vietnamese had at least perceived that there was substantial popular support in America for the war. One difficulty the United States had in Vietnam was that America is such a diverse, open country with a free press that it is impossible to pretend there is total support for controversial actions—at least not for very long. In the end, the North Vietnamese and Vietcong simply wanted to win more than we did and were willing to pay a higher price. It can be argued that they were more resolute and ruthless, but, in fact, we were at least as ruthless, simply not as resolute.

The *moral law* waxes and wanes. As the war in Vietnam intensified, the United States lost the fight to sustain its version of the *moral law*. American television screens were filled with graphic images of

pain and death. The My Lai Massacre proved—to our astonish-
ment—that our troops were capable of the most brutal savagery. For
the first time the true horror of war was brought into millions of living
rooms simultaneously on a daily basis. America's will to continue the
effort was undercut as this process continued. Our enemy was fully
aware of the conflict raging between different groups of Americans.
As Jane Fonda traveled to Hanoi and American streets and campuses
filled with antiwar protesters, the North Vietnamese knew they only
had to hold on a little longer and inflict sufficient casualties on our
troops so that demands for withdrawal of our forces would increase.
A related problem that weakened American capability in Vietnam is
that our political leaders imposed strategic limits on our military actions and forced our professional soldiers to fight a defensive war in
Vietnam. We fought not to lose rather than to win.

Fortunately, in this age of media and sophisticated propaganda,
even if the support does not actually exist, it is sometimes possible
to generate the impression it does. A contrary scenario unfolded in
the Gulf War between the United States, the U.N. allies and Saddam
Hussein's Iraq. The Gulf War quickly came to be perceived as a just
campaign against a brutal aggressor intent on military domination
of the Middle East. These beliefs and attitudes were not initially
representative of the feelings of the American people, most of whom
knew little or nothing about Saddam Hussein prior to his invasion of
Kuwait. Before Hussein's August 1990 invasion, eighty to ninety percent of Americans probably would not have been able to locate Iraq
or Kuwait on a map.

Because the *moral law* is so important, public opinion in the
United States was rapidly and carefully molded by the combination
of high pressure and sophisticated public relations and propaganda
campaigns orchestrated by the Bush administration and Kuwaiti-
funded public relations teams. The media were fed sensationalized
versions of atrocities. A Congressional vote was quickly pursued to
legitimize U.S. action and to squelch political dissent over foreign
military intervention in Iraq by American troops. The United Nations
was pressured into a vote that sanctioned the use of military force.
This allowed the United States to assume the high ground of the
moral law. The U.N. vote meant the conflict was no longer only the
U.S. v. Iraq, but the forces of a democratic world arrayed against a
brutal dictator. This sent an important message to both our allies and
our opponents.

Saddam Hussein, who had earlier been supported by some Americans and the Reagan/Bush administrations for defeating the detested Iran of the Ayatollah Khomeini, was now suddenly depicted by George Bush as a monstrous Hitlerian figure. Kuwait was this new Hitler's innocent, militarily raped, democratic, and freedom-loving victim. Atrocities—some real and others cleverly conceived by the well-paid propaganda machines of Hill and Knowlton, the U.S. Department of Defense, and Kuwaiti officials—were widely publicized. These allegations—some true, others unprovable, and some false—were transmitted throughout the world during Congressional testimony leading up to the vote to authorize U.S. military intervention.

This not only created widespread public support for U.S. involvement but was an attempt to communicate the fact of that support to Saddam Hussein. He was not listening, overrated his own capabilities, and refused to take the American posture seriously. His repeated pronouncements made it clear he thought the United States could not muster the political will or sense of *moral law* required to act against him, even though two decades had elapsed since our defeat in Vietnam. American assurances that military force was imminent weren't believed. Hussein's blustering and posturing about rivers of blood, secret weapons, and threats of annihilation played into our strategists' hands by intensifying the short-term American support necessary to mobilize and position our forces. A tinhorn dictator with a shaggy mustache and big mouth was insulting the pride of the world's greatest power. His threats backfired and Hussein himself helped form and coalesce the will of the American people. Saddam's misjudgments contributed greatly to his own defeat.

The Moral Law and Legal Strategy

The *moral law* is a basic part of legal strategy. As in military strategy, the importance of the *moral law* is not only in a client's actual level of commitment and resoluteness about pursuing a legal campaign—whatever it might require—but also is in a lawyer's ability to persuade opponents about the strength of the client's commitment to pursuing the case vigorously. In many instances, the projection of a powerful sense of *moral law* is a carefully crafted illusion, a lawyer's version of a public relations campaign designed to sell the opponent on the value of the case.

A lawyer's portrayal of a client's resolute spirit quite often has little to do with what the client actually wants. It is wonderful for the lawyer if a client is willing and able to see a case through to the end, but many times just the opposite is true. The required resources often don't exist, the stress is too great, and/or the risk of loss is too high. A client might, for example, have given her lawyer absolutely clear and final instructions to settle the controversy without trial, or it simply may be obvious to the lawyer or client after the trial preparation is done, that critical elements of the case won't be able to withstand scrutiny. If so, the lawyer and client know there is a barrier of timing or expense beyond which it would be foolhardy or counterproductive to proceed. In most instances, however, it is vital to keep the opponent in the dark, uncertain, and/or misdirected about this critical reality.

Because so much of strategy involves deception, a key part of the lawyer's task is to conceal the client's true spirit and desires, while projecting the strategic impression most appropriate to achieving the desired goal. This impression is often one of unyielding commitment to achieving a principled outcome of some sort—"whatever it takes!" The opposite can also be true, in which the client wants to take the case near or through trial but has reasons to be seen as cooperative rather than intractable during what may actually be a false or insincere settlement process. A false cooperative impression can lead opponents to reveal information about their cases that they would not be willing to share if they understood what the real motivation was behind the facade of cooperation. Or the lawyer may be playing a game for a judge or some other external decision-maker directed at generating the sense of reasonableness.

Impression management is a critical part of strategic behavior because it is an essential aspect of projecting the sense of the *moral law*. In a world where most of us prefer to conduct ourselves honestly, the need to deceive and create false fronts and impressions is a troubling aspect of being a lawyer. But it is essential in much of what we do. The primary reason lawyers restrict contact between opposing lawyers and their clients is that strategic leverage is needlessly given away to an opponent who senses the other client or the lawyer is unwilling to go forward, whatever the reason. If, for example, Frank Galvin had handled the case professionally in Example 1: *The Verdict*, he would have concealed the fact that his client would be happy with a reasonable outcome—or even a low settlement—and in no way wanted to go through the trauma, expense, or riskiness of a trial. Certainly he had tailor-made themes that would be considered compelling. A young woman who trusted the hospital and doctors lies comatose, never to awaken again. She has lost everything—as have those who love her. The case was very winnable and a competent attorney would have handled it far differently.

Additionally, if he had done his job properly, Galvin would not have put himself in a wretched situation and then, with his case severely damaged because he hadn't bothered to subpoena his most important expert witness, desperately telephoning the defendants' insurance company on the eve of trial and begging them to revive their lapsed offer. Because he had already rejected the offer and had insulted the judge and opposing attorney, it isn't surprising that the defense took his panicked last-minute collapse as representing extreme weakness. Their perception was accurate, but they also forgot what the Archdiocese would have preferred (i.e., a reasonable settlement), and ignored the fact that in the right case a jury can disregard even an incompetent performance by a victim's attorney and still do what is right. Lawyers are important, but juries still have the capacity to "do justice" and see through to the heart of a case in spite of the lawyers. The defense lawyers were enmeshed subjectively in the conflict and decided to go for the jugular. In doing so, they did not automatically lose, but they did keep a volatile battleground open when they had the ability to end the matter once and for all and on their terms. By failing to take what would have been an easy and extremely good settlement for the defense, they surrendered control to the jury and lost the war they had already (almost) won.

Impression management is also essential to erecting a protective screen between your client and the opposing lawyer. Cases can be lost if an opponent has the opportunity to "read" a client directly. Few clients are trained to hide their true feelings, fears, or beliefs. Observed by a skilled opponent, they will often reveal their real feelings, the truth of disputed facts even if it is to their disadvantage, and other strengths and weaknesses that can give the opponent important insights. Just as Sun Tzu says that a general can't afford to reveal his true plans to the enemy—or even to his own subordinates—a strategist cannot afford to give away this kind of critical information. The in-house counsel for the pharmaceutical company in Example 2 has to consider whether he should be involved directly with the opponents. Because he has important inside information that could destroy the company's position during negotiations, it is possible the opposing lawyers could bring up a matter during negotiations that would startle him into revealing something of substantial importance or make a response that is either a lie or does not ring true.

The revelation of damaging information not only occurs through clients, but can happen easily when several lawyers are representing a client and the attorneys haven't worked together enough to develop a common strategic agenda. Similarly, some lawyers have personality differences or competitiveness problems that mean they either compete with each other even when supposedly functioning as a team, or possess styles that don't mesh properly. Their incompatibilities can end up generating an internal disharmony that hurts the quality of representation.

Unintentionally giving away sensitive information also occurs when an unprepared, inexperienced, or unskilled lawyer isn't adequately in control of his or her strategic impressions. This can happen either when the lawyer is functioning as part of a team or handling an entire case individually. Just as there must be a high commander in a military context, there must also be someone in charge of any legal team. Whether we are engaged in a negotiation campaign or trial, this necessity of command requires that individual lawyers be able to suppress their egos and avoid the tendency of trying to show opponents how "brilliant" they are. Too many voices joining in a discussion can lead to unproductive confusion and can often result in the inadvertent disclosure of harmful information. It is important to hide disagreements within a team from opponents. Otherwise the opponent will exploit the situation. Of course there can be situations in which lawyers want to feign confusion or weakness, or to subtly and believably communicate disinformation, but that should only occur with a great deal of planning.

The unwitting exposure of critical strategic information is not only done by clients and uncoordinated teams of lawyers, but far too often by individual lawyers who reveal facts during negotiations or fail to respond effectively to an opponent's strategic probes. Skilled opponents can sense the false note an opponent sounds and use that valuable information to investigate further and direct their strategy. This happens regularly during depositions. The deposition is one of the few opportunities a lawyer has to deal directly with the opposing client rather than seeing past the barriers erected by the opposing lawyer. It is useful to visualize a deposition as an important interview of adverse parties—and often hostile witnesses—that allows what is often a lawyer's single most important opportunity to observe and evaluate opposing clients and critical witnesses, including assessing how they are likely to come across if there is a trial. The deposition also allows the lawyer to acquire more precise strategic information, to explore areas more broadly, to take chances he or she would not be willing to risk trying blindly at trial, and to pin down witnesses and opposing clients by forcing them to commit to a particular version of what occurred in the dispute.

Your skilled opponents have the same aim when deposing your clients and critical witnesses. This makes it very important to prepare your clients and witnesses thoroughly for their depositions, both so they make a convincing impression and to prevent them from betraying information of strategic importance to your case. This means that clients need to be educated about how to handle sensitive matters. Too many lawyers try to hold off thorough preparation until they feel the case may need to be tried or at least until they are closer to court-imposed deadlines that they can't avoid. In many instances thorough preparation comes too late, beginning at a point after the case has already been lost because discovery preparation was inadequate. The result is that cases are frequently won or lost on depositions, even though the attorney is not going to tell the client and it may be several years before inadequate discovery and tardy investigative preparation is manifested in the case's final resolution. But preparation for investigation and discovery—both for and against you—is how a lawyer creates the foundation for the ultimate outcomes in a legal dispute. If you prepare poorly or shabbily, without proper evaluation of the case, then no matter how much you do to try to recover in the later stages of the case you will have already lost if your opponent is competent. You will have allowed the foundations of your case to be built on sand. The problem is that it takes considerable thought, time, resources, and diligence to prepare a case properly and assiduously at the preliminary stages and too many lawyers simply don't do it for a variety of reasons, including economic pressures, overload, poor work habits, low expectations for the case, lack of skill, or laziness.

Thorough preparation should involve making certain that your client knows what the case is about, understands the desired approach, appreciates how important it is to listen to you during the deposition, and to follow your lead if you jump in. Obviously, an *moral law deals w/ the impression you give off!*

important part of this process is preparing your client about the *moral law* impression that needs to be generated. Otherwise your client can undermine the impression you are trying to communicate.

Heaven

def The second of the five constant factors is *heaven*. In Sun Tzu's system this idea represents the external, nonphysical conditions within which strategists must operate and to which they must adapt and learn to use. *Heaven* reflects the insight that all strategy involves intangible but quite real considerations that influence behavior, limit perception, create opportunities and dangers, and heighten and/or restrict strategic capability. In Sun Tzu's military strategy, *heaven* symbolizes such factors as *night and day, cold and heat, times and seasons.* Each condition represents elements that are not only dynamic, but tend to flow in cycles, rhythms and patterns. The strategist needs to know where in the cycle or rhythm of the situation the dispute is and how long the particular aspect will last, as well as when the next part of the pattern is likely to begin, its characteristics, and how it relates to or contrasts with the existing conditions. Each factor of *heaven* has specific characteristics and implications that must be taken into account when planning, maneuvering, and taking strategic action. They help form the conditions that make up an important part of the background context within which a strategist operates. Given the episodic and cyclical nature of these factors, it is obvious that timing is a critical element. Knowing where you are in a cycle or pattern will dictate action or inaction and tell you when to attack or defend.

essence of heaven

For the military strategist, the factors characteristic of *heaven* are obvious and extremely important natural phenomena. They have to do with the ability to move quickly or slowly, whether your forces freeze or swelter, when campaigns should begin, and when they need to be suspended or delayed before some natural force such as winter or a rainy season sets in. They force the strategist to not only deal with short-term conditions but with what lies ahead both in terms of micro-patterns and longer-term cycles.

Think of Napoleon wearing out his troops on the vast and frigid Russian steppes, chasing an enemy who keeps falling back because he knows his most powerful weapons are not military force, but starvation and the impending Russian winter. The Russian army could not have survived a direct full-scale battle with Napoleon's army, so a scorched earth strategy was used to deny the enemy the opportunity to replenish food supplies, and a delaying strategy was implemented that strung out the conflict until the savage Russian winter struck. Hitler was destroyed on the Russian Front in much the same fashion.

Heaven and Legal Strategy

For the legal strategist, *heaven* reflects such considerations as the timing of a particular phase of a legal controversy and the kinds of leverage that exist at one point that may not exist at another. This takes into account the combination of both formal and informal operations within virtually any legal process. For the legal strategist *heaven* means that there is a set of rhythms within most law cases that dictate whether it is possible, for example, to seriously pursue settlement or whether the timing is wrong to conclude the matter, regardless if one party desires or appears to desire to settle the controversy. You could even say that an "out-of-sync" or arhythmic settlement offer violates the natural "seasons" of a particular kind of legal dispute. In *The Verdict*, Frank Galvin violated the natural rhythm of settlement by not even contacting the defendant. His opponent was initially somewhat concerned by Galvin's failure to communicate because the rhythm of the situation was such that an attorney normally would have made some contact. Of course, Galvin could have failed to initiate contact because he was committed to trial, or was engaged in a strategy of attempting to convince the defendants he was. A lawyer in Galvin's position could be playing the negotiator's equivalent of "chicken," not wanting to be the first to initiate serious settlement contact and trying to hold out until the last possible moment. In doing so, he could be seeking to project a more powerful strategic spirit. Background research on Galvin by the defendants' attorney soon revealed, however, that he had personal and professional problems, and had seriously neglected the case. There were no hidden, powerful strategies. Galvin was just an incompetent drunk. The defendants then understood why Galvin hadn't followed the normal rhythm of the case.

The acquisition of this information about Frank Galvin by the defendants' lawyers was necessary because lawyers operate according to expectations and patterns. We seek to develop guides for decision-making based on assumptions that most factors and processes in a case will fall into predictable approaches. We worry when there appear to be deviations from the natural cycle because the other lawyer doesn't seem to be following the normal pattern. When something irregular happens, we need to understand the reasons for the difference. Is, for example, the case's "temperature" right for serious settlement overtures? If not, then regardless of what the opponent might say, it is very unlikely the case can be settled at this time. This means you must be always suspicious of your opponent's true intent. The reason for the deviation does not have to signal something ominous. If the offer is honest, rather than a strategic probe, the opponent who seeks to settle "out-of-rhythm" may be signaling inexperience, lack of adequate preparation, fear, ignorance of the case, a hidden agenda in relation to which damage control is being attempted, or incompetence.

The opponent may also be attempting a preemptive strike with a tantalizing offer because he knows something about the case that makes it a good strategy to get rid of the problem quickly while the chance exists to do some damage control. For many corporations who have a pattern and practice of an activity in an area, there may be, for example, other cases that would surface if this one is allowed to go further. An early lucrative offer to a plaintiff may be an attempt to "buy" the package before the larger situation explodes.

There may be predictable costs of business behavior that have already been built into the expense equation and the particular plaintiff may "win" because he or she is fortunate enough to fit into the parameters of the year's balance sheet. A defendant can be operating according to an agenda the plaintiff has no way of discovering. The pharmaceutical case described in Example 2 could be an example of this approach, complete with a covenant by the plaintiffs' lawyers not to take other cases, and a confidentiality agreement as part of the settlement. This approach raises serious questions for both the plaintiff and defense attorneys in regard to a lawyer's primary responsibility to his or her client, versus the moral and ethical responsibility to others who might be injured or killed by the concealed actions of a defendant. After the litigation process is initiated by the filing of a complaint, and particularly so if there is the potential of a class-action suit, the court in such cases is obligated to consider the implications of confidentiality agreements when others' life or health might be endangered. This means the defense lawyers could try to take early, prelitigation settlement action in an effort to avoid judicial intervention. Awareness of the patterns of intensity, conflict, barriers, and opportunities that exist in legal controversies is central to the legal strategist's ability to understand and use the cycles of *heaven* to best advantage, and to also avoid their adverse effects.

Earth

Sun Tzu's *earth* represents the strategic implications of terrain in reference to its defensive and offensive qualities and potential. *Earth* also stands for the strategic dynamics, opportunities, and limits that are created, imposed, or allowed by the distinct qualities of specific terrain. Narrow passes, rocky ground, steep slopes, deep or fast-flowing rivers, bridges, ravines, swamps, mud, sand, vast plains, and so forth, all represent characteristics that can become resources or traps. Some kinds of terrain allow easier defense, bog down an opponent, permit rapid movement, channel an opponent into a specific direction, disperse troops, provide concealment for ambushes, conceal forces, or allow escape. As Sun Tzu indicates, in military strategy this includes *"distances, great and small; danger and security; open ground and narrow passes; the chances of life and death."* This also shows how Sun Tzu's strategic method is an integrated system because the connection between *heaven* and *earth* is obvious. As the cycles of *heaven* shift, they create different kinds of conditions on *earth*. Terrain which is dry and easy to traverse in one cycle or condition can become an entangling trap or a dangerous situation under a changed cycle. A dry riverbed can make traveling easy, but can become a deathtrap in a heavy rain.

Understanding the strategic implications of *earth* helps the strategist know where not to go, how to use natural advantages as either a shield or a weapon, and to recognize the importance of looking ahead to the implications of all movement and action. Strategic foresight requires knowing where action is likely to lead ultimately, not only the short-term implications of beginning a journey on what appears to be an easy path. The most accessible trail, for example, may lead to a swamp in which your army can be trapped. Taking what seems to be a much harder path can create a situation that makes it difficult for an enemy to follow, to mass superior force, and make the defense easier. The initial path of least resistance may well turn out to be the least productive and most dangerous.

Earth and Legal Strategy

For the legal strategist, *earth* translates into such considerations as vulnerability, court procedures, evidentiary rules, deadlines, discovery, defensibility of positions, timing of informal and formal movements, pretrial hearings, interlocutory appeals, and knowledge of the conditions within which an opponent must operate. It also includes resources—both your own and your opponent's—and whether they can be mobilized and brought to bear when needed. Similarly, the quality of the evidence available to you and your opponent is part of *earth,* because that helps tell you which of the other factors should be given emphasis. If, for example, you possess significant resources but are in a relatively weak evidentiary position, this should help you to realize the importance of wearing your opponent down so his willingness to negotiate is enhanced and you don't have to submit the dispute to a trial during which your position may become obviously untenable.

Much of legal strategy, particularly that of defense-oriented strategists, uses approaches that prevent the final joining of the conflict for as long as possible. Defense strategies are often aimed at wearing down plaintiffs, forcing them into defensive positions that require substantial expenditures of time and resources, in addition to creating diversions that deal with everything but what the case is really about from the perspective of responsibility, accountability, or right and wrong. Law cases, like wars, are about winning—not truth and justice. For a defendant, victory is often gained by delay, which causes attrition of the opponent's resources and consequently undermines the opponent's will to continue.

This "wearing them down" approach often works well, but it is dependent upon the plaintiff having inadequate resources to sustain the "war." In Example 2, involving the coverup by the pharmaceutical company, the plaintiffs are represented by a well-funded law firm that is quite content for the defense to use delaying tactics. The longer the defense stalls, the more plaintiffs surface. As more plaintiffs are identified, the greater the defendant company's exposure and the worse the defendant appears. The plaintiffs' outcome potential grows exponentially as the defendant uses classic delaying tactics, and so do the ultimate earnings of both plaintiffs' and defendant's lawyers.

Such a situation as described above, however, has tended to be the exception. As might be expected, there is an important difference in perspective between the plaintiff and defense-oriented attorneys. Plaintiffs generally want to fight and resolve the case, whether through negotiation or litigation. Plaintiffs' lawyers want to force the substantive action in a case because they tend to benefit from the outcome, while defense lawyers more typically benefit from the process. Generally, plaintiffs try to accelerate and compress the process to put pressure on the opponent and to move closer to the ultimate moment of decision. The best way for a plaintiff to do this is to be fortunate enough to be able to use the procedural power of the court to set clear timetables, limit discovery to reasonable terms, and have the process moved along by a firm judicial hand. Defendants in civil cases typically fight this strategy at every juncture.

Most large and wealthy corporate defendants are like Sun Tzu's concept of an army protected behind the walls of a fortified city with supplies sufficient to allow them to withstand a protracted siege. Sun Tzu warns of the ultimate costs of a prolonged siege, and this is often what a plaintiff faces when going up against a powerful corporate defendant. In war, the besieging force risks substantial losses, exhaustion of resources, exposure to cold and heat, and a waning of commitment and strategic spirit. Much the same process occurs in this type of law case. Defendants' use of conflict-of-interests motions, overwhelming discovery and "papering" the case (flooding the opponent with documents and motions), and constant challenges to plaintiffs' discovery efforts stretch out the timetable of a case and force the plaintiffs to use up resources at a faster rate. Such activities make it seem as if the struggle will never end and typically will undermine the plaintiffs' spirit and zeal when the conflict drags on interminably. This can create a greater willingness to negotiate a less advantageous truce, retreat, or give up entirely when resources run out. Sun Tzu warns us that there are cities that should not be attacked, and similarly, clear evaluation of the "supplies" needed to fight specific kinds of litigation campaigns is critical to a lawyer's responsibility to a client. If what the client wants cannot be achieved with the resources available, then don't begin the fight until and unless that strategic imbalance can be rectified. You are not doing clients a favor to recklessly waste their scarce resources when there is little or no chance of victory.

The Commander

Sun Tzu's idea of *the commander* reflects the qualities needed in an individual responsible for leading others into situations in which many are likely to suffer great pain, loss, and even death. In the more detailed description of Sun Tzu's principles that appears in the next chapter, he defines the characteristics of the best strategists or *commanders*, as well as the shortcomings or faults that lead strategists to defeat.

Sun Tzu uses the symbol of *the commander* to represent *"the virtues of wisdom, sincerity, benevolence, courage, and strictness." The commander* is distinct from a nation's overall leader or sovereign. In the war against Iraq, for example, George Bush played the role of the sovereign prince responsible for mobilizing political will and projecting a resolute spirit. Bush helped create and focus the power of the *moral law* by convincing the American people that we were entering a just war against a brutal tyrant. Norman Schwarzkopf played the part of *the commander*, the military leader and chief war strategist. Saddam Hussein blurred the lines between sovereign and commander, and by doing so (for his own reasons of political survival), contributed to the Iraqi defeat by intermingling politics and field strategy.

The Commander and Legal Strategy

In the context of the legal strategist, the idea of *the commander* generally applies to the lawyer. It takes on a variable character depending on the nature, power, experience, and sophistication of the client. More powerful and experienced clients may insist on playing a significant strategic role. This client participation will increase as legal costs escalate and corporations bring more legal expertise in-house. A significant number of clients, however, are still willing and even eager to give their attorney virtually complete strategic control of everything in the case. Many clients seek lawyers in the hope that a problem or difficult situation that is creating great stress for them can be resolved. Because an important part of their desire centers on the need to seek relief from stress, they are happy to dump it all on the lawyer and forget about it for as long as possible.

From the perspective of the pharmaceutical company's house counsel in Example 2, another problem is that there is an almost inevitable tension between the incentives and perspectives of the corporation and those of the outside law firms to which it might refer the case. Generally, it isn't a matter of bad faith, but law firms involved in the defense of corporate clients understandably tend to want to maximize the value of the case to the firm. Such firms have extremely high overhead expenses and require substantial revenues to "feed their habit." For a variety of reasons—including the need for revenue—the initial approach of many corporate defense firms begins with a glacier-like perspective. Their expectation is that the real action will occur years after the case is begun—if at all. This leads to a total preparation perspective that has the convenient side effect of producing the highest number of billable hours for the firm. This involves painstaking and exhaustive research and analysis, even though some of it may be entirely unnecessary or redundant "overkill." It also involves a deliberate strategy of imposing significant transaction costs on opponents in the hope that the plaintiffs' resources will be exhausted and their willingness to accept a lesser settlement, or just give up and go away, is increased.

If the pharmaceutical corporation is able to identify and confront its real interests at an early point, it may find its needs and perspectives are quite different from this classic strategy used by large defense firms. No matter what happens, the corporation's interests are well-served by a clear evaluation of the down-the-line consequences of quick versus slow action. A realistic evaluation could show that a strategy of cooperation with potentially injured parties and avoidance of litigation are the most cost-effective ways to proceed.

The corporation generally will not have the internal expertise to make these judgments, and the law firms that represent such defendants rarely have either the expertise or the economic incentives to do so. The corporation can't see clearly because it is subjectively involved in the situation. The law firms have profit-oriented incentives and financial needs that can influence their judgments. Many large defense law firms are strategic dinosaurs that lack the flexibility and adaptability that is so critical in this new world of litigation in which plaintiffs' firms have grown rapidly in scale, sophistication, aggressiveness, and expertise. Such defense firms will increasingly find themselves applying outmoded strategies to a litigation world that no longer exists. In that new world, smaller, plaintiff-oriented firms are forming collaborative partnerhips with other firms both to share expertise and to create what in the business world would be thought of as a combination of a matrix-based management and an enhanced economy of scale. They are also "outsourcing" their research and investigative tasks by:

(1) hiring experienced lawyers to work only on specific projects;

(2) reorganizing departments to reflect tasks and assignments concentrated into areas in which there are substantial numbers of clients; and

(3) greatly increasing their access to sophisticated information sources and high-level expertise.

Consulting

One way to deal with the inherent dilemma of the corporation's and law firm's self-interest and lack of diagnostic expertise is to have law firms that specialize in diagnosis and strategy rather than direct representation. Such consulting organizations as Arthur Andersen and McKinsey & Co., are common in the business world. In law, there is a need for equivalent mechanisms through which both defendants and plaintiffs can obtain early diagnoses of their situations by experts whose profit incentives don't conflict with their clients' best interests. Without the perspective and disinterested approach of such evaluative systems, too many cases simply take too long and cost defendants and plaintiffs much more than they should.

The legal strategist must understand that the initial client vision of the lawyer as savior will often be a temporary illusion. It is an illusion because the lawyer often can't do everything the client wants, or can't do it for the price the client can afford. It is also an illusion because the client's attitude is only a short-term emotional phenomenon that grants initial power and trust to the lawyer, but is related primarily to the client's short-term need to reduce stress. The client will often become dissatisfied with some aspect of the case's outcome, such as fees and expenses or the terms of a settlement, and later turn against the attorney. This means the lawyer needs to counsel clients as to their best interests, let the clients make the ultimate decisions in cases, and insist on clients' understanding the implications and consequences of their choices.

The specific nature of *the commander* can vary depending on the type and scale of practice. Large law firm practices operate under different rules and strategic realities than are commonly found in solo or smaller-scale law practices. Similarly, specialized law practice represents different strategic realities than are commonly found in a general practitioner's office. Specialists can more easily evaluate and handle complex cases within their specific areas of expertise because they have already developed the strategic intellectual capital. The general practitioner, on the other hand, may need to invest too much money and time trying to "get up to speed" in an unfamiliar area. There is a much greater chance of the generalist being unaware of critical moments in a complex and specialized case, or spending far too much time in background preparation. A strategist unfamiliar with the characteristics and considerations of a particular area of law practice doesn't know the rhythms, people, patterns, textures, issues, pitfalls, or the various outcome potentials of the type of case well enough.

Each type of lawyering involves practicing law, but each is quite different in its approach, assumptions, tactics, expectations, and available resources. For example, representation of large, well-funded institutional clients takes on a different character from that of impoverished or even middle-class clients. The big firms live by diversion and delay. As many large, defense-oriented law firms know, well-funded clients allow them to use a strategy in which they don't have to worry about expending resources and can therefore impose significant costs and burdens on opponents. With large clients, the lawyer might be compared to the commander of the "big battalions." Their strategies play to their strength, which is the ability to apply significantly superior resources in a relatively crude fashion and take advantage of their opponent's weaknesses.

Access to resources has a significant impact on legal strategy. The lawyer who is forced to operate with scarce resources—whether in a defensive or offensive role—becomes more akin to an isolated guerrilla warrior than a general commanding an army. Many plaintiffs' lawyers are forced to operate in this way, as are public defenders with significant caseloads, as well as other public interest and criminal defense lawyers. If they are good, these guerrilla lawyers become adept at identifying and targeting an opponent's weaknesses. They learn how to operate on a shoestring to minimize expenses, and how to make the hard decisions involved in evaluating a case in order to understand what is worth doing and whether it has a realistic chance to succeed.

Done well, this can be a more efficient and surgically precise process that minimizes costs while maximizing results. It has an inescapable air of triage, where decisions are made about which cases are most likely to be profitable and or winnable, and therefore are favorites for the lawyer's attention. For lawyers in private practice whose financial well-being is dependent on being able to sell their time and expertise, it is necessary to make tough decisions about whether to take a case. Often, this results in frustration on the part of potential clients who have been harmed and have a legitimate case, but cannot afford the price of the legal services required to vindicate their rights. Nonetheless, the lawyer's cost-benefit analysis of a case is a necessary and proper part of practice, and one that leads to more efficient handling of the cases that are selected.

On the other hand, a bargain-basement approach to practice with a volume-oriented strategy can also result in very low-quality preparation of cases. Specialization, coupled with mass production of cases within that specialization, can easily lead to failure to evaluate each case on its unique merits, and the tendency to see individual clients as members of a generic class. When this occurs, many individual clients will be shortchanged, while others will be unfairly benefited.

The guerrilla lawyering approach—whether efficient or deficient—is very different from the massive D-day type assault often used by large firms in an effort to smash their opposition. In the latter situation involving large firms, the case is almost never handled by a single lawyer, but is managed by a lead counsel in charge of a team of lawyers and other experts. The large firm process involves a team of lawyers assigned to a wide range of tasks, such as discovery and document review, motions and research, settlement, and trial, if the process ever goes that far.

A lawyer "commanding" a team of lawyers in large, complex litigation—whether defensive or offensive in nature—requires a different range of strategic skills and qualities than are generally needed by an individual practitioner. The individual who is the exceptional trial lawyer often will not be the best person to manage a litigation team. Not everyone has the skills needed to manage complex litigation. Lawyers in charge of litigation teams need management skills that allow them to pull together diverse groups of lawyers, experts, and investigators, keep everyone focused, committed, and efficient, mediate conflicts and soothe egos, while still not becoming entangled in the process. The litigation team leader needs to be able to rely on the skill and judgment of others, and to organize and synthesize an enormous range and volume of information.

In two recent cases in which friends of mine were represented by large defense firms, they were both dismayed at the failure of the firms to consult with them, or to adequately coordinate their internal processes so that each lawyer working on an individual aspect of the case was aware of the relation of his or her activity to the case theory and strategic approach. In each situation, the law firms received several million dollars in fees and expenses, achieved what the clients and other knowledgeable lawyers considered highly questionable outcomes, and left the clients feeling angry and shortchanged. In one of the cases, a well-known national firm charged over $3 million in legal fees, and ended up with an unappreciative client.

The past decade has witnessed the emergence of larger-scale plaintiffs' law firms specializing in mass-tort litigation. This is a new phenomenon. For perhaps the first time in American legal history, a plaintiff-oriented litigation mechanism has been forged that operates on a scale capable of balancing the power of enormously wealthy defendants and the powerful and well-connected corporate law firms that have traditionally represented them. For example, look at the *Cipollone v. Liggett Group* case, in which plaintiff Rose Cipollone sued a tobacco company for her almost forty years of smoking, addiction, and lung cancer. After years of litigation the law firms that represented the Cipollones had spent over $6 million and only obtained a verdict of $400,000. And that award was reversed on appeal. Few law firms can afford to take such a financial hit, and this has traditionally inhibited the ability and willingness of ordinary lawyers and small law firms to take on powerful and wealthy opponents who will stop at nothing. This imbalance has begun to shift, although not without some questionable side effects.

The burgeoning plaintiff-oriented, mass-tort practice represents a revolution in American law practice. It fills a competitive gap and creates some balance in the process, but certainly is not all good. Plaintiffs' firms who have made the "big time" must continually generate cases to stay alive or to maintain the lifestyle and earnings levels to which they have become accustomed. For the most aggressive of these firms, a kind of feeding frenzy with an uncontrolled appetite occurs. As their scale of operation is increased, their demand for earnings and profits becomes greater. This means they are naturally driven toward creating the next series of lucrative cases. Before one major area of tort litigation is completed (e.g., Agent Orange, asbestos, or silicone implants), the groundwork must be laid for the next campaign or there will be too much downtime. This "opening up" of potentially lucrative litigation areas is now being pursued in the context of tobacco litigation based on the tobacco companies' alleged

[handwritten margin note: opening up potentially lucrative areas of litigation]

conspiracy to heighten the addictiveness of cigarettes. It is almost amusing to note "informational" television announcements paid for by plaintiffs' law firms concerning the addictive nature of cigarettes and how the tobacco industry has been manipulating the content in an effort to "hook" young people into the lifetime use of their deadly products. Under the guise of educating the public, these ads are being sponsored by plaintiff-oriented law firms to begin the process of creating a public perception among people who are potential clients and jurors, and to attract clients who are likely to decide the sponsoring firm possesses the expertise they need. It is amazingly cynical (although certainly no worse than the advertising tactics of the cigarette companies), and is a strategically interesting use of media both as propaganda and as a client-recruiting device at a very early stage of the "tobacco wars." Other "fertile fields" include DES, suits involving Upjohn's Halcion, and the rapidly emerging area of electromagnetic field litigation.

In the area of potential litigation against tobacco companies, an alliance has emerged between many of the most powerful plaintiffs' law firms in the United States. In an interesting revelation of the plaintiffs' lawyers' mindset, one of those lawyers, when commenting on the distinction between the approaches of his coalition and that of the public interest groups that have fought the tobacco companies for years, captured the essence of the change. He said that the anti-smoking advocates "just want to get the message out. We [the new plaintiffs' group] just want to kill them [the tobacco companies]. If our method works, there won't be any need to get the message out."

While such language signals a powerful strategic overture, the more dismal reality is likely to be one in which the plaintiffs' firms don't really want to "kill" the tobacco companies. That wouldn't be in their interest. The plaintiffs' firms are not public-interest mechanisms, but aggressive businesses in their own right. The firms want and need to generate a series of lucrative lawsuits and enormous settlements, company by company, so they can maximize earnings. Why would they want to put a lucrative deep-pocket out of business, when they can feed off the tobacco companies for a decade or more?

Method and Discipline

Sun Tzu's concept of *method and discipline* stands for the attention to procedures by which a military strategist organizes, administers, and acts with intensely focused coherence even under great pressure. This includes a military unit's or army's efficiency, its quality of communications, training, ability to follow orders and act with speed, power, and precision. It also includes the ability to adapt to changing conditions, and to invent new tactics and strategic responses when those conditions dictate or allow. For Sun Tzu's military strategist, *method and discipline* includes such considerations as *"the marshaling of the army in its proper subdivisions, the gradations of rank among the officers, the maintenance of roads by which supplies reach the army, and the control of military expenditure."*

Method and Discipline and Legal Strategy

For the legal strategist, *method and discipline* translate into considerations concerning how lawyers approach cases, their degree of efficiency and inefficiency, attention to or neglect of details, the quality and availability of such critical resources as secretarial, investigative, and research support. It also includes the extent to which the lawyers waste energy, the quality of case-tracking and monitoring procedures, the lawyer's organizational ability, and the efficient use of available, and often limited, resources. An incredible array of computer software has now been created that can help lawyers do much of the information organization, review, and recovery of data in a case. These tools can be very important in assisting the legal strategist who knows what he or she wants or needs. They can replace a great deal of the labor-intensive aspects of organization and retrieval of information about the case, research, billing, forms, and law office management itself. Properly understood, the information systems increase the efficiency of a good lawyer, and can make a difference in the profitability of a law practice.

But the informational tools will never replace what leading business strategist Kenichi Ohmae of McKinsey & Co. has called the "mind of the strategist." Equally critical are first-hand experience, and the lessons to be gained from direct observation of the legal "enemy." Technology is a means of saving time and labor, and enhancing what you are already capable of doing. It is not a substitute for the creative and insightful human who is at the center of the strategic process. This is made clear in the next chapter, in which Sun Tzu's strategic principles and techniques are presented.

Five
Sun Tzu's Strategic Principles and Techniques

"The general is skillful in attack whose opponent does not know what to defend; and he is skillful in defense whose opponent does not know what to attack."
Sun Tzu, *The Art of War.*

Sun Tzu's approach to diagnosis and planning allows the strategist to understand many of the advantages and disadvantages of a strategic situation in advance of the actual conflict. His approach makes it possible to identify strengths and vulnerabilities, evaluate an opponent's capabilities, assess the relative balance between the opposing sides, and decide on the viability of specific strategies to be used as the controversy unfolds. Sun Tzu's diagnostic methodology helps the strategist understand when, where, and whether to fight, and which strategies have the best chance of working. It tells what areas you are likely to be forced to defend and which potential weaknesses or strengths need to be reinforced or expanded. It tells how to position and focus resources for maximum effect.

But the *five constant factors* and the *seven considerations for victory* are only the beginning framework of a strategic methodology. They tell us much about where to begin, what to take into account, and what kinds of considerations tend to lead to victory or defeat. Planning and diagnosis are essential aspects of strategy but the real function of strategy concerns the ability to take effective action, and the wisdom to refrain from counterproductive action that harms the strategist's interests. Diagnosis and planning are critical preconditions to effective action—but strategy is entirely about achieving desired goals. The strategist must act at some point, and that requires much more specific knowledge, as well as a wide range of understanding of tactics, human nature, and the ability to concentrate and apply force and leverage.

69

Sun Tzu's principles and techniques are presented in this chapter. Strategy involves intelligent choices about action and inaction, but the ability to make those choices requires acquisition, interpretation, and refinement of strategic knowledge on which the choices of action or inaction are based. Many of Sun Tzu's specific approaches represent ways to acquire valid information prior to committing forces to action. Others have to do with information acquisition, control, and deception in the midst of conflict. His techniques are essential to evaluating and diagnosing, planning, probing, defending, avoiding, adjustment and adaptation, and attacking.

The quoted material in this chapter is taken directly from *The Art of War*. This is the only point in this book where the language of either Sun Tzu or Musashi is presented at length. It is being done here to allow the reader to capture the flavor of the concepts. A brief summary has been added before each point to help clarify Sun Tzu's meaning. Additionally, the material has been restructured to bring the pieces of Sun Tzu's thought into a more systematic pattern organized around principles. These principles include seemingly simple, but absolutely critical ideas, such as the need to define victory in the context of the specific situation, the characteristics of strategic excellence and ineptness, the acquisition of strategic knowledge, planning, the role of timing, surprise and deception, the function of spirit in strategy, and the uniqueness and power of strategic action. As with all strategy, implicit within many of the points is the need for the strategist to have a keen awareness of human behavior and motivation.

Strategic Excellence

Sun Tzu is not interested in mediocrity, crudeness, or clumsiness—even if you end up victorious. Anyone can bludgeon a weak opponent into submission, or expend resources when the ultimate goals could have been achieved more subtly, and with strategic wisdom. To Sun Tzu, victory is the critical object, but the elegance and sophistication by which victory is achieved are also important. Sun Tzu's insights into strategic excellence have an aesthetic quality. Balance, poise, efficiency, action or avoidance of action, patience, control, and precision in timing are all combined in the excellent strategist.

An important distinction between military and legal strategists is that while legal strategy is also about winning and achieving outcomes that favor your clients, unlike Ed Concannon's approach to law practice in *The Verdict,* there must be limits to your behavior. Otherwise you will end up as ominously dark as he did, a kind of antichrist of the law. The irony, however, is that in his own way Frank Galvin is at least as corrupt as Concannon, if not more so. Galvin won the trial verdict in spite of his incompetence. He not only did a totally unprofessional job, but committed a crime by breaking into a nurse's mailbox to obtain her telephone records so he could track down his key witness. He lied to his client and to witnesses. He misrepresented his identity. He refused what appeared at the time to be a reasonable settlement offer ($210,000), and then failed to communicate that offer to his client for personal reasons rather than being concerned with the client's best interests.

This idea of the limits of legitimate professional conduct is an intriguing ethical and moral dilemma for the legal strategist. For Musashi and Sun Tzu, there were no limits. Anything was appropriate as long as it helped to defeat the opponent. This has long been the case in warfare, although international conventions have been created in an attempt to restrict some of the worst forms of barbarism. While law is at least theoretically different in terms of setting behavioral limits on lawyers, the lawyer's ethical obligation to zealously represent a client tends to cloud the issue.

If you take away Ed Concannon's use of the spy and his apparent intimidation of one of Galvin's expert witnesses (a Doctor Gruber who conveniently disappeared to a remote island rather than staying around to testify as agreed) then much of his behavior was consistent with what a lawyer is supposed to do when representing a client. Much of what Concannon did reflected strategic excellence, although ultimately he let his pride and arrogance blind him. He was apparently unaware of his client's alteration of the victim's hospital admission record. He didn't knowingly put on perjured testimony. I have little doubt that he would have been willing to do so if his clients told him the truth about what occurred, but he didn't face this problem because he didn't know. Otherwise, as dark as Ed Concannon seems, he handled the case in the way a zealous lawyer should. This, in itself, is a message about the role of the effective lawyer and the tradeoffs it can demand.

Concannon did make several serious mistakes that cost him the case. Ironically, they can be tied to his unethical behavior. One mistake was that he came to rely too much on the intelligence his planted spy was feeding him. Instead of using his own skills, he trusted someone who ultimately betrayed him. He spent too much time playing to the younger associates in his law firm, revealing his ego as much as his skills. Frank Galvin, on the other hand, was the worst model of a lawyer. He was unprepared, negligent, and unprofessional. He had little idea of the worth of his case, and engaged in both criminal and unethical behavior. Galvin won, but he was a sloppy, pathetic, professional embarrassment.

If Sun Tzu were speaking directly to a legal strategist and evaluating the quality of how a case was handled he would not only look at the outcome, but would be very concerned with how it was achieved, at what costs, its timing, and would want to know what actions were necessary. This idea of excellence is the same as that of professional craft and pride in one's work on behalf of the client. This is obviously the ultimate meaning of a lawyer's professionalism—achieving the best results for the client as efficiently and with the least waste or expenditure of resources as possible. Sun Tzu captures the elements of both excellent and inept strategists in the following passages:

> Supreme excellence of the strategist: *"[T]o fight and conquer in all your battles is not supreme excellence; supreme excellence consists in breaking the enemy's resistance without fighting."*

> The five faults common to imperfect strategists: *"There are five dangerous faults which may affect a general: 1) recklessness, which leads to destruction; 2) cowardice, which leads to capture; 3) a hasty temper that can be provoked by insults; 4) a delicacy of honor that is sensitive to shame; and 5) over-solicitude for his men, which exposes him to worry and trouble."*

> Six calamities caused by a bad strategist: *"[A]n army is exposed to six several calamities, not arising from natural causes, but from faults for which the general is responsible. These are: 1) flight; 2) insubordination; 3) collapse; 4) ruin; 5) disorganization; and 6) rout."*

> Adapting your strategy and tactics to the particular qualities of the enemy: *"He who can modify his tactics in relation to his opponent and thereby succeed in winning, may be called a heaven-born captain."*

> The most skillful strategist: *"[T]he skillful leader subdues the enemy's troops without any fighting; he captures their cities without laying siege to them; he overthrows their kingdom without lengthy operations in the field."*

Strategic excellence lies in winning with ease: *"What the ancients called a clever fighter is one who not only wins, but excels in winning with ease."*

Positioning oneself to make defeat impossible: *"[T]he skillful fighter puts himself into a position which makes defeat impossible, and does not miss the moment for defeating the enemy."*

Concealing your underlying strategy: *"All men can see these tactics whereby I conquer, but what none can see is the strategy out of which victory is evolved."*

Pragmatic Definitions of Victory

Too often we get caught up in a conflict and forget that it is only a means to an end. Sun Tzu tells us how to recognize and concentrate on our goals, outlines what is involved in defining the terms of victory in the situation with which we are engaged, and offers a variety of approaches that increase the likelihood of success and reduce the costs of the campaign, or, for our purposes, the case.

Defining the specific terms of victory for your client, and your opponent, is important because deception, false impressions, and hiding behind masks and illusions, are key elements of strategy. Both you and your opponent will be constructing false images of positions and desires in an effort to achieve desired goals. Understanding the terms of your victory, and the most likely terms of your opponent's victory, helps you hold your perspective against the illusions and the distorting pressures generated by the heat of conflict. Being anchored in this way gives you a secure place from which to perceive, and this helps you see through the illusions.

Think of the examples presented in Chapter Three. A central aspect of each case involved the need to identify the terms of a client's victory. Frank Galvin never even had a sense of what his case was about. Because he had no idea of what it was worth, the jury had to ask if it could increase the award beyond the maximum requested in the complaint. In the pharmaceutical case, one of the first things the corporation must do is figure out what is in its best interests. This is likely to be the only way it might be able to avoid an overwhelmingly expensive and damaging process. In the third example, in which the company ignored the warnings about a defective pressure-release valve, the plaintiffs defined their victory in reasonably realistic terms,

the defendants failed to do so, and an indignant jury surprised everyone by breaking the particular jurisdiction's pattern of past jury verdicts in a way that couldn't have been predicted by either side. Even
though strategy is goal-driven, the process of setting goals is quite
imperfect. The point that strategy is goal-driven is reflected in Sun
Tzu's following observations:

> Victory, however defined in the particular situation, is the only
> purpose of strategy: *"In war let your great object be victory, not
> lengthy campaigns."*
>
> Five essentials for victory: *"There are five essentials for victory: 1)
> he will win who knows when to fight and when not to fight; 2) he will
> win who knows how to handle both superior and inferior forces; 3) he
> will win whose army is animated by the same spirit throughout all
> ranks; 4) he will win who, prepared himself, waits to take the enemy
> unprepared; 5) he will win who has military capacity and is not inter-
> fered with by the sovereign."*
>
> Knowing yourself and the enemy is essential for victory: *"If
> you know the enemy and know yourself, you need not fear the result of
> a hundred battles. If you know yourself but not the enemy, for every
> victory gained you will also suffer a defeat. If you know neither the
> enemy nor yourself, you will succumb in every battle."*
>
> Gaining victory through the enemy's weakness: *"To secure our-
> selves against defeat lies in our own hands, but the opportunity of
> defeating the enemy is provided by the enemy himself."*
>
> The functions of defense and offense: *"Security against defeat
> implies defensive tactics; ability to defeat the enemy means taking the of-
> fensive."*
>
> Victory through no mistakes: *"Making no mistakes is what estab-
> lishes the certainty of victory, for it means conquering an enemy that is
> already defeated."*
>
> The timing of victorious action: *"[T]he victorious strategist seeks
> battle after the victory has been won, whereas he who is destined to
> defeat first fights and afterwards looks for victory."*
>
> There are hopeless battles for even the most masterful strate-
> gist: *"There are roads which must not be followed, armies which must
> not be attacked, towns which must not be contested, commands of the
> sovereign which must not be obeyed."*

Indirect methods are essential for victory: *"In all fighting, the direct method may be used for joining battle, but indirect methods will be needed in order to secure victory."*

Using the enemy as your own strategic tool: *"How victory may be produced for them out of the enemy's own tactics—that is what the multitude cannot comprehend."*

Adapting to the enemy's purpose: *"Success in warfare is gained by carefully accommodating ourselves to the enemy's purpose."*

The strategist begins the process of strategic analysis by asking where the case should be when it is finished. Another way of saying this is, "What would be a victory or a win in the specific case?" What does your client want to achieve? What does your client need to achieve? Much of what you do as a lawyer is based on developing a pragmatic and realistic sense of what you are trying to achieve. You then design your strategy to achieve your goals. This seems a very obvious premise, but far too many lawyers don't do it.

Winning is at the heart of strategy, but the real nature of victory in a specific case is a slippery phenomenon. Part of winning is knowing you have won. Knowing whether you have won or lost requires that you understand the meaning of victory. This is neither as easy nor as obvious as it sounds. Go back to Sun Tzu's description of the five essentials for victory (i.e., knowing when and whether to fight, the ability to handle forces, a powerful *spirit*, preparation, having strategic capability without excessive interference from the sovereign). The combination of these factors becomes a complex process requiring great insight, skill, and experience. Nonetheless, at least it tells you the factors that will make a difference in the outcome—if you are capable of understanding and mastering them.

The ability to define goals and objectives includes knowing not only the conditions of a complete victory, but the importance of the smaller and more intermediate wins that increase the probability of your ultimate success. Victory must be defined in terms of what is realistically achievable, given the skills and resources available to the strategist, compared to those within the control of the opponent. The strategist cannot afford to be deceived by the lure of ideal or even highly desired goals. Of course, the desires of a military leader, sovereign, business executive, or a lawyer's client to achieve a specific end must be taken into account when creating strategic goals, but the strategist fails if the desired goals are not realistic.

The lawyer's job is to educate the client about the case's reality, and to help the client determine what outcomes are desirable and realistic. Clients often don't know what they want. This is part of defining the specific terms of victory and defeat. Going into a negotiation, for example, some clients will insist they don't want to go to trial. Divorce clients will often say, "Do whatever you want in talking to the other side, but I am not willing to go through a messy and humiliating divorce trial." Or they may tell their lawyers they want to be vindicated in court, and that they are willing to fight to the end no matter what the cost might be. The problem is that either client may have something he or she wants hidden from public scrutiny or from the other side.

The strategist must help the client see that what is desired may not be achievable or, if it is, that it can be won only at enormous cost. This is among the most important aspects of strategy. Humpty Dumpty could not be reconstructed. A lost life cannot be reanimated. A shattered relationship cannot be put back together and changed back to "the way they were." Without a realistic and pragmatic definition of goals and the terms of victory, other strategic considerations are irrelevant. The strategist must therefore ask at the beginning of the strategic process, What is it that we seek to achieve? What does our victory look like? Where do we want to be when this is done? What price will the process exact, and how much of that price are we willing to pay to achieve our ends?

Consider the outcome of Example 1, *The Verdict*. At the end of the story, Concannon is defeated and Galvin is redeemed. In an ironic reversal, the woman who spied on Galvin for Concannon is on her way down the path of despair and self-loathing from which Galvin has apparently been saved. We don't know what Concannon is experiencing because he sold his soul many years ago. To paraphrase what he tells his spy Laura when she is in his office feeling terrible about what she is doing, "Our job isn't to try hard or do our best. Our job is to win and that's all that matters. It is winning that pays for all the luxury and power that the firm represents and that you like." It is easy to see Sun Tzu and Musashi saying such things, and that fact brings out an important and necessary distinction between lawyers, sword-fighters, and military strategists.

It also highlights the fact that Galvin had his own goal of personal redemption that confused his loyalty to his client. Concannon lost because he wanted to show off and crush and humiliate Galvin for refusing to settle. The judge had his own goals, which included helping the defendant win through his trial rulings and punishing Galvin for insulting him during the pretrial conference. The defendant doctors had the goal of covering up what they had really done by blaming the victim. While the defendant Archdiocese had the goal of justice, as it conceived it to be in its own minimalist terms, it also had the goal of not looking bad publicly while keeping its losses to a reasonable level. Ultimately, the Archdiocese turned over the decision-making to its insurer and lost its soul in the process. Each participant in the drama operated from a different frame of reference. It is the lawyer's job to recognize this and to take advantage of the nuances rather than exacerbate the situation.

The Client's Goals and Resources Drive Your Strategy

What your client wants to achieve is a good place at which to begin your strategic assessment, but that isn't the end of the analysis. Acquisition of the strategic information needed to make intelligent judgments about achievable goals and directions is an essential part of the process. Are your client's various goals realistic in the sense that they could be achieved with the right combination of resources? If the goals are realistic, how can they be achieved with the least expenditure of energy, resources, time, and money? These questions help you define the terms of real victory in the specific situation. Other important questions are: Who are my friends? Opponents? Potential allies? Who will be the decision-makers? What resources are available to help you achieve the desired goals? Will it cost more to achieve your client's goals than the outcome is worth? Is the client willing to pay to achieve what he or she sets out as the desired outcome? Regardless of what a client tells you at the beginning of the case, will he or she continue to be willing to pay the price as litigation costs and attorney fees mount and there is still a chance of losing? These questions and others are addressed in greater detail in the specific considerations of negotiation and trial found in Chapters Ten and Eleven.

While we should begin the strategic process by determining what our client wants to achieve, the client may desire an unrealistic, unreasonable, excessively expensive, unaffordable or improbable outcome. Even if the outcome is achievable given the expenditure of sufficient

78

amounts of professional time and client resources, the client may not be able to pay what is reasonably required to win the case. The problem of an injured party being unable to afford the price of justice is a common dilemma for members of the legal profession. Many lawyers in private practice take a percentage of their cases *pro bono,* or for substantially reduced fees, but even this does not satisfy the demand or need for legal services. This creates significant resentment among the general public whose legal needs go unsatisfied, who expend significant sums for legal services that produce compromises and ambiguous outcomes, or who must capitulate to opponents because they cannot afford the cost of legal services. The fact that other professionals also don't give away the bulk of their professional services without charge doesn't prevent the ever-increasing resentment of lawyers.

The client's goal may be less than your professional judgment tells you is reasonably attainable. If an offer is made that you communicate to your client, he or she may want to settle at a considerably less advantageous point than you consider to be in his or her interest. If Frank Galvin, for example, had done a competent job of representation, he might have determined the settlement value of the case to be in the $1.5 to $2.0 million range and that there was a 75 to 80 percent probability of a $3.0 to $3.5 million verdict. If Galvin had communicated the defendant's $210,000 offer to the plaintiff's representative, what would Galvin have done if she said, "take it"? Assuming a significant difference between your client and yourself, if you haven't educated your client as to the outcome probabilities of the case—based on your best professional judgment—and if you settle for a great deal less than you think you could realistically achieve, you have lost the case from a professional perspective, even if your client feels satisfied. A troubling aspect of such a situation is that it involves differing attitudes toward risk-taking by both the lawyer and client, ones that in extreme cases may be in conflict. A lawyer might well be willing to accept the greater risk involved in trying for significantly larger amounts because of the nature of the contingency fee arrangement or simply because the case is only one of a large number of cases. The individual client with one chance at victory is likely to be in a different frame of mind, particularly in a case such as this in which the client's representative, the victim's sister, was from a working-class family.

Your job is to obtain an outcome in appropriate cases that represents the best resolution. The opportunity to achieve that outcome depends on your ability to evaluate, distinguish, justify, cope with stress and ambiguity, and persuade. This is why you are being paid. If the plaintiff in *The Verdict* accepts the $210,000 offer, one reason might be that Galvin failed to educate his client on what was a realistic outcome. The victim's sister may, however, simply decide that this is what she wants to do, that this amount represents all that is needed to achieve her purposes, and that to take more would be a kind of sinful profiting from the terrible thing that happened to her sister. The ultimate choice is your client's, and if the reasons are valid, the client has the complete right to accept or reject the settlement. Practically speaking, however, if there is a large difference between the action you recommend and that chosen by the client, put your advice in writing and have the client sign the document. Otherwise a client's memory can become highly selective.

The Importance of Defining Your Opponent's Victory and Resources

Just as important as defining the terms of your victory is knowing what your opponent considers a victory. We have already noted Sun Tzu's observation that, *"If you know the enemy and know yourself, you need not fear the result of a hundred battles. If you know yourself but not the enemy, for every victory gained you will also suffer a defeat. If you know neither the enemy nor yourself, you will succumb in every battle."* Obviously, the promise of perfection if you "know" the enemy and yourself is somewhat overstated, particularly in law because there are many ambiguities, never perfect knowledge, and the frequent need for intelligent risk-taking. The idea of critical and extensive strategic knowledge working to greatly enhance the probability of your success does, however, remain entirely valid as a basis for making the right strategic decisions and increasing the likelihood of winning through being able to more realistically define the terms of an attainable victory and the best pathways to that outcome.

In *The Verdict*, for example, Ed Concannon had extensive financial resources while Galvin was virtually broke. Concannon had a large team of lawyers and investigators at his disposal, and time to prepare totally in addition to possessing absolute ruthlessness. As is too frequently the case, however, he also had a client who covered up the truth. At the end, this exploded on him and his client. Along the way, however, Concannon intimidated witnesses, planted favorable media stories, and paid a woman lawyer a considerable sum of money to seduce Galvin so she could relay inside knowledge back to Concannon. The woman developed an intimate relationship with Galvin in order to reestablish herself with Concannon's firm, but eventually stopped short of telling her boss a critical piece of new information that Galvin had discovered. This is why Caitlin Costello Price's unexpected rebuttal testimony destroyed the defense case so completely.

Knowledge of your opponent's desires and goals gives you significant insight, added leverage, and increased control. It doesn't make sense to engage in the most intense aspects of conflict unless you can't achieve your goals through other strategic paths. Often, the easiest way to win what you want is to give your opponents something they value highly. But you must be able to figure out what it is that your opponent values. This is reflected in Sun Tzu's urging that we win by accommodating ourselves to the enemy's purpose. This won't work with a stupid or overly greedy opponent, but it must be explored before you go too far into a strategic conflict. If you are forced to fight, rather than engage in the legal system's version of diplomacy, then as Sun Tzu says, "*be terrible*" in your onset—but be terrible only when necessary.

Experienced strategists who understand the strategic implications and realistic value of a case can often resolve a dispute with a relative minimum of effort. This is possible because they have the ability to see past the preliminary and intermediate moves most lawyers muddle through. They can bypass those stages and go directly to the endgame. The process can be akin to a chess match between Grandmasters who completely understand the ultimate implications of each move. Upon reaching a certain point, they are able to visualize how the game will turn out. Rather than waste time, they capitulate or acknowledge a draw without bothering to waste time with the intermediate moves that lead to the already known result.

Trials and negotiations are not as precise as chess matches, in which the outcome possibilities are contained within the confines of a chessboard, but there is still a level of expertise that legal strategists who have mastered the "game" achieve that enables them to recognize whether there is any reason to continue within a range of acceptable solutions. After they have exchanged critical information, these experienced strategists can often reach a relatively quick and amicable settlement because they know approximately where they are going to end up. Whether they take a thousand steps to complete the journey, or do it in two or three "giant" steps, they know they will reach the same place—or one so close to the other's that the incremental difference is not worth the cost to pursue it.

For lawyers who are being paid an hourly rate, one of the main problems is that there can be a subtle disincentive to settle quickly and efficiently because of the resulting loss of income. Many lawyers do possess the knowledge, experience, and ability to see how the case is likely to be resolved, but they keep fighting because it is in their own financial interest—even if it may be contrary to their client's. A shift to a by-the-job rate for lawyers is one way some corporations are attempting to alter this incentive situation. Some litigation firms have eliminated hourly billing or time-based fees, instead agreeing on a total-job price with a client. Other highly specialized litigation firms are emerging that are able to concentrate resources and evaluate cases in ways that are more concrete and accurate than an ordinary firm. In this way, market pressures are driving law firms to be more responsive to clients who are increasingly concerned with legal costs. By using a specialized legal firm, corporate clients can know how much they are going to pay for legal services, and don't have to establish contingency accounts to cover the chance of being hit with unanticipated legal fees that are far higher than expected.

An important question in evaluating any case is whether there is a way to achieve your desired goal (or come close) while giving something of significant value to your opponent. If this is possible, rather than simply seeing negotiation as a "zero-sum game" in which you must take or give everything and your opponent must either win or lose, you should be able to see that you can alter the equation. Not all situations allow for such a strategy, but many do. If you make it possible for your opponents to achieve an approximation of their needs and goals, you may be able to convert what is originally seen as a "zero-sum game" into a mutually beneficial "positive-sum game." Or you may be able to design an outcome that seems mutually beneficial to your opponent.

A settlement of a dispute between Microsoft and STAC Corporation, after a patent infringement verdict in favor of STAC, which had sued Microsoft for using STAC's disk-compression technology, reflects the ability to create mutual benefit for two opposing corporations while giving each disputant something it values highly. Both Microsoft and STAC ultimately valued a different outcome than what was decided by the trial jury—Microsoft gained control of the technology, while STAC received profits on its invention and also long-term investment. Arguably, the Microsoft/STAC dispute should not have been allowed to degenerate into the full-blown hostility it did, but could have been a situation in which each side could obtain positive outcomes or at least prevent something negative from occurring. Each company was much more likely to benefit from exploring such options rather than wasting more money on lawyers. Unfortunately, as we will see in the subsequent discussion of the paths of strategy and the function of trial, the parties were only able to come to agreement after the jury reached a verdict in favor of STAC. Until then, it was a *David v. Goliath* situation in which the relatively small STAC was stalemated by the immensely wealthy Microsoft.

Helping Your Client Define Victory

Clients and lawyers can have unrealistic or ambiguous expectations of the extent and probability of financial return or loss. This can be a particular problem in the early stages of a case when imagination runs rampant and discovery hasn't yet begun. Inexperienced clients who have seldom—if ever—been involved in the litigation process often have no idea of the real costs of the legal process. Most clients with legal problems or needs have seldom gone through litigation and consequently have no sense of its costs and demands.

Many business clients, on the other hand, have become increasingly sophisticated and knowledgeable about costs and have begun to set up mechanisms to review, evaluate, and reduce their legal costs. Corporations have begun to bring a larger share of their legal needs in-house and have increased the role and responsibility of corporate counsel. Some have even begun to use in-house litigators to resolve disputes. Corporations are also paying closer attention to the billing practices of the private firms they use and are seeking audits and explanations for the fees and expenses they are being charged. This has proved extremely embarrassing to several firms as audits have uncovered padded bills and partners' personal expenses charged to client accounts.

Given most clients' lack of knowledge concerning the costs of the legal system, the lawyer must be certain clients understand the operation of the fee contract. The most frequent ethical complaint clients make against their lawyers has to do with the ambiguities of fee arrangements and the lack of any clear explanation about fees and expenses. The problem is caused not only by clients' lack of familiarity with the cost of legal representation, but also by the fact that many legal costs depend on how hard the opponent fights and how long the case drags on. This is often not within the control of the lawyer.

Clients commonly experience "sticker shock." If a plaintiff accepts an offer of $350,000 in settlement in a contingent-fee case, the lawyer will usually be entitled to receive at least one-third of the recovery depending on the contract, plus expenses for such things as discovery, investigative services, telephone, postage, copying, travel, expert witness fees, and so forth. To the extent a structured settlement is part of the deal, one in which the defendant's payments are made over a period of time rather than immediately, the lawyers often take their fee from the beginning payments rather than as the money is paid out over time. Even if everything is paid up front, $150,000 could be reasonably taken out of the $350,000 award, with the plaintiff receiving $200,000. This sounds like a huge deduction, but without fees, rent is not paid. Secretaries and receptionists quit. Creditors dun. Spouses leave. Bankruptcy is declared. The temptation to "borrow" client funds "just until some money comes in," may increase. Law is a profession, but it is also a practical, highly competitive business that must be conducted as such. Overhead costs, hidden costs and indirect costs eat into lawyers' gross incomes. For a single-lawyer law office, a lawyer who requires a $100,000 net annual income must generate at least $200,000 worth of gross revenue. This doesn't even begin to take into account the unrecoverable expenses many lawyers put into a case during the process of investigation and initial development. At $125 per billable hour, this requires the equivalent of nearly 2,000 billable hours of work for which the lawyer actually collects from the client or opponent. If we assume 50 weeks per year of legal work, this means 40 hours per week of collectable billable hours specifically assignable to clients' cases must be charged.

Because not every moment can be spent on matters that are billable to clients, and not all bills are fully collectable, 65 to 70 hours per week of work may be needed to achieve 40 billable hours. Of course, many lawyers have discovered that they can almost magically enlarge their billable time by using billing units in which the minimum unit billed is, for example, one-quarter hour. Even if only two or three minutes are actually spent on a telephone call relating to a client's case, the lawyer bills for the complete unit. If a lawyer sched-ules telephone calls in bursts and makes 5 to 10 brief calls on behalf of various clients, he or she could conceivably bill a total of 1.5 hours to those clients even if all the calls only took a total of 15 to 20 minutes. Lawyers learned this lesson from auto mechanics and doc-tors. Many doctors have walked through hospitals saying, "Hi, how are you?" to all their hospitalized patients and then billed the insur-ance companies for full visits with fifty patients that might have taken a total of two hours. If the reports of rampant Medicare fraud are true, some doctors bill without even actually visiting their patients.

If the client is familiar with the real costs of legal representation, he or she can make informed judgments about whether to proceed, and how far to push a dispute. This includes knowing how much a dispute is likely to cost in both fees and expenses. It is impossible for a client to make informed judgments about a pragmatic victory without knowing how much of the client's resources should be risked to achieve the victory and the probability of a positive outcome.

Knowledge, Planning, and the Sources of Strategic Information

Sun Tzu tells us: *"If you know the enemy and know yourself, your victory will not stand in doubt; if you know Heaven and know Earth, you may make your victory complete."* Sun Tzu's approach to planning is that of a continuous process in which the strategist does not create a single plan, but is constantly adapting, altering, reevaluating, probing, testing the quality of knowledge, and rethinking the approach to be taken. He speaks of the need to acquire detailed information in "real time," not only to continue planning, but to recognize the moment when strategic action is required if victory is to be gained or defeat avoided. Strategic planning is a fluid process aimed at acquiring the best information directly from the raw source, as well as from alterna-tive sources so that it can be verified. Consider Sun Tzu's following observations on strategic planning:

The strategist plans continually: *"The general who wins a battle makes many calculations in his temple ere the battle is fought."*

Lack of planning causes defeat: *"The general who loses a battle makes but few calculations beforehand."*

Be always aware of opportunity and danger, plan for action continually: *"[W]hat enables the wise sovereign and the good general to strike and conquer, and achieve things beyond the reach of ordinary men, is foreknowledge."*

The strategist seeks direct knowledge of the enemy: *"Knowledge of the enemy's dispositions can only be obtained from other men."*

Gather intelligence continually, be always prepared, victory or defeat can occur in the briefest moment: *"Hostile armies may face each other for years, striving for victory which is decided in a single day. This being so, to remain in ignorance of the enemy's condition...is the height of inhumanity."*

The strategist must seek to know everything: *"If you know the enemy and know yourself, your victory will not stand in doubt; if you know Heaven and know Earth, you may make your victory complete."*

A strategist needs special skills of evaluation and control: *"The natural formation of the country is the soldier's best ally; but a power of estimating the adversary, of controlling the forces of victory, and of shrewdly calculating difficulties, dangers and distances, constitutes the test of a great general."*

Lack of forethought by a strategist leads to defeat: *"He who exercises no forethought but makes light of his opponents is sure to be captured by them."*

The strategist must acquire an enormous array of information through a wide variety of senses, processes, evaluations, and strategic decisions long before the dispute is resolved. In a military context, the sources of information include history, maps, scouts, patrols, satellites, spies, intelligence gathering systems, direct observation, and so forth. The military strategist is continually seeking to verify and cross-check information through direct observation, because there is no substitute for hard data gained from personal senses. Anything else can be disastrously misleading, deceptive, and hypothetical. Information from direct observation helps cut through assumptions, hopes, and illusions. You can still be fooled, but you can also perceive things that can't be understood through any other method of information acquisition.

The best information is often that which your opponent is unaware you are seeing. The problem is that you may only think the opponent is unaware. "Red herrings" and disinformation campaigns are intended to take advantage of this belief. They are designed to make you think you have acquired critical knowledge about your opponents that takes on great significance because they don't know you have it. The problem is that your adversary may have been leaking the information to you as a diversion, or with the intention of sending you off on an unproductive or destructive tangent. For the strategist, nothing and no one can be fully trusted. Everything must be checked out in as many ways and from as many different directions and sources as possible. This is the mistake Ed Concannon made in Example 1. He became overly dependent on the information his spy was leaking to him about Frank Galvin's activities. Because it had proven reliable several times he trusted it—to his downfall. This is one way to set up an opponent.

In law practice, the legal strategist acquires information from such sources as interviews with clients and other witnesses, investigation, discovery, site visits, expert analysis of the evidence, past behaviors of opponents and others relevant to the case, opponent assessment techniques, and knowledge of human nature and human behavior. These sources also include awareness of the tendencies of the key decision-makers, discovery of apparent and real chains of command, the case's physical evidence and exhibits, scientific and technical studies, public records, newspapers and journals, and computer analysis of diverse data.

Patterns and trends in arguably similar situations play important roles in aiding the strategist to decide on strategic courses of action. Ask yourself, for example, if you were representing either Deborah Anne Kaye or the defendant hospital in *The Verdict*, where would you begin in order to determine how much you should seek or how much you might be responsible for paying—depending on your assessment of probable liability? In the book version of *The Verdict*, the jury ultimately returned an award of $5 million. Given the levels of verdicts today in cases in which defendants have covered up their negligence, and a patient has suffered brain damage, paralysis, or been rendered comatose, a jury could easily return a verdict in the tens of millions. A New York jury recently returned a verdict of $47.3 million (reduced to $30 million for present value) in a case in which a newborn baby suffered brain damage when doctors failed to respond adequately to an obvious emergency situation. Another New York jury gave an $8.8 million verdict for retardation injuries and a paralyzed arm caused by loss of oxygen to the brain at birth. Such verdicts must be factored into a lawyer's estimations of a case's outcome potential during the processes of diagnosis, strategic planning, negotiation, and trial. One of the obvious and important messages to take from these two examples is that in evaluating your case you must make certain (to the best of your ability) that your client hasn't done something outrageous, and always look for signs of outrageous behavior by your opponent's client.

A significant source of information is obtained by talking to other people experienced in some aspect of the same type of case or situation, including other strategists. These people are among the most helpful sources in providing perspective and valuable insights. A brief period spent with knowledgeable people can save a tremendous amount of time through avoidance of blind alleys and wasted resources. For a lawyer, discussing matters with the kinds of people who will be deciding the case is an invaluable source of strategic information. It is particularly important to include people who aren't lawyers. Non-lawyers are more likely to give you the kinds of reactions you would receive from jurors or other critical decision-makers. Lawyers tend to look at cases from a too legalistic and technical perspective. Non-lawyers, on the other hand, often approach the problem from a fresh viewpoint, as people who don't have special technical knowledge and professional biases, and can help provide a reality check to help lawyers guard against their own subjectivity.

talk to others

This approach is necessary because a serious problem for any legal strategist is that, after being immersed in a case, a lawyer too often comes to see it subjectively. This is why lawyers have begun to use mock jury trials in case preparation. They hire ordinary people to serve as jurors, because bringing in the perspectives of "real" people (i.e., nonlawyers) helps to determine how best to "sell" the case to their peers. This approach identifies the strengths and weaknesses of the legal "sales pitch," and the lawyer as "pitcher." The failure or success can be in the plot, the script, the actors, or some combination. It might be saved by a rewrite or recasting, or it could possibly demonstrate that the production is doomed to bomb.

To Become the Enemy

It isn't enough to study your opponent. Acquiring essential strategic knowledge requires that you must become your enemy. You don't simply prepare your side of a contest, but need to visualize the entire case from the perspective of your adversary. This allows you to see yourself and your weaknesses and strengths in a different light. To "become the enemy" means we must know how the world functions. Then we put ourselves into the perspectives and frames of reference of our opponents in order to see into the opponent and into ourselves. Ask yourself such questions as:

- What are my opponent's strengths?
- What would he or she perceive my weaknesses and strengths to be?
- How would the opponent evaluate our side?
- How is he or she likely to think I or my client can best be manipulated?

Your enemy is one of your most important sources of knowledge, but the concept of "enemy" is multifaceted and complex. It includes not only the opposing lawyer, but the opposing client. It even includes current allies or neutrals, because they have the potential to become opponents if the balance of the case shifts for some reason. In the Agent Orange and asbestos litigation and the resulting settlements, for example, plaintiffs with different levels of exposure or different manifestation periods are often at odds over how the money paid in by the defendants is to be allocated and distributed. They were allies as they fought to convince the companies to pay for their injuries or diseases. But allies in the struggle can easily become enemies in the distribution after the initial victory is won. They may fight viciously over the terms of distribution of the fund or benefits of victory—the "spoils of war." The Soviet Union was our enemy prior to Hitler's invasion of Russia, even signing a nonaggression pact with the Nazis. After Hitler's invasion, the Soviets were our military ally until the end of the war, and then returned to being our enemy for two generations of the Cold War following their seizure of the Eastern European bloc.

The concept of "enemy" also includes potential adversaries, and those who declare themselves to be neutral. The world is ruthless, and allies or seeming friends may be using you as a stalking-horse. A neutral posture can be a sham, or only a temporary position. Shifts are made as the stakes change, or deals are cut by you or your opponents. Potential adversaries can be standing on the sidelines, hoping to step in after you and your opponent have been exhausted. Rather than expend their own resources, they are letting you use up yours.

"To become the enemy" means literally to put yourself in a state of mind so that you are able to develop your opponent's strategy. Put yourself in the opposing lawyer's place, although even that isn't enough. This also needs to be done with clients and witnesses. Your clients will often lie to you, so you can say, "Look, I believe you, but it doesn't matter if I believe you. It doesn't even matter whether you believe in your case, because we aren't making the final decision. You are paying me and retaining me as your lawyer. I believe you, but I need to present this situation to you from the perspective of what the other side is going to say, and how they are going to look at it. What matters is what is going to happen if we have to go to court and offer the facts, claims, and explanations you are giving me. As it stands right now, you are going to lose—and lose big."

Knowing Your Enemy and Yourself

No matter how perceptive we are, everyone is deceived about something at some time. Often we are deceived because we want to be deceived, or at least want to avoid confronting something unpleasant about ourselves or our preferred vision of things. There are many things we want to believe about ourselves, about the world, and other people. Self-deception is an important coping mechanism for everyday life. It allows us to blur the harshest edges of reality. We create illusions to mask reality, to retain our cherished beliefs, and to make us feel better. The strategist cannot afford to have illusions. There is a price to pay for this clarity. But if you want to be a strategist, it must be paid.

The strategist must transcend his or her illusions, false beliefs, and self-deceptions because once we learn to go beyond our own illusions we can perceive more clearly and deal better with others and control any attack our opponent makes. As a strategist, if you need to believe in something, then it is possible for you to be deceived by others who discover your illusions and dependencies. This is the essence of strategic control: the understanding and control of self. You become vulnerable because you don't want to give up your beliefs, which give you comfort and security. The strategist must try to not be deceived, and to avoid deceiving herself, so that she is able to look into her opponents and know what they are doing, rather than being misled by strategic illusions. When the strategist does this, she has the ability to see through an opponent's strategy to the reality.

To Become the Decision-Maker

Although the issues are discussed at length in subsequent parts of this book, it is vitally important to consider the nature of the decision-maker you must influence or persuade in the process of achieving your goal. Among lawyers' strengths and weaknesses is the fact that they are trained skeptics. They won't or can't buy into another lawyer's emotional or punitive arguments. That's why there are juries. One of the reasons there are different outcome probabilities for each strategic path—trial, negotiation, mediation, arbitration—is primarily because it is very difficult for a plaintiff's emotional and thematic intensity to be taken seriously by a defense-oriented opponent. This difference relates to the distinct nature of the decision-makers in each process. The defense lawyers in Example 3, in which two workers were disfigured and maimed because of a defective pressure-release valve about which the defendant had been warned, refused to settle, and ended up with a jury verdict more than eight times greater than what plaintiffs would have taken in settlement prior to trial. The defense lawyers and their clients simply couldn't accept the probability and potential for such an outcome.

Throughout the various settlement paths you are forced to work through lawyers and clients. Each works according to different assumptions and burdens of proof or persuasion. Lawyers have their own jaundiced and often economically self-interested views of the world; clients are also subjectively caught in their own conceptions of what should happen. Increasingly, judges have become involved in settlement negotiations in order to force the lawyers and clients to face reality. One of the problems with this, of course, is that it is the judge's reality—rather than the jury's—and this judicial pressure can cause problems of its own.

Both you and your client need to be able to see how people who are not subjectively involved in the case will evaluate the facts and the witnesses. To do this, you must become the decision-makers. Put yourself inside the analytical, motivational, experiential, and emotional worlds of the people who will decide the case and look at it through their awareness. When you do this, you will know how to adapt your strategy to present it to those decision-makers in a way they will understand and accept as valid.

The decision-makers include juries, judges, administrative boards, agency personnel, bailiffs, and so forth. It includes the principals on the other side of the dispute or opportunity, because they will ultimately decide if there is to be a settlement or a deal of some kind. How will they view the terms, and the people? Why will they see something as acceptable or offensive? Regardless of what they might like to do personally, do they have a constituency they have to appease, placate, or impress? Putting yourself in the place of the decision-makers requires knowing everyone who has an important decision-making connection with the case, and the conditions under which they will, or must, function when making their determination. This requires evaluating the case with respect to understanding the people empowered to make the decisions that will substantially affect the case's outcome. The trial lawyer must ask, for example, "If I use this witness, what is the jury going to think about this person?"

The identity and characteristics of the ultimate decision-makers vary depending on which strategic path you are using to resolve the controversy. In a negotiation, for example, the immediate decision-makers are the opposing lawyers and their client or clients and you and your client. Often an insurance company will be a key decision-maker, regardless of the apparent parties in interest. In *The Verdict*, the insurance company was a major player, and this ultimately cost the defendant because the company representative rejected the plaintiff's last-gasp settlement overture on the eve of trial. The concept of client is not simple or singular. Regardless of the captions in a complaint, and the rules of professional responsibility, you must put the "client" in context. This requires knowing who actually has formal and informal authority, who has to pay the money, what monetary and nonmonetary values they hold, and to whom they are listening and on whom they rely. Similarly, you need to understand the potential collateral consequences for the "client" that reflect other obligations, opportunities, embarrassments, motivations, or consequences that on the surface appear unrelated to this specific case or situation.

In many disputes for which people use lawyers, there is the invisible looming presence of the "decision-maker of last resort." This influences the perspectives of the negotiators. Obviously this refers to the judge, jury, or binding arbitrators, and the inherently risky nature of the process. Much of a lawyer's task as a legal strategist includes developing a sense of how those decision-makers of last resort are likely to resolve the controversy. This includes questions of allocating liability, responsibility, and consequences. To do this you must step back from your adversary perspective and look clearly at the evidence

look at evi d from
↓

and people in the case from the viewpoint of those decision-makers. Part of this involves enhancing your ability to look at the case with fresh eyes, but it also ties into the kinds of information you are seeking to acquire. This is why judges' past decisions in similar cases are useful, and why presenting the case to real people (i.e., nonlawyers) as an advisory group can provide you with important insights as to critical strengths and weaknesses.

Dealing With Your Client's Negative Information in Strategic Planning

Part of strategic planning and intelligence gathering is to trust no one completely. Clients are often hiding something or have what they consider a dark secret they are afraid will be exposed. They don't reveal it to their lawyer until and unless investigation brings it out, or it is exposed through discovery. What they fear will be revealed may or may not be directly related to this case. Divorce clients are not likely to want allegations of adultery made public. Many others simply don't want to go through the substantial stress and emotional trauma of trial.

One of my clients, the plaintiff in a personal-injury case, had serious tax problems involving failure to file tax returns for a significant number of years. He was afraid this would come out if the personal-injury case ever went to trial or even progressed significantly into discovery. During settlement negotiations we were careful to act in a way that communicated we were willing—even expecting—to go to trial. But I knew my client wouldn't risk his tax problems being exposed. This meant he was willing to take a lower settlement than would have been probable if the case were taken to a point near trial. The problem was that if the defendant's attorney even sensed the plaintiff wasn't willing to go to trial, there would be little chance for a substantial recovery through a negotiated settlement.

Ultimately, the plaintiff wouldn't budge concerning his desire to settle at what would otherwise be a too early point, and this altered the timing of our settlement strategy by compressing and accelerating it. Because of this, the settlement was significantly lower than his injuries would otherwise dictate. His fear of possible criminal prosecution, or being subject to substantial civil penalties and back taxes, was something he could not overcome. He wasn't willing to take a chance, and it was his right to make the choice. His settlement valuation included the fact that he put significant value on preserving his privacy and secrecy. This was part of that particular client's definition of victory. The extra 30 or 40 thousand dollars we could most likely have obtained through using "eve-of-trial" brinkmanship, was less important to him than the risk that his tax problems would be revealed.

Another client wanted a substantial settlement, but also didn't want the case to go very far. Although not certain of her true motivations, I suspected that there was a good chance she had worked during her claimed period of disability; that her personal doctor padded the medical records regarding the frequency of her required therapeutic treatment, both to recover more in medical insurance and to increase the medical expense figures to create a more substantial settlement; and that since the plaintiff was in a cash-only business, the defendant's discovery might have brought closer scrutiny of her actual cash flow and unreported income than she wanted. We ended up with a good settlement, but not as high as we would have obtained had we ridden the process to a point closer to trial.

This highlights the fact that your own client can be your case's worst enemy. Clients frequently tell lies and half-truths, and omit critical information. Many clients are, in essence, following their own strategic paths in which they treat you as someone entitled to information only on a "need-to-know" basis. They, of course, decide what they think you need to know. Providing you with complete truth and honesty about what they have done or failed to do is often not part of the process, at least not until they totally trust you, or it becomes absolutely necessary because your investigation has made you suspicious. Then a client, or witness, may simply shift to the next level of deception, ambiguity, and equivocation, which they hope is beyond your awareness—or at least your ability to disprove. Sometimes they may just lie straight out and dare you to disprove them.

Clients haven't accepted the validity of the American Bar Association's Code or Model Rules of Professional Responsibility. They aren't worried about getting disbarred, and are operating according to whatever principles of behavior they follow in their own lives. Don't let your feelings be hurt because a client lies to you or fails to tell you everything. I was recently talking to a young lawyer who had returned from her first plea-bargaining meeting with a prosecutor. She was representing her first criminal client, and had spent a large amount of time researching and preparing arguments on behalf of her client.

But the prosecutor produced information showing that the defendant had lied to his young attorney. In addition to feeling totally offended, professionally embarrassed, hurt that her client had lied to her, and that her time had been wasted, this young lawyer was trying to discover why it had happened. She, after all, felt she was trying to help the defendant, and was totally committed to representing him zealously. When I asked her whether it made sense to think that someone who had spent his life as a hustler and con artist, who was willing to rob, beat, rape, or murder another person, would hesitate to lie to her or not tell her everything, she began to understand that you have to be realistic about the nature of the people with whom you are dealing. She started to understand that most clients see the lawyer as nothing more than a tool through which they are seeking to achieve their own results. As has been mentioned, a lawyer is his or her client's instrumentality. You may see yourself as a person. They see you as a means to an end.

In any event, regardless of the existence, cause, and source of such constraints, the legal strategist can't afford to let the opponent know about these limitations. The hard question is what can be done when the strategic image you must project is so completely different from the conditions set by your client. If the lawyer allows his knowledge of the client's real desires, conditions, and instructions to interfere with his strategic spirit, and comes across too passively or weakly, a skilled opponent is likely to sense something is wrong and try to force the issue. When an opposing lawyer in a personal-injury case starts attacking the weak points—perhaps your plaintiff's preexisting back problems from before the accident—you must be prepared to respond convincingly to sell what at least appears to be a solid trial case.

In this case involving a client's back injury, and my suspicions about her honesty, we never had to deal with the issue of whether the client was actually willing to go to trial. The opponent's insurance company accepted that she was willing to do so because it fit into its expectations, and bought the premise that she was. At a critical point in the discussions, a clear and convincing explanation of what would happen if the case were tried was used to send the message that we would try it if necessary. Because we obviously understood the important aspects of the case and articulated them convincingly, why wouldn't we try the case if a reasonable settlement wasn't reached? Such a representation is distinct from the issue of whether I was authorized to go to trial with the particular client, or actually would go to trial if a satisfactory settlement wasn't reached. In normal circumstances we would. In a system based on confidentiality and zealous representation, an opponent simply isn't entitled to this information and the truth may suffer. The possibility of a trial, whether real or simply believed by the opponent to be a realistic option, is an integral part of generating and sustaining the pressure that is responsible for settlement.

There are penalties to be paid when a client's deceptions come back to haunt you. Whether corporate in-house counsel or law-firm litigator, part of developing your defense strategy requires you to look closely at your case and discover what particular kinds of factual situations are likely to explode on you when handed to a jury or other critical decision-makers. The worst cases, such as when there has been suppression of information concerning the consequences of pharmaceutical products, as was alleged with silicone-breast implants, create a significantly enhanced probability for punitive damages as well as an increase in the likelihood of plaintiffs being awarded larger amounts of the "softer" categories of damages, which are largely discretionary with the jury. These include such damages as those for pain and suffering, the value of the harm to health, to quality of life, or harm or mutilation to the plaintiff's body.

In the silicone-implant situation, for example, the group of defendant companies created a settlement fund in excess of $4 billion in an attempt to satisfy plaintiffs' claims. The settlement soared to this level after discovery of documents reluctantly produced by the defendant companies, which revealed there had been a coverup that had lasted for almost 20 years. Thousands of innocent women had suffered side effects from the implants that could have been avoided if the companies had been honest. The callousness that this coverup represents had the potential for generating such jury hostility that, if the cases were tried to juries, the total damages would likely far exceed the $4.25 billion fund set up by the defendants. A Texas jury, for example, recently awarded a woman $5.2 million in one case involving a leaking breast implant. A Nevada jury returned a plaintiff's verdict of $3.9 million compensatory damages and $10 million punitive damages in a similar case. A thousand such Texas awards would equal $5.2 billion, and close to half a million women filed damage claims against the settlement fund in the class action.

A $4 billion settlement sounds enormous, but is a great settlement deal for the defendants. The $4 billion is obviously several orders of magnitude below the defendant companies' cumulative potential liability. The silicone defendants were going to lose huge amounts of money. The only questions were when and how much. Given the trends and probabilities, $4 billion now seems embarrassingly low. That is one reason the original settlement agreement has fallen apart, and it is unclear what will happen. There have been several recent medical studies that have down-played the health effects from silicone implants, but in the Nevada case mentioned earlier, the new studies were introduced and the jury ignored them. Given the nature of litigators and the high-stakes game being played out in this area of litigation, members of the plaintiffs' bar have questioned the good faith of the researchers involved in the studies, even though the scientists are working for the country's most respected institutions.

A coverup also happened in the asbestos cases, where it became known that Johns Manville (and other companies that either used or manufactured asbestos) suppressed information for decades that revealed they knew the health dangers from asbestos. This is almost certainly why Owens Corning was hit with a $54 million punitive damage judgment in the three asbestos cases mentioned earlier. It is why cigarette companies now are concerned about the potential for tens of billions of dollars in liability if it is proved that they deliberately enhanced the chemical addictiveness of cigarettes while simultaneously denying cigarettes were addictive. The cigarette companies used all their weapons in an attempt to stop the FDA from classifying nicotine as a drug, even though internal memoranda obtained from at least one company clearly demonstrate the industry's knowledge of the addictive effects of nicotine and the ammonia-based enhancement techniques the companies used to increase nicotine's effects.

Recognizing an Opponent's Strategic Patterns

Both Sun Tzu and Musashi tell us it is dangerous to be predictable or to use the same approach more than twice in succession. Sun Tzu says, *"The student of war who is unversed in the art of varying his plans, even though he be acquainted with the five advantages, will fail to make the best use of his men."* Applied to legal practice, this can mean that it is dangerous when other people have access to certain types of information about us, such as, "this person bluffs up to this point, makes it look like they are going to court, and then backs off and settles 99 out of 100 cases." Or perhaps, "They usually raise their final pretrial offer with a 25 percent increment after the jury is sworn in and the selection doesn't appear to be clearly in their favor, or after the second or third witness if the opponent's presentation is coming across reasonably well." Such insights can win the case for you, or lose it if you are the one who is unaware about how predictable you have become.

An increasing number of lawyers and insurance companies are keeping files on the ability and effectiveness of opposing lawyers. As sophisticated computer information systems make it easier for attorneys to identify individual tendencies about lawyers with whom they have never dealt, they will access information on opponents that enhances their own strategic analysis.

Some of this information, at least in generic terms, will be readily available. Much of it, particularly the most specific and individualized, will be kept secret. You will not know that you have begun to exhibit predictable tendencies. You won't be aware that intelligence files are being kept on you, revealing how you handle cases and how you should be handled. An opponent may come to know your patterns, tendencies, favorite techniques, finances—both personal and professional—better than you. They will be able to ignore your deceptions and wait patiently because they know what you will do and where you are going.

On the other hand, strategy is about deception and how to fool an opponent by leading him to expect one course of action and then capitalizing on his expectation by doing something else. A significant advantage can be gained by surprise. The NFL's Washington Redskins used such a strategy in a key playoff game. As the television analysts described how the team had run to a specific point every time during the regular season, the Redskins faked that play and went another direction for a touchdown—untouched. The opposing team had obviously identified the same tendency as the expert analysts because its defense congregated on the point to which Washington had run in every other similar situation during the entire season. The lesson is that you can use your patterns and repetition of specific tactics to set up an opponent's expectations. Then when everything is on the line and you are going for the ultimate win, vary your tactic and win by the unexpected move. You may have fooled the opponent deliberately by creating the pattern, or you may simply have come to recognize you had fallen into the pattern and decided to take advantage of it. As the Redskins' example demonstrates, the predictability of your pattern can become a strategic weapon in which you create the expectation that you will do the same thing again and cause your opponent's strategy to be set up to counteract it. Then you vary your approach and your opponent will be defending at the wrong place, or at the right place but at the wrong time.

Converting Planning to Action

Preparation, awareness, and planning eventually give way to action. Focusing and unleashing our energy when the right time has come is part of this. So is the need to recognize the right timing of action, the idea of efficient versus wasteful action, and awareness of the variety of forms that action takes, both when used by us and against us. What is involved in taking effective strategic action is captured in the following principles offered by Sun Tzu:

The many sides of strategic action: *"The skillful tactician may be likened to the shui-jan. Now the shui-jan is a snake that is found in the Ch'ang mountains. Strike at its head and you will be attacked by its tail; strike at its tail, and you will be attacked by its head; strike at its middle, and you will be attacked by head and tail both."*

Do nothing without purpose: *"Move not unless you see an advantage; use not your troops unless there is something to be gained; fight not unless the position is critical."*

Caution and judiciousness in strategy: *"If it is to your advantage to make a forward move, make a forward move; if not, stay where you are."*

The power derived from actually engaging the enemy: *"On the day they are ordered out to battle, your soldiers may weep, those sitting up bedewing their garments, and those lying down letting the tears run down their cheeks. But let them once be brought to bay, and they will display the courage of a Chu or a Kuei."*

Lengthy campaigns exhaust spirit and resources: *"When you engage in actual fighting, if victory is long in coming, the men's weapons will grow dull and their ardor will be damped. If you lay siege to a town, you will exhaust your strength."*

The importance of being an unpredictable strategist: *"[T]he student of war who is unversed in the art of varying his plans, even though he be acquainted with the Five advantages [the five essentials for victory] will fail to make the best use of his men."*

A strategist uses the enemy's resources whenever possible: *"[A] wise general makes a point of foraging on the enemy."*

Avoid bluster, pretense and inconsistent behavior: *"To begin by bluster, but afterwards to take fright at the enemy's numbers, shows supreme lack of intelligence."*

Use of the opponent's vulnerability and creating surprise in strategy: *"Appear at points which the enemy must hasten to defend; march swiftly to places where you are not expected."*

Being unpredictable and selecting from the infinity of strategic methods and tactics: *"Do not repeat the tactics which have gained you one victory, but let your methods be regulated by the infinite variety of circumstances."*

Understanding spirit and timing in strategy: *"[A] soldier's spirit is keenest in the morning; by noonday it has begun to flag; and in the evening his mind is bent only on returning to camp."*

Beware of deception and illusions used by opposing strategists: *"Humble words and increased preparations are signs that the enemy is about to advance. Violent language and driving forward as if to the attack are signs that he will retreat."*

Understanding advantage, balance, and inferiority in strategy: *"If equally matched, we can offer battle; if slightly inferior in numbers, we can avoid the enemy; if quite unequal in every way, we can flee from him."*

Probing the enemy to acquire strategic information: *"Rouse him, and learn the principle of his activity or inactivity. Force him to reveal himself, so as to find out his vulnerable spots."*

Following the path to victory: *"If fighting is sure to result in victory, then you must fight, even though the ruler forbid it; if fighting will not result in victory, then you must not fight even at the ruler's bidding."*

Avoiding costly attacks on the enemy's strength: *"To refrain from intercepting an enemy whose banners are in perfect order, to refrain from attacking an army drawn up in calm and confident array—this is the art of studying circumstances."*

Seize or threaten what the enemy values: *"Forestall your opponent by seizing what he holds dear, and subtly contrive to time his arrival on the ground."*

Always leave an outlet for the enemy to escape: *"When you surround an army leave an outlet free. Do not press a desperate foe too hard."*

The strategist must always be ready to recognize and seize opportunity in the midst of adversity: *"If, in the midst of difficulties we are always ready to seize an advantage, we may extricate ourselves from misfortune."*

Understanding and taking advantage of the opponent's vulnerability: *"When asked how to cope with a great host of the enemy in orderly array and on the point of marching to the attack, I should say: 'Begin by seizing something which your opponent holds dear; then he will be amenable to your will.'"*

Flexibility, adaptability, and unpredictability: *"By altering his arrangements and changing his plans, he keeps the enemy without definite knowledge. By shifting his camp and taking circuitous routes, he prevents the enemy from anticipating his purpose."*

Relentless, properly timed aggression: *"[T]he good fighter will be terrible in his onset, and prompt in his decision."*

Energy and action: *"Energy may be likened to the bending of a crossbow; decision, to the releasing of the trigger."*

Six
Musashi's Method:
The Book of Five Rings

"The Way of the warrior is resolute acceptance of death."
Musashi, *The Book of Five Rings.*

While Sun Tzu's system outlines how a military strategist approaches a potential conflict, Musashi is much more oriented toward the individual strategist. Sun Tzu provides the emphasis on structure, planning, large-scale campaigns, and political reality. Musashi, while professing to offer this, is in fact most useful for visualizing what the strategist in action must do. Taken together, their insights are powerful. Each approach has obvious implications for lawyers who combine the need to design and implement campaigns to protect and advance their clients' interests, and must also be able to execute the tasks individually. Unlike Sun Tzu's general or commander, Musashi's strategist is simultaneously general and foot soldier. This is the situation in which most lawyers find themselves, one in which they are responsible not only for the underlying strategy but for direct "hand-to-hand" interaction with opponents and others. Musashi offers many advantages to the lawyer who is responsible for such an undertaking. It is also why a synthesis of the insights of both strategic masters is so critical.

This chapter presents what I consider to be the basis of Musashi's system. It continues the discussion of the structure of *The Book of Five Rings* begun in Chapter One, and then presents the nine basic elements of Musashi's *Way*. The nine elements provide the basis for the strategist's ability to take strategic action. The first of Musashi's five *"rings"* is the *Ground Book,* in which he sets out the underlying principles of strategy reflecting the strategist's essential state of mind and the foundation of the method that must be followed by the strategist as she sets forth on the *Way*. This includes strategic spirit, perception, discipline and training, the distinction between strategy and technique, and what Musashi calls *resolute acceptance of death*.

The *Water Book* is Musashi's second *"ring."* It presents insights into the nature of strategy, how it must be learned and practiced, the individual's state of strategic awareness and perception, the centrality of the strategist's spirit, and the importance of being in control of oneself and the opponent. Water is a particularly important symbol because it represents adaptability, flexibility, and power. Water can be a trickle or a flood—seemingly trivial or immensely powerful. Water is change and adaptation. Water is hard as ice, hot as steam, potentially volatile and explosive when under pressure, or tranquil as a forest pool. Water can conceal much beneath its surface. The changeable nature of the strategist and the conditions of strategy are therefore represented in this *"ring"* of Musashi's strategy.

The *Fire Book* is the third *"ring."* In it Musashi moves more to the basic principles of strategic action. The *Fire Book* deals with the strategist's behavior in the midst of individual combat and battle. It involves intensity, ferocity, and the ability to consume. It explains how to control events, when and how to attack, and the means of responding to the conditions of struggle in ways that increase the probability of gaining victory. Fire is the spirit of winning, the energy of combat. Coolness and balance are always essential, but the strategist must also be able to attack and defend with the greatest intensity, as well as take whatever action is needed to damp, douse, or avoid the fire of an opponent's spirited assault.

The *Wind Book*—the fourth *"ring"*—is primarily concerned with Musashi's critique of others' approaches to strategy. While at times it seems almost like a salesman's attempt to denigrate competitors' products and elevate his own to preeminence, it offers important insights concerning our tendency to follow narrow schools of technique rather than be open to the broad range of flexible approaches necessary to a total understanding and application of strategy. *Wind* represents the force of tradition and how we allow ourselves to be deceived and limited by rigid adherence to a particular approach or school. An important part of Musashi's system is understanding the teachings of all schools, while following none. This will be seen more clearly in the discussion of the nine elements. Musashi emphasizes broad and diverse learning that focuses on achieving desired outcomes, overcoming the limits of specific techniques, and controlling oneself and the opponent. As with the other *"rings,"* he emphasizes the ideas of strategic "seeing" and "perception" as critical means of penetrating the masks donned by opponents and avoiding being deceived by their clever strategies, posturing, and maneuvering.

The fifth and final *"ring"* is reflected in the *Book of the Void*. The *Way* of strategy derives its power from the *Way* of nature. In Western thought a *void* is only a vacuum or emptiness. But for Musashi the *void* is as real and integral as the concept of zero in mathematics. Just as zero is a nothingness that makes the system possible, the *void* is the source of great power and natural rhythm. When we learn to join with it—and in fact we are already part of it—we become able to focus and apply our power. The *void* in Musashi infiltrates and permeates the other four books or *"rings"* of strategy. The *void* is everything within which all else takes place. It is the song of the universe, the background power—that which makes it all work.

The Nine Elements of Musashi's *Way*

Musashi describes nine points a strategist must master to achieve the *Way*. They are:

1. *Do not think dishonestly.* don't deceive yourself.
2. *Become acquainted with every art.*
3. *Know the ways of all professions.*
4. *Distinguish between gain and loss in worldly transactions.*
5. *Develop intuitive judgment and understanding for everything.*
6. *Do nothing that is of no use.*
7. *The* Way *is in training.*
8. *Perceive those things which cannot be seen.*
9. *Pay attention even to trifles.*

These nine points are the foundation of an integrated system—they create the *Way* of the strategist. Musashi's nine points reflect the strategist's holistic approach to knowledge, awareness, and action. They represent the great range of knowledge a strategist needs. This knowledge isn't limited to external information or hard data. The strategist's knowledge includes reliance on a greater range of human senses and faculties than we normally use. This should not be thought of as some kind of mysticism, but the knowledge reflects the kinds of awareness attained when an individual integrates perception, intellect, self-control, and experience within a disciplined system. Knowledge of human nature—and of self—are critical parts of this awareness, which is gained by increasing the quality of the information being processed. This is achieved through greater alertness, focus, and concentration, by becoming more aware of the power of intuitive understanding, and by gaining access to the sources of our natural human power. Finally, Musashi's nine points of strategic mastery include not only acquiring information, but being able to recognize and discriminate among different types of information, to identify the implications of knowledge and action essential to achieving the strategist's desired goals, and to take action.

Do Not Think Dishonestly

The inherent paradox in *do not think dishonestly* is that strategy is inevitably dishonest. For both Sun Tzu and Musashi, strategy is premised on deception, trickery, taking advantage of others, spies, fooling people, and masking your intentions. Deception is an integral part of strategy. If, for example, your client gives instructions to the effect, "Come back with a settlement on these terms or don't come back," this creates important strategic constraints you don't want your opponent to discover. Or what if your client tells you, "We can't risk the exposure of taking this case to trial. Fifty other cases hang on the outcome of this one. We can't afford the publicity because it would hurt our sales too much. So whatever strategy you use, I want this case settled, but I don't want to pay more than $3.5 million."

Think back to Sun Tzu's warning that the general must keep his true plans secret even from those closest to him. Deception as to your real terms of operation and your intentions and goals is an inevitable and necessary part of strategy. This is the only way to ensure that your opponent will not be able to spy out your true intentions. Consider the impact of the spy's betrayal of Frank Galvin's plans in Example 1. Until she withheld the final piece from Concannon, Galvin was stymied at every turn. If your opponents discover your real conditions of operation they will have the knowledge needed to control you and shift the probable outcome more in their favor. Access to the secret knowledge of your case—even if only suspected by your opponents—gives them greater leverage, which can't always be overcome, regardless of how much innate strategic ability you might possess.

This is why it is so important to keep your inner knowledge and aspirations secure, and to conceal your desired outcomes from your opponents. Otherwise, you will have unwittingly provided your adversary with the proverbial Archimedean lever by which you can be manipulated. The strategist can't count on the spy "getting religion" or falling in love with him as Laura does with Frank Galvin. In the real world, Laura would tell Ed Concannon what Galvin discovered through Caitlin Costello Price, and Concannon would convince the judge to either limit or exclude the testimony of the admitting nurse before she ever takes the stand, or he would make a surprise settlement offer and get out before any more damage has been done.

Musashi's warning, *do not think dishonestly,* doesn't mean you should not deceive your opponent. The strategist must deceive opponents. Instead of honesty to others, Musashi means don't deceive yourself, and don't think dishonestly when you are acting as a strategist. Don't become entangled in the strategic illusions you are creating to fool others. See clearly into things, perceive their essence. Have no illusions about yourself, people, justice, your client, or your opponent.

This means Musashi's definition of dishonesty is quite different from what we would generally consider moral or ethical. Being a strategist inevitably involves dishonesty of the kind involved in manipulating and deceiving other people. This is what lawyers do and what any strategist takes into account. The strategist is an advocate, and an advocate strives to achieve his goals at the expense of his opponent. Nearly 2,500 years ago, Aristotle recognized that the fundamental nature of an advocate's rhetoric involved elevating one's own position while weakening that of the opponent. The task has not changed—the strategic game is still intrinsically manipulative and deceptive. An ordinary person would call much of this behavior dishonest, or at least of a questionable ethical or moral nature. The strategist must address this dilemma because the strategic approach clashes with many belief systems about truth, honesty, and openness. Because we can become obsessed with and consumed by the steady diet of deception and manipulation, there is a need to put limits on the dishonesty of our strategic behavior. This behavior must be relegated to the "arena" within which lawyers compete. It can be troubling even then, but is potentially destructive if allowed to seep outside its legitimate context.

Become Acquainted With Every Art

Musashi's next point is to *become acquainted with every art*. Being a master strategist requires an enormous information and knowledge base. For the legal strategist, it means you must learn the insights and methods of an extraordinary range of other disciplines. The most important part of the practice of law is an understanding of humans and human nature—knowing what people think, know, desire, fear, and want. Anyone who wants to master strategy must seek knowledge from a wide variety of sources and in many different areas. This is necessary because the practice of law is a reflection of the problems and needs of society, and of the people within that society. Literature, religion, ethics, history, science, philosophy, war, psychology, sociology, economics, and so forth are attempts to capture what humans are all about, and to understand the nature of the universe we inhabit and our place and responsibilities within it. These areas of knowledge are continually and unpredictably relevant to a large part of law practice and strategy. If we are unaware of this diverse knowledge base, then we are ignorant of strategy.

The previously mentioned concept of *all things with no teacher* reflects another set of important insights. The insights are, if you as a person are too narrow; or if you follow just one school of thought; or if you become trapped inside the teachings of any one school; or if you read only law as opposed to books on psychology, philosophy, science, politics, ethics, morality, religion, and so forth; or if you have only that limited kind of experience—then you can't know what you need to know to be a strategist. This is part of Musashi's urging to become acquainted with every art.

Know the *Ways* of All Professions

Not only is it necessary to seek voraciously after knowledge in the general sense, it is essential that the strategist know the *ways* of all professions. Musashi means that we should know the mission, the method, the secrets, the flaws, the assumptions, the techniques, and the values of the various professions, including how they work and why. If we know this, we can identify strengths and weaknesses and be able to attack or defend critical points.

As a legal strategist, think about the importance of knowing the methods and underlying principles relied upon by economists, doctors, psychologists, statisticians, pathologists, chemists, police, and so on. We must know them to be able to "use or abuse" them. This knowledge of the ways of other professions is something we synthesize and integrate into our own knowledge base. It then becomes part of our own way. Consider a lesson from the O.J. Simpson murder case. The trial lawyers needed to understand statistics, chemistry, forensics, medicine, DNA methodology and its limits, police procedures, the psychology of spousal abuse, intricacies of human nature, and much more that they never heard mentioned in law school. Lawyers on each side had to master the inner details, assumptions, and outer limits of these disciplines to contend with witnesses, create themes and strategies, and evaluate the truth and falsity of all aspects of the case. Nor can the lawyer's knowledge be superficial if the case is to be presented or defended effectively.

Distinguish Between Gain and Loss in Worldly Transactions

A fourth aspect of Musashi's way is to learn to *distinguish between gain and loss in worldly matters.* This principle has to do with the strategist being able to know the nature of what is a realistic victory, and to be able to discern what is valued highly enough by an opponent that obtaining or defending it will enhance the probability of reaching agreement and concessions. In other words, look at the big picture. Know the world. Have real experience. Don't be too abstract. Know what people value, not only as individuals but as part of institutions. What is important to them, to others, to you, and to your clients? Why is it important? How do you know it is important?

Knowing what people value as gain or loss relates to Musashi's point that, *"The way of strategy is based on overcoming men."* As a lawyer you are in a competition to win, to gain advantages for your clients in terms of worldly matters. This means you must be able to define what victory is in the specific situation and create strategies that help you achieve it. We are manipulating people to achieve victory and avoid loss. This is generally defined in terms of tangible, concrete outcomes that are measurable in worldly terms. But understanding gain and loss is not simply an all-or-nothing, "zero-sum game." Often, more can be gained by a legal strategist who is willing to allow opponents to share in the gains. Otherwise, the short and longer-term costs of the process can exceed the gains, either from the financial or nonfinancial perspective. Human nature is an integral element, because making people feel good and allowing them to save face has much to do with winning; both with winning now, and being able to win in the future by not making enemies who will be intent on avenging themselves on us or our clients. This was one of Frank Galvin's mistakes in *The Verdict*. He got lucky, but made an enemy of the judge who will be waiting for the chance to get even. Any practicing lawyer knows there are times you must stand up to a judge, but also that you must be aware of the enormous discretionary power judges possess and must never gratuitously alienate those who wield that power. Galvin stupidly took a cheap shot at his trial judge and will eventually pay for it, as will his future clients.

Develop Intuitive Judgment and Understanding for Everything

Another of Musashi's principles is the need to *develop intuitive judgment and understanding for everything*. But what is *intuitive judgment*, and why is it important? Musashi begins with the recognition that not everything is neatly rational. Such qualities as guts, instincts, subliminal perception, along with the distillation of experience that allows you to anticipate, recognize, and react to stimuli seemingly without thought, are all attempts to describe real human abilities that operate on the edges of our conscious rationality. Being able to adapt almost instantaneously and to make quick decisions are integral skills of the strategist. In terms of the ability to gain an edge and succeed in conflicts, the best strategists are able to make quick decisions without thinking about them explicitly before acting.

Strategists do this by developing their intuitive powers to a heightened degree. They learn to allow what some would call their "body-mind" to take over in conditions of great stress, intensity, and conflict. When we do this, it isn't that we are not thinking when we perceive, act, and react, but that our rational minds are more fully integrated with our physical and emotional selves so that a deeper, more visceral form of thought operates on richer and more holistic levels than when we are functioning within the limits of linear, explicitly conscious rationality.

A very simple example of this "body-mind" process is a dancer beginning to learn a new dance. The dancer has to go through a conscious thought process that might sound something like, "Hey, my feet are supposed to go here, and my partner over there. But we keep bumping into each other." A dancer who has to go through this type of conscious mental dialogue has not yet mastered the intricacy of the dance. On the other hand, an experienced dancer has instantaneous recognition of cues and the ability to make virtually simultaneous reactions in time with the music. If you have to think about what is happening and how you should respond, your timing, rhythm, and positioning are already flawed. While the dancer is thinking about what he or she is going to do, the movement becomes out-of-sync with the music because the timing and rhythm are off.

The master strategist is like a dancer who has fully internalized his or her art form. Such a dancer knows the depth, characteristics, and parameters of the stage on which he or she works. The dancer knows where others involved in the performance will be at what time. The dancer knows the lighting and music, and can feel and respond to the audience and play to that source of energy. The dancer knows the air, surrounding scenery, and the floor underfoot, feels the time between beats, and uses the power of expression and presence. Such awareness is part of mastery—regardless of the specific discipline.

Whether a dancer, musician, athlete, sword-fighter, or legal strategist, the only way we will be able to act quickly enough is to have developed intuitive judgment for the type of situation with which we are dealing. In Musashi's terms we must have trained constantly to make quick decisions, and must "teach our bodies strategy." The legal strategist's task is often more complex than that of dancers or musicians following a choreographed sequence or musical score that they have practiced or performed many times. Closer parallels to the legal strategist's task are musical jam sessions in which the musicians take inspiration from each other, improvisational theater, or the flamenco dance form, which has a symbiotic relationship between dancer and guitarist and singer in which each creates rhythm, tone, mood, inspiration, and variation for the other. Whether artist or lawyer, functioning on that improvisational and reactive level requires the substantial knowledge base already described as being essential to strategic mastery, but that knowledge base must also be extended through experience, creativity, and a commitment to continued learning. All this is still not enough. The legal strategist, like the dancer, must train continually and constantly practice, visualize, and evaluate what he or she is doing and needs to do. This leads to Musashi's next point, that the *Way* is in training.

The *Way* Is in Training

There are many levels to Musashi's idea that *you must practice con-stantly.* The counterpoint, of course, is that "there is no fool like an old fool." Experience is essential to the strategist's development, but many people don't learn from their experiences. They repeat the same mistakes forever. You can't learn strategy by simply reading, talking, or thinking about strategy. You must do it and apply it and think about it and apply it some more and think about it and evaluate what you've done and gain from that experience. Becoming a strategist is not simply acquiring experience, but having the ability to learn from that experience, which is filtered, interpreted, critiqued, and refined through a constant commitment to drawing out the fullest meaning from what has occurred. You can't learn strategy without constant practice, but practice itself is not enough and experience without insight is insufficient.

As a strategist you are training your entire being to perceive, as-sess, and act, not simply observe. You are training to be able to func-tion through the integrated power of your mind, body, and emotions. No amount of intellectualized information can do this for you. The teacher can only guide, introduce, critique, and facilitate. Each strate-gist must make his or her own personal leap to the level of perception, awareness, and ability to act that is essential to the master strategist. This process is continuous and takes years of study, thought, practice, experience, and action.

Training and intuitive judgment are intimately related. Much of your training is intended to internalize your knowledge and experi-ence in such a way that you are able to perceive and act intuitively. Intuitive perception, judgment, and corresponding action are not en-tirely mysterious processes. In many ways they are learned and ratio-nal. The intuitive rationality, however, operates on more subtle levels, and with a richer complex of our intellectual and emotional resources than does conscious reason. It requires that we train ourselves to experience similar strategic realities, so that we can recognize the characteristics of the present challenge and react to them intuitively in ways that seem instinctive but really aren't. In other words, if we have seen the specific type of situation before, or at least experienced something sufficiently similar that it fits closely enough into our intu-itive patterns of perception that we are continually creating, refining, and extending into analogous contexts, then we see its essential nature and where it must almost certainly lead.

Training to recognize the appropriate timing of strategic situations is fundamental. Timing is a critical element not only of your assessment and strategic analysis but your action. The most elegant intellectual understanding of an opponent is meaningless if you can't convert it to effective strategic action. Musashi says, *"You must train day and night in order to make quick decisions."* But how do you do this? How do you train to adapt? How do you learn to respond quickly and accurately? How do you know how to take advantage? How do you decide when you should attack?

Lawyers are often a beat or two behind an action situation's strategic rhythm because there is an inevitable time lag between our perception, and the quickness with which we take corresponding action. There is delay between the time an event happens, a lawyer's perception of it, and our ability to react. This often happens, for example, with objections during trial. But that is just the most obvious example. Lawyers hear something but sit and think for too long—which could be only a half-second or less in some situations—before reacting. A mistimed response, however, can be all the opponent needs to realize an error has been made or information revealed.

The essence of effective strategic action is in being able to anticipate and then respond quickly. Seize the opportunity when it is there. Know when the opening is false. Train yourself to make quick or perfectly timed decisions, including the decision not to respond. Train yourself to adapt. Being proficient at timing requires that you put yourself into situations in which speed and intensity are heightened, and you must practice functioning effectively in those situations. There is no substitute for testing yourself under equivalent situations and then evaluating why you were able to function with the proper skill and timing, or why you failed.

Practice simulations, no matter how real they are made to seem, aren't enough in themselves, however. They can help immensely, but no one can be a true strategist until he or she has had the opportunity to apply his or her ability to real situations in which there are serious consequences for being wrong. In the fire of battle we have only ourselves to rely on. No simulation can create the same pressures as those situations that involve the consequences of failure or the rewards of success that are real and substantial. But simulating strategic situations is still extremely important and enables one to better evaluate strengths and weaknesses.

When functioning at advanced levels of skill, our brains are incredible tools. They are capable of making instantaneous jumps and transitions, and are able to recognize patterns while the patterns are still in the process of becoming or forming. Our brains are capable of functioning far faster than computers, and in ways that are infinitely more varied and complex. Developing this potential to the highest level takes constant practice, training, and experience. This requires a combination of knowledge, experience, practice, focus, and a balanced spirit.

As a lawyer engaging in trials and negotiations, you strive to reach a point at which you don't have to consciously think about what you are doing. The goal is to no longer have to go through a process of conscious linear logic in which you have to think, *"I see that she made an offer here and I think she's doing this, and her strategy is probably this, and so on."* By the time the lawyer has figured all that out analytically, the movement has become out-of-sync and has a corrupted rhythm. Intuitive judgment is the key concept because the strategist must respond quickly to avoid loss, or to take advantage of opportunities. When Musashi talks about *seeing into* your opponent, the *seeing* to which he refers is the ability to understand humans well enough to sense clearly and instantaneously what is happening, sometimes even before the other person is aware.

Perceive Those Things That Cannot Be Seen

Related to the idea of intuitive judgment are Musashi's principles of developing understanding for everything and learning how to perceive those things that cannot be seen. Such perception is obviously easy to describe and difficult to do. Musashi's concept of perception represents an important process through which the strategist takes in the data on which his or her judgments are based. When you know humans, what they value, how they act and why, and are able to function intuitively, then you can see past other's masks and illusions. When you have studied in the way required of the strategist you will be able to perceive the structure, rhythm, and timing of the strategic context. Factors and details that confuse others will be clear to you.

Listening and seeing are two of the most basic skills of any strategist. Although most people think they are listening to what others are saying and are seeing what is going on around them, they really aren't listening, seeing, and perceiving in the way that is essential to strategists. The process we use in our general life tends to be incomplete. The strategist needs to operate on a more complete perceptual level.

Musashi tells us that the strategist masters two methods of seeing, what he calls *perception* and *sight*. He observes that *perception* is strong, while *sight* is weak because it is too specific and narrow. *Sight* in essence is the trees, while perception includes the forest and the trees. He says:

> *"Perception consists of concentrating strongly on the enemy's spirit, observing the condition of the battlefield, fixing the gaze strongly, seeing the progress of the fight and the changes of advantage.... In single combat you must not fix the eyes on details.... [I]f you fix the eyes on details and neglect important things, your spirit will become bewildered and victory will escape you."*

This obviously means the strategist must focus beyond the immediate while still knowing detail and applicable timing. The strategist must see beyond the artificial and the deceptive. The strategist must perceive all about him. The strategist learns to *see* with his entire being and senses. In Musashi's words:

> *"When you become accustomed to something, you are not limited to the use of your eyes. People such as master musicians have the music score in front of their nose[when they play], or [master sword-fencers may] flourish swords in several ways when they have mastered the Way, but this does not mean that they fix their eyes on these things specifically, or that they make pointless movements of the sword. It means that they can see naturally."*

Part of the ability to *see naturally* is derived from a great amount of experience. Through the combination of experience, practice, and reflection, the strategist develops the ability to perceive an opponent's essence more accurately. Musashi observes:

> *"In the Way of strategy, when you have fought many times you will easily be able to appraise the speed and position of the enemy's sword, and having mastery of the Way you will see the weight of his spirit. In strategy, fixing the eyes means gazing at the man's heart."*

Heightened levels of perception require a combination of intensity, focus, knowledge, experience, and method because the strategist needs to hear more, understand more, and see more. It takes considerable training and commitment to achieve this kind of perception.

Knowledge is essential to heightened perception because when we know the significance of things we can see them more clearly and recognize when something that ought to be present is absent. Although this logic admittedly sounds circular, the simple fact is that we don't perceive the meaning of things because we don't know what they mean. Once we know what things mean and what to look for, we will truly *see* them.

Much of strategic perception is derived from understanding the special language of nonverbal communication. Nonverbal language involves such details as posture, how you react to stimuli, as well as how quickly or slowly you react, how and when you tilt your head, how you use your eyes, when you move back or forward, nervousness and displays of anxiety or your lack of anxiety, inattention, when you underline something or take notes, and much more. Tone of voice, amount and direction of eye contact, how unsure or certain we seem when problems suddenly arise, whether we become upset or angry, and what triggers those reactions are all part of nonverbal language that can be perceived.

A skilled strategist can read the meaning of these nonverbal cues. Certainly this awareness is fundamental to litigation and negotiation. Many people are skilled verbal liars. They control the intonations of their voice and project sincerity and believability. But even if you are adept on verbal levels of communication, you can give yourself away nonverbally. It is more difficult to deceive people on nonverbal levels, particularly if they are looking at you. If what is being said on the verbal level is incongruent with what is perceived on the nonverbal level, then the incongruence can be translated into terms useful for strategy. Is someone speaking words that communicate confidence, while the posture, position, or movements of their body, or their tone of voice is signaling hesitance and fear? What does the lack of "fit" mean between verbal and nonverbal cues, and between inconsistent nonverbal responses? We must learn to recognize the different levels of messages, and develop tests to discover which message is likely to be closer to the truth. This is why the legal strategist needs to have a full understanding of the case, so that cues and implicit messages can be interpreted in a heightened context of probability and significance.

But interpreting the significance and meaning of nonverbal language is only part of the strategist's task. The strategist also uses nonverbal language to send messages to clients, opponents, witnesses, judges, and juries. Because we tend to believe the impressions we obtain from others' nonverbal cues, the strategist who communicates effectively on nonverbal levels can be extremely persuasive and deceptive. This insight is also important in terms of determining the meaning of an opponent's nonverbal communication. All information must be cross-checked and evaluated. Nothing can be taken as true. A master strategist is quite capable of sending false messages that are perceived as being "more likely true" precisely because they are being transmitted on the nonverbal level. The likely truth must be put in context, and everything an opponent does should be distrusted.

Lawyers frequently miss nonverbal signals during the intensity of a trial or negotiation. The conflict's intensity, the high stakes at risk, and the almost instantaneous rapidity with which we must recognize cues, interpret them into terms useful for decision-making, and implement appropriate responses, cause us to function inadequately on the complex levels of perception, communication, and action. Additionally, lawyers and witnesses sometimes say things during discovery, investigation, negotiation, and trial that could severely damage their cases. Often the opposing lawyer isn't listening to the nonverbal cues. Sometimes the lawyer on the same side isn't listening and gets surprised when it is brought out later. *Listening* is one of the strategist's most fundamental skills, and one of the most difficult to master. We hear the person speak the words and see the movements, hesitations, emotional cues and nuances, but still don't perceive what they really mean. Listening, watching, absorbing, and knowing all that is happening is essential to being a good lawyer and an effective strategist.

One of the most basic reasons we don't listen with the complete awareness required of the strategist is that we tend to be so self-centered we think no one else has anything of importance to say. We are the center of our universe. Others exist only for our use and benefit. Others are important only in reference to us, and so it doesn't matter if we listen to them as long as they listen to us. This self-centered attitude is doubly troublesome for the strategist, because when it exists not only are we not listening to what others are saying, we may be revealing too much about our own case in an effort to impress people.

Another problem is that we often fixate on our planned action to such an extent that it dulls our sense of what is actually occurring. Even though it looks as if we are listening, we are just waiting for the other person to finish making noise so that we can voice our own statements. We are waiting for the moment we can jump in. We are so focused on what we have decided we want to say, or have planned to say, that we fail to hear what is actually being said.

Most of us feel fear, nervousness, and tension when we enter into conflict or a stressful situation. One way we manage the stress of conflict and performance is through structure, organization, and planning. Such preparation is important, but when we allow the fear and structure to control us—as we often do—our thorough planning becomes a crutch. This means the hypothetical conflict or stressful situation for which we have prepared dominates our awareness, and we are blocked from listening to and perceiving the real conflict.

Our ability to perceive is easily disrupted, particularly in very threatening or accelerated and intense situations in which instantaneous perception and action are required. This can occur even if we are otherwise good observers in nonthreatening situations, or in contexts with evenly paced and predictable rhythms—even if they are intense. Stress, and the tendency toward overreliance on a plan of action, often inhibit our ability to perceive clearly. What military strategists call the "fog of war" blocks our ability to perceive accurately and prevents us from making the instantaneous decisions needed to function effectively in conflicts. This concept stands for the combination of stress, fear, emotion, uncertainty, and chaos that is generated by intense conflict. The roughly equivalent condition can affect lawyers and witnesses during trials, but many of the same pressures can also be characteristic of certain phases of negotiation.

In operating within the "fog of war," the problem is in how we perceive and react in situations in which timing, outcome, pressure, and so forth are intensified, compressed, disjointed, and accelerated. In such situations, many people still function in a kind of slow motion, or continue to react at regular speed when they should have shifted to "fast-forward." Similarly, many people function well in intense situations as long as the rhythms are predictable. But much of strategy involves surprise, and creating deliberately altered conditions by which the opponent intends to throw you off balance, and then gain an advantage when you are startled. The strategist must anticipate the unexpected, and be able to overcome being surprised. The strategist also needs to be able to impose stresses on the adversary and to seize advantage when an opening is created.

Anticipation and focus are key to strategy. The perception of timing, rhythm, and flow is essential. The strategist's perception is a total awareness, one highly concentrated on specifics and details, while encompassing everything happening around you, within others, and within you. This special kind of perception is both detail-specific and "big-picture" aware. You must see all the pieces of the mosaic, as well as be able to perceive the entire "field" of conflict. Recognizing the patterns, signals, and limited set of options to which an action must inevitably lead enables you to react before the opponent's action is underway. This often happens at trial with both direct and cross-examination. Rather than waiting until the opponent causes damage with a questionable statement or line of examination, and then trying to rely on a relatively useless curative instruction from the judge, approach the bench and make your point about the potential for prejudicial impropriety. Cut short your opponent's path. Trials demand a level of concentration probably not achieved in anything else a lawyer does. They involve total focus. In what seems to be a paradox, this total focus allows you to see the forest and the trees simultaneously, as well as what they have been and will become.

Think about Mark Fuhrman's original testimony on cross-examination in the Simpson murder case. Given the nature of the police culture in major U.S. cities, the harshness of the task facing street cops, statements by several people about Fuhrman's prior use of racially derogatory statements, and his request for disability retirement due to job-related stress produced by working in the ghettos and barrios of Los Angeles, it was nearly inconceivable that Fuhrman had never used racial epithets. His denials were not likely to be true. Foresight—as well as hindsight—should have told the prosecutors that Fuhrman's denials were not true. He and the prosecution would have been better off to have admitted on direct examination that there were occasions when he had used what has come to be known as the "N" word. It was easy for defense lawyers to see past the illusion because they knew his denials almost had to be false. Prosecutors apparently thought they should accept Fuhrman's version because their prior experience in trying the average criminal case led them to think all they had to do was put a police officer on the stand, have him testify with the standard "cop-speak" that characterizes a police witness, and that the jury would buy the story. What was rarely mentioned in the various assessments of the trial was that the prosecutors were very inexperienced trial attorneys, not because of the number of trials they had under their belts (which was substantial), but because the typical criminal case is a "gimme" for the prosecution, a "slam-dunk," or a "piece of cake." Urban prosecutors rarely go up against really good, well-funded, prepared attorneys, so such prosecutors as Marsha Clark and Christopher Darden may have tried and won 100 jury trials, but that doesn't really matter. Their experience is roughly equivalent to a paraplegic running 100 meters against Carl Lewis. When such prosecutors with their "vast" experience have to try a case against a team of sophisticated defense lawyers, they often lose because they really don't know what they are doing.

Pay Attention Even to Trifles

If you observe everything and make certain all your loose ends are taken care of, you are far less likely to be surprised. *Trifles,* or seemingly small details, surprisingly often are pieces of the signals or data we need in order to understand what is going on. An opponent may have control of his or her illusions but there can be small, seemingly insignificant items that allow us to see the hidden truths. Remember that most of what we do as legal strategists involves reconstructing a past reality to make it seem favorable to our client's interests. Or we are projecting a future reality (i.e., the deal) that appears to be beneficial to the negotiating parties. In either situation there is an element of illusion.

It is almost impossible, however, to make the illusion perfect. Our job is to perceive the imperfections and know what they mean. Consider the Simpson case again. Only a totally thorough analysis of every piece of evidence in the case revealed the tiny strands of imperfection that could be added up to create arguments of reasonable doubt. One expert witness was forced by the defense to admit a statistical error. Another noted that a video of evidence in Simpson's home was not in the proper time sequence, allowing the defense to suggest there was something devious in the State's record-keeping. In most criminal cases these details would be overlooked, as well as others in the Simpson case concerning such factors as dryness of blood samples on swabs, defects in evidence-gathering techniques, and much more. Because everything in that case was examined with incredible intensity, it offered a paradigm of how defense counsel should approach trial evidence. Of course, virtually no criminal defendants have the resources needed to allow their lawyer to prepare a case with such thoroughness, nor do they have such an extraordinarily cooperative judge as Lance Ito, who essentially allowed the defense lawyers to say or do whatever they wished—often on the most tenuous of foundations.

The excellent strategist understands the significance of the small and often invisible incongruities that the ordinary lawyer doesn't notice, either because of perspective, or lack of time and resources. How many times has someone lamented, "I didn't think it was important," after some small thread led to the unraveling of an entire scheme? Similarly, if you pay attention to small threads and *trifles* in your own case, the opponent is less likely to be able to unravel your strategy. Signals about the *trifles* often occur on the nonverbal level of communication. Understanding nonverbal language is one of the best ways to "see into" someone else. Something an opponent does or doesn't do may seem insignificant at first, but in fact could be one of the most important ways they unconsciously reveal useful insights about their real intentions, apprehensions, and desires.

Do Nothing That Is of No Use

The last of Musashi's nine principles is the need to *do nothing that is of no use*. Everything you do should be for a reason that advances your case. Your opponents will be attempting to divert you into tangential activities that waste your time and resources, and keep you from focusing on how to win your case. Don't waste time, be inefficient, dither around, or fritter. You may choose to seem to be doing these things, but be sure it is only because of the impression you have chosen to make, and that there is a reason for your actions. The corollary is that the strategist seeks to suppress the opponent's useful actions while encouraging, provoking, or allowing the opponent's useless actions. Of course, this simple statement belies an extremely complex process involving anticipation, recognition, assessment, judgment, decision, action, and reaction. It also requires the strategist to be able to distinguish between useful and useless actions, and to react in an appropriate and timely way.

Seven
Musashi's Strategic Principles and Techniques

*"In strategy it is important to see distant things as if they were close
and to take a distanced view of close things."*
Musashi, *The Book of Five Rings.*

Fundamental Attitudes of the Strategist

Sun Tzu begins with the ideas of what is necessary for the excellent general to achieve success, and Musashi describes the characteristics of strategic excellence. Some of his observations were revealed in Chapter Six. In this chapter, Musashi's concepts of strategic action and attitude are developed. These include the strategist's fundamental attitudes, the functions of rhythm and timing, intuitive understanding and constant training, the importance of the balanced strategic spirit, and what Musashi calls *resolute acceptance of death*. The concepts also include strategic perception and sight, surprise, anticipation, and the centrality of controlling an opponent while not allowing the opponent to do the same to you.

Control of self is one of the most vital aspects of an effective strategist. To achieve self-control a strategist must learn to channel and suppress ego, anger, hostility, fear, and sometimes even the most obvious manifestations of competence. You may be the best-looking lawyer in the world, but what counts is being the most effective lawyer. Ed Concannon, for example, ended his case still looking like the epitome of the powerful trial lawyer, while Frank Galvin could only stumble his way through to the end of the trial. But the jury awarded the victory to Galvin's client. Galvin came up with the single most important witness who exposed the falseness of the defendants' denials. In spite of Galvin's overall ineptness, this is what mattered in the

SELF CONTROL

121

end. Effectiveness is measured only by the outcomes you achieve. Don't fall into stereotyped preconceptions of the "lawyer" and seek to terrify opponents or convince them you are exceptional simply because your ego demands everyone recognize your extraordinary brilliance.

In fact, failure to control the self in the beginning phases of cases or the tendency to try to dazzle opponents often means you are educating your adversaries by revealing your best strengths (for which they will have time to develop defensive strategies), or reflecting their own weaknesses back to them (ones they would not necessarily have discovered if you hadn't provided them with the insights). You may want to seem brilliant at times, but do it because you have made a decision as a strategist that the projection of such a spirit will enhance your client's outcome. Don't do it because your ego requires that you impress people.

All this means that the ultimate test of the quality of a legal strategist's representation of a client lies in the outcome actually achieved. Like Sun Tzu, Musashi tells us that winning is the ultimate purpose of strategy. But while there was an aesthetic component to Sun Tzu's method, Musashi is driven by the stark nature of hand-to-hand combat and its central principle of individual survival. For Musashi there is nothing but winning. His entire system is geared to victory.

While Musashi's admonition is to *do nothing without purpose,* many lawyers are so full of pride and ego that they try to impress everyone with how good they are. Other lawyers are fearful, and bluster in the mistaken assumption that if they talk all the time an opponent can't beat them—the strategic equivalent of whistling past the graveyard. It may help you deal with your own fears, but often weakens your case. In situations in which it is inevitable that there will be a long negotiation process, and a substantial amount of information needs to be obtained from an opponent in order to evaluate the best path of action, don't grandstand by seeking to intimidate, impress, or apply pressure. At least don't do so until the time is right.

It is often better to "sneak up" on an adversary. Stalking behavior is common in the animal world. A predator silently and patiently moves in on the prey before exploding into an attack only after finally reaching the right position. Great care is taken during the stalk to avoid signaling the potential victim of either your presence or your deadly intent. Attention is paid to wind, shadows, terrain, concealing cover, and timing. The animal that shifts to the attack too soon, commonly fails to achieve the goal and goes hungry. The attacker that makes a misstep or does something that warns the target too early loses out. Much of strategy is like this. Musashi tells us, for example, that application of raw force is not the way to win, but that we will win more often through subtlety and misdirection. For example, Peter Falk's Lieutenant Columbo is a caricature of the strategist's ability to sublimate ego to achieve the desired outcome. Columbo is himself a kind of predator, one who hides his dangerousness behind a clever illusion of the bumbling fool. The nonthreatening impression Columbo projects is a combination of carefully selected physical characteristics and strategic spirit. The detective is rumpled and food-stained. He drives a horrible old car. His slow, seemingly confused manner of talking causes his smug targets to take him too lightly. They know instinctively that such a person couldn't possibly match their intelligence and cunning. The villains continually underestimate him, always to their chagrin and eventual downfall. His adversaries don't understand that he is stalking them, using their pride and ego against them until the moment is right to strike. Supposedly clever criminals never take Columbo seriously until they are in jail, then must spend years wondering how such a fool could have gotten lucky enough to put someone as smart as them behind bars. Like Sun Tzu and Musashi, Columbo is the master strategist who knows that only the outcome matters, and projects his illusion to conceal his tough-minded tenacity.

Some of Musashi's most important points concerning how the strategist approaches situations are captured in the following statements. They are discussed subsequently, largely in the context of the examples introduced in Chapter Three and the *Clark v. Mega* fact pattern. While several reflect observations that have been mentioned earlier, it is important to see how they might be applied to specific legal contexts.

- See the whole of being and action.

- Develop the spirit of not being defeated.

- Overcome a lack of innate strategic ability through discipline and constant training.

- The strategist's attitude is resolute acceptance of death.

- The strategist goes beyond the confines of technique.

- The strategist continually cultivates the spirit of adaptability.

- The strategist knows self and others.

- The strategist uses rhythm and timing.

- When the conflict is underway, the strategist seeks to dominate the opponent relentlessly.

- The strategist strives to crush the opponent when the opportunity exists.

- The strategist avoids being predictable.

- The strategist doesn't repeat the same technique more than twice in a specific conflict.

- The strategist seeks to make an opponent his or her own.

- The strategist becomes the enemy.

- The strategist knows that only the outcome matters.

- The strategist visualizes and stays focused on the desired goals.

- The strategist understands others' techniques and principles.

- The strategist avoids a rigid spirit.

- The strategist knows the danger of relying only on strength.

- The strategist understands that strategy often works best through subtlety rather than direct applications of strength.

Rhythm and Timing as the Basis of Strategy

A brilliant strategy at one point in time is a foolish blunder at another. Musashi tells us that all five parts of *The Book of Five Rings* are concerned chiefly with timing and rhythm. He offers these words:

> *"From the outset you must know the applicable timing and the inapplicable timing, and from the large and small timings and the fast and slow timings find the relevant timing, first seeing the distance timing and the background timing. This is the main thing in strategy. It is especially important to know the background timing, otherwise your strategy will be uncertain."*

Other aspects of his timing system are premised on observations such as:

- Constant practice is required to master strategic timing.

- Understanding background timing is fundamental.

- Weapons and timing are interrelated.

- Timing rises and falls.

- The strategist needs to know the opponent's timing, and then strike unpredictably with a timing that surprises the opponent.

The Art of War reflects that same kind of understanding that timing is inside virtually everything we do. Sun Tzu captures some of this in his observation that, *"Rapidity is the essence of war; take advantage of the enemy's unreadiness, make your way by unexpected routes, and attack unguarded spots."* This implies the combination of timing, rhythm, and surprise. Musashi goes beyond this and tells us that timing is the basis of all strategy. This is similar to the insights contained in Sun Tzu's concepts of *heaven* and *earth,* once we understand they represent cyclical phenomena related primarily to timing, cycles, and rhythm. Let us see how these ideas fit into trial.

Trials follow a rhythm and cycle, both in their overall structure and flow, and in the specific contexts of day, persons, and tasks. There are different energy and attention characteristics for each day of a trial, ones in which jurors are more likely to be paying attention, or are bored, tired, or preoccupied with other concerns. Experienced litigators take account of such considerations in determining when to offer key witnesses, how long to continue questioning a witness so the direct examination is the last thing the jurors hear before recessing until the next day, and when jurors are likely to be least attentive—such as when they are digesting their lunch—and therefore might not pay attention to an opponent's cross-examination points. No one can control all these factors, but each can be important during trial, and each operates according to an identifiable and predictable rhythm.

The *rising and falling* timing to which Musashi refers is found in all varieties of strategy. Think about the meaning of what he calls *background timing:* the turning of seasons, light and dark, tides, and weather. There is an inexorable rhythm to such processes, and the strategist needs to adapt to and internalize these rhythms rather than contradict them. Such awareness underlies Musashi's strategic thought. Although much more is said about these considerations in the specific contexts of negotiation and trial, think about the many factors that go into the background timing of a lawsuit. *Background timing* has many aspects, but consider that as the disputants exchange demands and proposals and each engages in attempts to convince the other side of the weaknesses of their position and the strength of his or her own, both know that the case is moving forward toward completion and decision, if not by mutual agreement then by some independent decision-maker. In litigation, this underlying rhythm sets the structure and rules within which the dispute flows. Ultimately, the pressure builds sufficiently to produce settlement in most cases—regardless of the posturing each has practiced along the way. Legal disputes are outcome-driven, and no matter what any of the lawyers or clients assert during the process, there will be an outcome if the process is allowed to move along.

Timing and rhythm in all their dimensions reflect a complex combination of widely divergent considerations. These include not only the background timing mentioned above, but reactive timing, defensive and offensive timing, natural timing, the rhythms followed by humans and human institutions, and the timings imposed by the informal and formal rules of the legal process. Understanding timing and rhythm is integral to planning your strategy because strategy involves many such timing-based actions as drawing in an opponent through overtures or feints, attacking, probing, responding, and taking control of the interaction.

Visualize the following hypothetical interchange between Concannon and Galvin: "Frank, look, I know you've been having trouble with your witnesses. The case is in terrible shape and it's not going to get any better for you. We have the witnesses, the evidence, and the resources. It's only two weeks until trial and you know you're going to get killed."

Galvin has to decide how to respond. Concannon could have been trying to insult him sufficiently that he would respond in a way that would provide Concannon insight into Galvin's attitudes or level of confidence. He could have been simply stating an obvious set of undeniable truths and daring Galvin to challenge them and prove him wrong. He could have been waiting for Galvin to attack Concannon's witnesses in the hope that if he had overlooked something Galvin would bring it out by trying to convince Concannon that his own case wasn't as good as he seemed to think. Galvin needs to make all these assessments virtually instantaneously because the timing of his response can be as critical as its substance. So Galvin's lightning-quick, alcohol-fogged mind selects his strategic response: "Ed, you're so full of crap the Tidy Bowl man couldn't help you. You know damn well that it almost doesn't matter what I do at trial just as long as I get the pictures and story of Deborah Anne Kaye to the jury and keep repeating that this poor girl put her soul and life in the hands of the defendants, went into the hospital whole and alive, and came out a goddamned vegetable!"

Concannon now has to make his own decisions about what to do. He sought information and acquired some that was very useful. He has to decide if Galvin is bluffing, whether this response is one that temporarily reflects Galvin's anger at Concannon's attacking tone of contempt, or represents Galvin's true attitudes. His problem is that the assertion from Galvin is too accurate a description of what a strong opponent—even one with a relatively weak evidentiary case—might very well have decided is the best approach to take if there is to be a hope for a substantial financial victory. The jury could react just as Galvin describes and now Concannon must think about how much risk to take. He also knows that with the trial only a short time away he is going to have to make his decisions soon. We will return to this dialogue later.

While Musashi refers to *background timing* and *rising and falling timing* to express critical ideas, they aren't impenetrable concepts. An economist might, for example, use the ideas of macro and micro timing as well as various business and investment cycles to reflect the distinction between broad and long-term structural aspects of a system or process and more specific and limited processes. The specific timings and rhythms that exist within each element of a system and process, as well as those that reflect human behavior should also be taken into account. The legal strategist utilizes the timing of the legal system through procedure and rules, the timing of discovery and motions, predictable settlement rhythms, the identifiable pressures of the periods before and during trial, and the timing of post-trial and appeal. While the negotiation and trial rhythms are set out subsequently in considerable detail, think of the rhythms through which clients and lawyers go as a case is pursued, negotiated, brought near to trial and settled, or tried and possibly appealed. Throughout those processes there are considerations of timing that are formal, predictable, and fixed because they are dictated by law and rules. These factors represent some of what Musashi would call the *background timing* of the case.

Knowing the structure of a case's *background timing* helps the lawyer to keep everything in context. The defensive strategist learns to use this structural timing to good advantage in a lawsuit; using it to deflect an opponent's efforts, and hiding behind it while developing the case, acquiring information, and mobilizing and positioning forces. The attacking strategist not only must understand all this but also understand the importance of generating pressure that alters some of the more malleable elements of *background timing*. This includes being able to convince the opponent that you are aware of factors that put their case at great risk, for instance, the plaintiff firm in the pharmaceutical example might offer to explore ways by which a substantial settlement could be achieved in exchange for the firm not taking on any more of these types of clients or sharing its knowledge and expertise with other law firms. Such an overture by the plaintiffs' lawyer might well be in "good faith" (if that term can be used to describe a situation in which the plaintiff is agreeing to keep knowledge of risk and harm from others who might be at risk), or the offer might be intended as a probe to see how serious was the extent of the defendant's concern and probable overall exposure. If the offer was in "good faith," then it could result in the normal stretched-out defense timing being truncated and the background timing altered.

There are also more informal considerations of timing and rhythm. These are much more idiosyncratic and changeable by human choice, but they are real and important. The best chance the pharmaceutical company in Example 2 has to settle—short of trial—is if its leadership, including the in-house counsel, has the wisdom and intelligence to make the tough outcome calculus and act on that judgment before the case gets very far along in the litigation process. If possible, it would even be preferable to resolve the various disputes and claims during the prelitigation or pre-filing phases. If the defendant company offered $10 to $15 million to the plaintiffs at a sufficiently early stage, it might be able to settle the worst of the cases. Covenants not to sue on behalf of other similarly situated clients, as well as agreements about secrecy could be part of the settlements.

In its ongoing Halcion litigation, for example, Upjohn reached a settlement with one plaintiff, a key component of which involved a secrecy agreement with the plaintiff's firm. Given that the firm was considered to have the most knowledge and expertise about Halcion, Upjohn paid a premium—but removed its strongest opponent from the game. At a minimum, Upjohn altered the overall group of potential plaintiffs' timing and access to expertise by buying the opponent and neutralizing the most effective plaintiff-oriented law firm. An early, but still substantial, settlement might be the only relatively inexpensive strategy for the pharmaceutical company, although such a strategy is unlikely to be a viable option in Example 2. Other cases will happen, news always leaks out, and it would be immoral—as well as extremely damaging—to the company to try to conceal problems of this nature.

Strategic insight involves being able to know what the timing is at any particular point, where it is going, when it will get there, what effects it will have, how it can be influenced or used to your advantage (if at all), and when to get out of the way or be flattened as a consequence of your feeble and futile attempts to counteract a case's powerful natural rhythm. One example of timing, already suggested, is that you must give your opponents something valuable before they have invested so much money and time into the case that they no longer have an incentive to settle. The pharmaceutical case in Example 2 represents a potential case that could use such a strategy. Once a lawyer has taken steps that impose extremely significant costs on opponents those opponents have much less reason to settle, at least not on terms that don't reflect the changed costs. They have already "bitten the bullet," paid a significant price, and the lawyer caused it by forcing them to fight. Their incentive to settle is greatly reduced, unless there is another significant strategic escalator built into the process that will impose substantially heavier costs or consequences if they don't compromise.

What if the pharmaceutical manufacturer in Example 2 wants to settle early on, but is afraid the plaintiffs' law firm is using tactics that aren't really aimed at settlement but instead are intended to obtain concessions the firm can use in other cases against the manufacturer? The plaintiffs' law firm may not even want to settle its best cases prior to trial, because its lawyers hope to use the verdicts in those cases to leverage the negotiated or trial outcomes of other cases and also obtain high-profile publicity that attracts additional clients.

What if you hear from a reliable source that the plaintiffs' law firm has already spent close to $5 million of its own money on case preparation? What are likely to be its reasons for doing so? You have enough experience to know that the firm will do so only because they see a cumulative total outcome potential for the cases they are handling running into the hundreds of millions, or even billions, of dollars. This approach is becoming increasingly common in mass-tort situations. The plaintiffs' firm in Example 2 may be willing to make a substantial investment in the initial case preparation because the process creates intellectual and strategic capital. There are significant economic incentives for the firm to amass the facts, develop the strategies, and create and refine the processes that will allow for greater efficiency and reduced expense in handling future cases of the same kind. The lawyers are building their expertise, strategies, and sophistication in the specific area. The firm can decide to specialize in the particular type of mass-tort case, can sell its knowledge to other lawyers, or associate with other attorneys in exchange for a percentage of the recovery in their cases.

Controlling the Opponent's Timing

Musashi's *strategist* is far more aggressive than Sun Tzu's *commander*. The strategist controls the opponent by understanding human vulnerability, motivation, values, and sources of leverage. Musashi's nine elements are designed to provide the strategist with the knowledge needed to understand and apply these strategic insights. This awareness allows the strategist to control the opponent's timing. Because timing and rhythm are so critical to success or failure, Musashi tells us to control the opponent's timing by our actions. When attacking action is necessary, strike fluidly, unexpectedly, and relentlessly to destroy the opponent's balance. This allows the strategist to forestall the opponent and take the lead. Doing this requires that the strategist control the opponent by anticipation.

Other aspects of Musashi's system for controlling the opponent includes the recognition that the strategist controls the enemy's spirit and is not controlled by the opponent. While Musashi recognizes the importance of adaptability and flexibility, he does so within a dimension of relentlessness. There is no passivity in his system of action. He voices this in the following terms:

> *"By their study of strategy, people of the world get used to countering, evading, and retreating as the normal thing. They become set in this habit, so can easily be paraded around by the enemy. The Way of strategy is straight and true. You must chase the enemy around and make him obey your spirit."*

The goal of control by anticipation is further reflected in his statement:

> *"In contests of strategy it is bad to be led about by the enemy. You must always be able to lead the enemy about. Obviously the enemy will also be thinking of doing this, but he cannot forestall you if you do not allow him to come out.... The spirit is to check his attack at the syllable 'at...,' when he jumps check his jump at the syllable 'ju...,' and check his cut at 'cu....'"*

Many of Musashi's techniques are aimed at achieving the result of preventing the opponent's *coming out*. His point is that in doing so, the strategist blocks attempts to gain enhanced strategic position and greater momentum. This is why Musashi tells us that:

> *"The important thing in strategy is to suppress the enemy's useful actions but allow his useless actions. However, doing this alone is defensive. First, you must act according to the Way, suppress the enemy's techniques, foiling his plans, and thence command him directly."*

Musashi emphasizes the importance of understanding the difference between defensive "attitudes" and the offensive strategies he feels are needed for victory. In many situations "the best defense is a good offense." He says, however, the successful strategist cannot afford to rely primarily on defensive attitudes, warning:

> *"[Defensive] attitudes are for situations in which you are not to be moved. That is, for garrisoning castles, battle array, and so on, showing the spirit of not being moved even by a strong assault. In the Way of dueling, however, you must always be intent upon taking the lead and attacking. Attitude is the spirit of awaiting an attack."*

Trial and other forms of litigation "combat" are the time to move to the offensive. So is the closing stage of negotiation if you judge there is a reasonable chance of achieving a favorable settlement. Defensiveness in those contexts tends to result in losing.

Taking the offensive requires that the strategist perceive the opponent's weaknesses and strengths and then maneuver to take advantage. Go back to Sun Tzu's heavy emphasis on planning, on the acquisition of valid strategic information, and the intelligent conversion of that knowledge and planning to effective strategic action. A great amount of strategy involves assessing the opponent, yourself, and the conditions under which the strategic interaction must unfold. Because so much of strategy involves application of timing and rhythm, perceiving the opponent's rhythm becomes a critical aspect of forestalling and controlling the opponent. First learn the enemy's approach and timing, test the opponent's rhythm, take steps to influence, disrupt, or alter that rhythm when possible, and then attack unexpectedly using a timing of your choice rather than one suited to the opponent's needs.

When you have done this successfully, it is important to perceive the collapse of your opponent's rhythm and seize the opportunity to react. Sun Tzu tells us that opponents may face each other for years without an opening, but that they must always still be poised to seize the opportunity to gain victory in a single moment. Musashi tells us:

> *"The enemy sometimes loses timing and collapses. If you let this opportunity pass, he may recover and not be so negligent thereafter. You must utterly cut the enemy down so that he does not recover his position."*

For the lawyer this is obvious. As lawyers we have all experienced moments in negotiations and trials when we, our opponent, or a witness is off balance or when the pressure is such that he or she is particularly vulnerable. If we aren't alert, there can be a loss of a valuable opportunity that cannot be recaptured, or we can lose the case through our own weakness or failure to protect our witnesses at critical moments. I know from a personal perspective that there have been moments in many negotiations when I felt that a particular situation had reached a point at which there wasn't going to be a settlement. Because I actually enjoyed going to trial this didn't bother me, but I often found myself soon realizing that the opponent had been bluffing. I would terminate the negotiation in response to their position. The first few times this happened, I was surprised when either right then and there—on the spot or within a day or two—the opposing lawyer expressed a change of heart and offered something considerably better, often after "conferring with the client." But even though this happens in negotiations, the point is that the process of negotiating a settlement really can collapse because the lawyers aren't communicating on the same wavelength, or are playing games that go awry and from which the dispute can't be retrieved. In the negotiation situations just mentioned, I terminated the negotiations and intended to try the cases. If the other lawyers had not altered their positions, we would have tried the cases or they would have had to increase their offers even more when the day of trial arrived. If a case has decent settlement potential, then it is in the interest of both sides to deal with each other more honestly and/or openly during the negotiations. In the end, it saves everyone a lot of time, money, and wasted energy.

People are resilient, and while there are often moments of weakness and vulnerability, we are all capable of holding on and weathering the storm. Just when it seems we are on the verge of giving in, we rebound and come back even stronger. There are moments in many negotiations when one side is ready to take a deal that isn't the best that could be achieved, but the other negotiator doesn't see the cues and fails to take advantage of the situation. When that happens, settlement isn't reached and the opportunity is wasted. Every negotiator has experienced moments such as this when a deal is in the balance but isn't reached even though it was possible and the right action would have tied it all down. Then, the opportunity having not been seized, the timing and emotional spirit of the situation changes in ways that sometimes make it impossible to either "do the deal" at all or results in a significantly different outcome.

An increasingly popular way in which traditionally defensive legal strategists are controlling a potential opponent's timing is through the use of preemptive strikes before the other is ready to act, or by shifting the game from one of public discourse to the more expensive forum of litigation. Preemptive attacks designed to alter a case's traditional rhythms are an increasingly important part of legal strategy for lawyers who in the past have relied on defensive strategies or reactive strategies to protect their clients' interests. SLAPP suits (Strategic Lawsuits Against Public Participation) have become common weapons. The tobacco industry's suit against the State of Florida's legislative effort to obtain reimbursement for Medicaid health-care expenditures is an example of an aggressive-defensive strategy on an extremely high-stakes level. Rather than falling back into the defensive attitude, which Musashi describes as appropriate to withstanding prolonged sieges, and waiting for the assault, the lawyers are seeking to control the opponent by launching aggressive attacks.

An increasing number of people and organizations whose proposed actions are being challenged by public-interest opponents or concerned citizens are using SLAPP suits to make preemptive strikes. As reprehensible as these suits seem to people involved in public-interest activities, they are the strategic equivalent of the aggressive-test litigation and citizen-suit strategies that have been used for years by public-interest lawyers. The SLAPP-suit strategy effectively suppresses complaints by citizens concerned with being sued either for exercising their right to free speech and/or petitioning the respective governmental institutions concerning matters they consider important. While citizens usually can't afford the expense of attorney fees, for the powerful opponents who are increasingly bringing the suits the fees are just a relatively small cost of doing business.

Apart from the SLAPP strategy, most lawyers generally don't want to intimidate their opponents at a too early point in a controversy because such an approach may simply motivate the other side to work harder or fight more savagely. Instead, many lawyers prefer to lull opponents into a false sense of security that causes a busy adversary to allocate time and resources to other matters. This is equivalent to the stalking behavior mentioned earlier. If you expend your attacking energy too soon, or from too great a distance, the prey escapes and time and energy have been wasted. People who feel they are being attacked or pushed too hard—particularly if they are professionals—resist with greater intensity, reinforce their defenses, or figure out how to escape the planned trap. Few well-trained professionals will simply "cave in" to pressure.

On the other hand, clients often decide that a battle isn't worth pursuing when their opponent attacks without mercy early in a conflict and imposes significantly higher economic costs than anticipated or predicted. This may be a preemptive attack that exhausts or greatly reduces the attacker's resources, but inflicts great damage to opponents at a point when they are still attempting to mobilize their "political" will to support the growing conflict. A no-holds-barred assault can cause opponents to hesitate and even decide it would be wise to avoid any further struggle. As long as they don't know the attacker's true capabilities and resource limits, they may withdraw thinking, "If it has cost me this much already, then the eventual cost of fighting will be catastrophic." Even though the attacker may have used up essential long-term resources in the all-or-nothing short-term assault, if the other side is unaware of the severity of the depletion they may overestimate the remaining capability. These are the kinds of games lawyers and clients play, and they depend upon generating impressions and weaving illusions.

A preemptive strike need not take the form of unrelenting overt aggressiveness, but will often benefit by being "open," seemingly cooperative, and even gentle. For the pharmaceutical company in Example 2, ethics, morality, and strategic wisdom suggest the desirability of at least attempting to control the emerging dispute's timing by developing cooperative approaches. Whether the company fights or cooperates, the payout is going to be substantial, and past a certain point it will become increasingly expensive and probably counterproductive to fight. A cooperative posture has the potential to increase the likelihood that a class-settlement pool can be set up with limits put on the company's absolute liability.

The toughest part for a defense strategist faced with this kind of situation is knowing how hard to fight and for how long. The pharmaceutical company can't just roll over and play "soft" from the beginning. If it does, slavering packs of aggressive plaintiffs' law firms will attack without remorse. This is what happened to DuPont in the Benlate litigation. Only after DuPont decided to fight—a decision reached after paying out hundreds of millions in settlements—did it actually begin to win. Ironically, and in a development I hope is not true from the standpoint of ethics and law, DuPont's success is under attack, and the company is reported to be under investigation for allegedly withholding critical information about Benlate from government scientists. Of greater significance for lawyers, apparently so is one of the law firms that represented DuPont.

As Musashi indicates, anticipation and control of an enemy's timing is critical to effective strategy. Even though it is often dangerous to impose significant costs on an opponent, it is also sometimes necessary to "fire a salvo" or even wound an opponent to gain his or her attention and to convince that person you are serious. Often opponents may think you are bluffing, weak, or afraid of them. You may have to "bloody the bully's nose" so they know something about the consequences of their action or continued inaction. Musashi said to always be intent on *cutting* the opponent. Doing this is dangerous in the sense it may be the spark that sets off an explosion or even a full-scale war. But with some opponents you have to be seen as resolute, firm, and completely willing to carry out what you threaten or they won't take you seriously.

One of the ways a strategist controls an opponent's timing is by disrupting the enemy's rhythm. To achieve this disruption, Musashi urges that you must move the opponent's attitude, suggesting, *"This can be done by attacking where his spirit is lax, throw him into confusion, irritate, and terrify him. Take advantage of the enemy's rhythm when he is unsettled and you can win."* A boxer or almost any other intense competitor employs such processes and tactics. Probe, probe, jab, feint, disrupt, learn the opponent's rhythm and techniques, force the opponent into your rhythm, deceive, set up a tendency or discern the other's tendencies and timing preferences, unbalance the opponent, and then attack.

Control is often subtle. The strategist engaged in conflict does not act hastily but applies and generates the proper rhythm and timing. This includes being able to project your strategic spirit in such ways as to influence your opponent's timing and rhythm. Musashi puts it in the following words:

> *"When your opponent is hurrying recklessly, you must act contrarily and keep calm. You must not be influenced by the opponent. Train diligently to attain this spirit."*

On the other hand, if your adversary is unsettled or acting unwisely, you may want to push the response even further in that direction. While you don't want to be out of control, if the opponent has "lost" it, there may be the possibility of gain by exacerbating the situation.

I stated earlier that there was little of the aesthetic in Musashi's system, but that point was somewhat overstated. It is in the master strategist's ability to absorb and use the elements of timing and rhythm that we can find Musashi's essence and style. The skilled strategist has elegant rhythms. Musashi's strategist knows that rhythm—not speed—is the essence of action. He advises:

> *"Speed is not part of the true Way of strategy. Whatever the Way, the master of strategy does not appear fast.... Unpracticed runners may seem to have been running all day, but their performance is poor. Really skillful people never get out of time, and are always deliberate, and never appear busy."*

This is the essence of the master strategist, whatever the discipline. The strategist is always in control of self and part of that control is the integration of the strategist's being with the rhythms of nature and the specific strategic situation.

The Balanced *Spirit* in Strategy

While Sun Tzu developed the concept of the *moral law*, Musashi uses that of strategic spirit, emphasizing the importance of the strategist possessing a determined and calm spirit. Musashi says, *"Win with your eye and beat men with your spirit, the spirit of not being defeated."* Spirit represents the inner attitudes we generate or experience in carrying ourselves in life and in conflict. *Spirit* operates on multiple levels. The most important is the true *spirit* Musashi says the strategist must possess to be effective. This *spirit* is a critical source of power, energy, confidence, focus, and balance. He tells us that it is necessary to have a poised, balanced, and constant inner *spirit* so that we are not distracted by uncertainties and surprises. The centered, inner *spirit* of the strategist is the plane on which we anchor ourselves, both to engage with the conditions we encounter and to remain aloof in order to see with greater clarity the events swirling around us.

Why is *spirit* so important to the strategist? After all, we like to think of ourselves as creatures of reason and intellect, not animals who recently climbed out of the ooze and just learned to stand erect and light fires. The fact, however, is that after several thousand years of recorded history during which we have been told by philosophers that we are creatures governed by reason and intellect, we have become blind to our biological, animalistic natures. The master strategist knows that we are biological beings who react to ancient genetic signals imprinted in our brains. We remain governed by a deep layer of instinctive patterns and primordial reactions, which dictate much about how we respond to nonverbal stimuli.

The biological nature we try so hard to deny means that we can be influenced, confused, swayed, persuaded, and made to feel apprehensive by the nonverbal behaviors of our opponents, and the tension of stressful situations. We can trust another person, not necessarily because that person is trustworthy or sincere, but because he or she knows how to communicate at the perceptual levels on which our feelings of belief in another's degree of honesty, sincerity, or truth are generated. Such stimuli bypass our largely superficial systems of rational thought and perception. A projection of a strategist's spirit that penetrates to these deeper, more biologically based and instinctive levels, can therefore affect us in ways we are not even aware.

We reveal our *spirit* not only through our eyes, but other forms of nonverbal communication and miscues in timing and knowledge. That is the reason for Musashi's urging to perceive those things that cannot be seen and to develop intuitive judgment. We read each other's spirit through posture and nonverbal cues transmitted by our bodies. The messages we send with our eyes, voice, and bodies are among the most important aspects of reading and being read, not only by our opponents but other important decision-makers in our cases. Our eyes are one of the most important windows to both truth and falsehood. Our eyes can create the impression of confidence and power even when we are a mass of quivering fear beneath the surface. In one of my early trials I was doing a cross-examination in which I felt nervous, flushed, stupid, and inadequate. I survived, and was quite surprised when several lawyers who had been in the courtroom during the examination congratulated me at the next recess about how well it had gone. When I told them how completely nervous I had been, one said, "Well, it sure didn't show because you looked like you totally had it together up there." Those words taught me that no matter how we feel on the inside, there are ways to conceal the worst of it and project a much more powerful impression. Part of the lesson is that if we appear to be confident—even if we are not—our opponents will often begin to question themselves and to feel less certain about the winnability of their case. The ability to project confidence and sincerity to the members of a jury is an equally important aspect of a trial lawyer's performance.

Realization of this vulnerability and opportunity is integral to the power of the strategist, both in our understanding of how others are manipulated, and defending against others' attempts to influence us on deeper levels. This is why the legal strategist learns everything possible about how and why humans operate, and about understanding human nature in ways that lead to productive outcomes for the strategist's clients. This knowledge becomes extremely important when communicating with jurors and in negotiation. Much of what jurors perceive in judging a case comes to them on this deeper level. They are using their experience and common sense, but they also relate to the lawyers, clients, and witnesses on much deeper, emotional levels. They hear their tones, see their posture, decide whether they are good or bad, and if they are telling the truth or lying much in the same way their ancestors would have evaluated someone 20,000 years ago while huddled in a cave.

A balanced *spirit* is central to Musashi's strategist. This is reflected in his observation:

> *"In strategy your spiritual bearing must not be any different from normal. Both in fighting and in everyday life you should be determined though calm. Meet the situation without tenseness yet not recklessly, your spirit settled yet unbiased."*

This leads to the point that the strategist must be constantly vigilant. Musashi uses these words, *"Even when your spirit is calm do not let your body relax, and when your body is relaxed do not let your spirit slacken."*

Strategy involves the ability to cause people to think certain things are true, when in fact they are illusions. While the strategist must attain a balanced, centered *spirit* in all he or she does, he or she must also be able to manipulate and project the external signs through which others think they perceive the strategist's true *spirit*. Warfare and strategic conflicts are based on being able to conceal your true intentions until the proper moment. Control of your projected spirit—strength, weakness, uncertainty, knowledge, confidence, willingness to fight to the death—is a critical part of the strategic process. So is seeing and recognizing your opponent's true *spirit*.

A balanced *spirit* is essential because it helps conceal true feelings. Lawyers are like animals who sense fear, weakness, or vulnerability in their prey. Opposing lawyers often attack when they sense you don't feel strongly about your case. Remember the dialogue between Concannon and Galvin when Concannon pushed hard and was surprised when Galvin fought back in a way that showed he understood the only real path to winning the jury trial? A lawyer's reactions to an opponent's probes, feints, and attacks can reveal true feelings. Whatever we know or suspect about Galvin's level of fear after years of being a bumbling drunk who hasn't seen the inside of a courtroom, a defense lawyer in such a situation would still have to respect the potential for an aggressive plaintiff taking such a serious personal-injury case to a jury. When we use probes, therefore, always remember that it is important to gain insights that help us make our judgments about whether we should proceed further or settle. Any information we can verify as having some degree of validity is useful strategic data, whether its import is good or bad from our perspective. If, in fact, you don't feel strongly about your case and this is revealed to the opponent, you have given away extremely valuable information.

This is why the centered, constant *spirit* Musashi describes is so important to maintain. A centered attitude in which you expect attack at any time, from any direction, and are prepared to cope with it, helps control, focus, and mask your true *spirit*, which may be strong or weak. Be like Sun Tzu's *shui-jan*, the snake of the Ch'ang Mountains that responds effectively regardless of which part of it is attacked. The centered *spirit* of readiness, and acceptance of the worst consequences, also helps to generate the strongest possible true *spirit*, even under the most difficult and trying circumstances. You understand how critical your *spirit* is, and shape it so that no one "gets" to you.

This is a main source of a strategist's ability to remain balanced, focused, and powerful.

On the other hand, no one is Wonder Woman or Superman. If you sense something bad is happening to you, step back from the situation and give yourself time and space to regroup. This may even require withdrawing temporarily from the specific interaction so that you can think it out, to regain control of yourself if you have been taken by surprise or need to refocus and reformulate your strategy, reevaluate your position in the case, or make decisions about the validity and direction of the case itself.

Musashi remarks, *"The spirit can become big or small,"* and that particular spirits can be passed on to your opponent. Choose the impression you need to create in order to cause your opponent to perceive you in the desired way. There are, for example, situations in which you may want to project an impression of neutrality, a nonthreatening aspect, weakness, defensiveness, cooperativeness, or unconcern. You may not want to come across as strong or overbearing. That stance could alarm your opponents or make them work harder because they realize they face a tough situation. In practice, when I knew the opposing lawyer was skilled or the person had an excellent reputation, it caused me to redouble my efforts. It wasn't that I didn't work hard in other cases, but when you know you are going up against a particularly worthy opponent it adds an extra level of challenge.

The converse to being nonthreatening is that you may need to slow down the opponent in order to buy time. You may be able to achieve this by projecting the impression of cooperativeness in which the other lawyer doesn't want to push too hard to avoid ruining what seems to be an easily achieved and nonconfrontational outcome at minimal effort and expense. On the other hand, sometimes the only way to hold the wolf at bay is to make it a little afraid of you even if it's relatively sure it can gobble you up. To achieve this short-term apprehension on the part of your opponent, you may have to seem sufficiently strong, confident, and aggressive that it puts your opponent on the defensive, and gives you time to flee to safety—or at least to get your defenses in better shape. In such paper tiger situations, while you may feel weak, you must project strength to delay or confuse your adversary.

Not only must your *spirit* be under your control, but an important part of strategy involves influencing your opponent's spirit. A small spirit projected by you causes many opponents to relax. When they see you as weak, afraid, and vulnerable, or content, lethargic, and disinterested, you won't be considered dangerous. They will feel you either aren't able to attack or are not prepared to attack. Similarly, your calm spirit can do much to soothe and placate an opponent's spirit that is heightened or intense. It's not mind control, but mood control.

Much of Musashi's strategy involves what he calls the *spirit of the void*. He describes it as:

> *"What is called the spirit of the void is where there is nothing. It is not included in man's knowledge. Of course the void is nothingness. By knowing things that exist, you can know that which does not exist. That is the void."*

It is obvious that the true *void* to which he refers is not coextensive with the vacuum of human ignorance. The *void* spirit is beyond the limits of a particular craft or school of strategy. The true *void* is understood by the strategist, if at all, only after years of practice and study. He continues:

> *"With your spirit settled, accumulate practice day by day, and hour by hour. Polish the twofold gaze perception and sight. When your spirit is not in the least clouded, when the clouds of bewilderment clear away, there is the true void."*

The spirit of the *void* is found in the *Way* of Musashi's strategist and he describes the benefits of its understanding:

> *"You will come to think of things in a wide sense and, taking the void as the Way, you will see the Way as void. In the void is virtue, and no evil. Wisdom has existence, principle has existence, the Way has existence, spirit is nothingness."*

Among other important observations made by Musashi concerning the more tactical applications of *spirit* are:

- The strategist releases a deadlocked *spirit* when necessary.

- The strategist uses feints and ploys to gain insight into the opponent's *spirit*.

- The strategist suppresses the opponent's *spirit* when it is clearly seen.

- The strategist defends initially with total aggressiveness to undermine the opponent's *spirit*.

• The strategist is able to project the desired *spirit* to the opponent to gain advantage.

The *Spirit* of *Resolute Acceptance of Death*

If a centered, balanced spirit is a fundamental part of being a
master strategist, how is it achieved? Musashi offers the idea of *resolute
acceptance of death* because he understood that the prospect of our own
death is so powerful that it frightens and weakens us. This concept
was an integral part of the samurai culture during Musashi's lifetime.
Musashi's strategist accepts his death ahead of time and in doing so
achieves the seemingly paradoxical result of increasing his chances
of winning. Musashi's message is that you can't be preoccupied with
death (or humiliation and failure) and still function at the highest
levels as a warrior or strategist.

Many people overestimate their opponents. This generates a self-
fulfilling prophecy that weakens a strategist's essential spirit. Musashi comments:

> *"In large-scale strategy, people are always under the impression that
> the enemy is strong, and so tend to become cautious. . . . In single combat
> also you must put yourself in the enemy's position. If you think, "Here
> is a master of the Way, who knows the principles of strategy," then
> you will surely lose."*

It is easy to misunderstand Musashi's intent. His principle of resolute acceptance of death is not offered as suicidal surrender to our
fate. *Resolute acceptance of death* is a concept of empowerment that leads
to heightened clarity and precision of thought and action. Musashi
knew that if he constantly worried about his death he would be restricting himself, instinctively holding back in his effort, and be insuf-
ficiently focused to achieve victory. Great power comes from the fact
that if you accept your death ahead of time, you don't have to worry
about it and be slowed down and weakened by your fear and apprehension. Accepting the consequences of failure frees us to be powerful and helps reduce the chances that we will fail. This attitude is
central to the litigator. Whatever machinations occur during planning
and negotiation, when the moment comes to walk to the courtroom,
all the illusions are stripped away and set aside. This is where the
litigator and the samurai become one and the conflict is fully joined.
When the moment comes to enter the arena all the preliminary game-
playing ends and the lawyer becomes part of a conflict with another

of the kind that has taken place for thousands of years, whether it is one of hand-to-hand combat, or law. To succeed in this arena requires the attitude Musashi calls *resolute acceptance of death*.

In legal strategy, *resolute acceptance of death* represents the idea of "death" as losing, or making a fool of yourself, being embarrassed, and having your various inadequacies revealed. As a lawyer, if you accept the possibility that the worst possible thing can happen to you, then you will find you can tolerate that outcome if it should happen, and get on with things. This means that you need to consider the possible outcomes in advance, accept them, and then do everything you can to win. It is a kind of ritual thought process through which to prepare yourself for conflict. Indian warriors who performed the Death Dance or equivalent rituals before battle were practicing this approach. Soldiers who are told to put their affairs in order before the battle are doing the same thing—clearing their minds and accepting the possibility of their death. Of course, we also owe it to our clients to understand what we are doing, and need to allow them to set the parameters for the limits of failure beyond which they are unwilling for us to go.

Part III
An Exercise in Strategic Diagnosis: *Louis Clark v. Mega Corporation*

Eight
Louis Clark v. Mega Corporation

*"It is the way of heaven to take from what has in excess in order
to make good what is deficient. The way of man is otherwise.
It takes from those who are in want in order to offer this to
those who already have more than enough."*
Lao Tzu, *Tao Te Ching.*

Musashi continually emphasizes that the process of becoming
a strategist requires the combination of experience, action, self-reflec-
tion, and constant practice. While there is no substitute for actually
doing strategy, a legal strategist can learn important principles and
refinements by working through the kinds of situations that are confronted in law practice. Much of the preparation and learning required
to become a strategist involves the ability to visualize and anticipate
situations, including variations on how they may unfold. The strategist is able to multiply experience and understand its extensions and
nuances. This means that strategic experiences are living texts the
strategist must learn to read, interpret, transfer, and extend into related dimensions.

Multiplying and extending the insights of experience is something
we are all capable of doing. At the point in my career when I was
regularly trying cases, every conceivable situation would run through
my mind as the time for trial approached. By the time the trial actually
began I had already been through it mentally at least three or four
times. When you approach a situation in this way, it is still possible
to be surprised, but far less likely. Similarly, after a lawyer performs
a professional task, one way to gain the most knowledge from it is to
"debrief" yourself by critiquing your performance and admitting not
only what went well but at what points you failed. This is an important

way to learn from experience. The process includes accepting the opportunity to learn from others' critical assessments of the quality of our performance.

Part of the learning process involved in strategy involves making judgments about what should be done and how we would do it. Now that we have begun to develop a preliminary understanding of Sun Tzu and Musashi, the following case scenario presents the opportunity to apply many of their principles in greater detail and depth. This chapter not only develops a case scenario but begins the process of working through a strategic analysis of how a situation such as this might be handled. By considering how this dispute should be handled—including deciding what goals are desirable and possible—and by assessing the competing parties' interests, the expense of various resolutions, and estimating the most likely outcomes, the legal strategist creates a systematic approach to the study of strategy.

Background Facts

Assume you are telephoned by Louis Clark, who arranges to come to your office to tell you about a problem at work. During the initial interview, you find that Louis Clark is 55 years old. He has spent 19 years at the Mega Corporation, and for the last five years has been Mega's vice-president for personnel and regulatory compliance. You get the impression he is a "good guy." He goes to church, has been married to the same woman for 30 years, and has two grown children.

Clark tells you there were no work-related problems until roughly two years ago. At that time, Mega came under new management led by what he describes as a young "hotshot," James Miller. From his tone, you can tell Clark doesn't think much of Miller, who is the son of Mega's founder and who took over the company when his father retired due to health problems. After receiving an MBA from Stanford, Miller worked briefly as a mid-level executive for several companies before his father brought him in as CEO of Mega. Miller is only 33 years old.

Clark says that, from the beginning, it was obvious the younger Miller and the new people he brought with him to Mega thought they knew everything. They made clear their feelings that the people who had been working at Mega before the new team arrived weren't worth much. Clark says Mega was a solid, middle-of-the-road company before Miller arrived, with a comfortable annual return. That middle-of-the-road approach wasn't enough for Miller, however. All the people he has brought in as senior managers have been between the ages of 30 and 35. Most had been students with Miller at Stanford Business School. Miller told the carryovers, including Clark, that they had better be prepared to work like never before—if they expected to stay. He said if they performed, and "got with the program," there would be jobs for them.

Clark says he did work hard—up to 60 hours a week—but he and Miller never hit it off. Clark thinks it is because of their age difference. While Clark admits Mega's earnings have gone up substantially in the last year, he thinks Miller has been cutting corners to achieve the results. Clark says that part of the "earnings" that have made the stockholders happy, and increased the share price, have been generated by Miller playing a little fast and loose with the company's pension fund. As far as Clark knows, there hasn't been any criminal behavior, but Miller is using pension-fund money in ways Clark thinks could endanger the workers' future. He can't provide details, but is worried that Mega could be hit with ERISA (Employee Retirement Income Security Act) underfunding claims when they are reviewed next year. He mentioned this fear to Miller about six months ago, but instead of talking about the problem, Miller made a remark about how only "old fogies" worry about such things and told Clark to "leave it alone." When Clark tried to discuss the issue further, Miller ignored him and started talking about something else.

Increasingly, Clark has felt frozen out of the management process since that discussion. Meetings are held without giving him notice. Also, memos have been issued about excessive consulting on company time. Clark admits he does some outside consulting, but says that many executives at Mega do the same thing, at least the people who are left from before Miller took over. He said the previous management encouraged such activities because they felt it kept Mega's people on their toes and helped to bring in new customers. In the last month, Miller has had several people talk to Clark about how he hasn't seen him in the office past 5 p.m. on Saturdays.

Clark is particularly concerned about an allegation made about him several months ago by one of the young women Miller hired recently. Several departments had an office party to celebrate the closing of a big deal, and quite a few people got a little drunk—including Clark. Like many others, Clark was dancing, and somehow he ended up with this woman. She suddenly pushed him away and, for reasons he still can't figure out, exclaimed, "You dirty old man, keep your hands to yourself!" Clark said he hadn't touched her except in dancing and he doesn't know why she said it. For several weeks, there were rumors at the company about the incident, and he was terribly embarrassed. Since then, the rumors have settled down, but several of the men on Miller's team have made comments such as, "Way to go, old man," and, "Not bad for an old guy." He has tried several times to talk to the young woman about what happened, but she won't speak to him. Last week he received notice by registered mail that she had filed an internal company grievance against him for sexual harassment. That notice made him decide things had gone too far and that he was in trouble. At that point he called you.

Clark says he thinks Miller is considering firing him. Miller has already discharged at least three executives who were only several years younger than Clark. One of them was allowed to take early retirement even though he was only 52, but the other two were simply let go, and are having a difficult time finding new employment. Clark has spoken with the three men and says they are convinced this happened because of their age. He says he doesn't know what to do about his own situation. He can't afford to lose his job and doesn't want to stop working full-time. He is doing a little consulting on personnel matters for some smaller companies, mainly on Saturdays, or at night, and on occasion, he will have lunch with a client. He estimates this consulting brings in about $20,000 a year and would like it to continue. At Mega he is earning a base salary of $115,000 this year, but the salary is generally supplemented by an annual executive bonus. The bonus can be as high as 25 percent of salary. Last year his bonus was $22,000. The executives have a fully paid health care plan that he estimates would cost $7,500 per year if he had to pay for it himself, and a $500,000 term life insurance policy paid for by the company. Senior executives also receive stock options in Mega that are geared to their salary level and Clark received 250 shares last year. Over the years he has sold some of the stock, but he still has almost 1,900 shares in a safe-deposit box. Mega is currently trading at $50 per share, up from $33 per share two years ago when Miller took over. Mega's executive retirement plan is based on an average of the last three years of earnings (the "Final Average Salary" or FAS), including the annual bonus, for the years immediately preceding retirement. Retirement usually is at age 62 and also includes continuation of full health coverage and the $500,000 life insurance policy.

Now that you know the background of your client, Mega Corporation, and the dispute, it is time to start defining victory for your client.

Defining Victory: Louis Clark's Range of Nonlitigation Goals

Assume you see merit in the case, and Clark agrees to sign a lawyer/client agreement. What happens next? Return to the basic questions all legal strategists should ask. What does the client want to achieve? How does Clark define victory? At the end of the strategic process where does your client want to be, and what is pragmatically achievable? What does Clark want? What does he need? What must he have? What are his primary goals? Are they realistic and achievable? What can he afford?

For the moment, suppose that Clark tells you he would really like to stay at Mega and have everything settle down so that he can work productively to retirement at 60 or 62. This means that rather than immediately analyzing the case from a litigation perspective, you need to think about Clark's best interests and desires in the context of the possibility of defusing the situation. This nonlitigation assessment of victory is often more difficult for lawyers than the analysis of litigation victory. This is because we, as lawyers, tend to think in an aggressive conflict-oriented mode in which law, procedure, burdens of proof, and damages are our specialized language—rather than as problem-solvers and conciliators who take human needs, emotions, less-expensive resolutions, and so on, into account. This tendency is why there has been such a push in recent years toward alternative methods of dispute resolution, particularly mediation and consensual arbitration.

Because Clark wants to remain at Mega, and it is not yet obvious whether that goal is possible, his lawyer should help him focus on articulating his goals, defining the nature of victory in the context of remaining at work, and assessing the probability and priority of different goals. After this is done, you can work together to develop a strategy to determine whether any of the goals are achievable, and at what cost. This obviously requires a significant amount of information acquisition before knowing what to do. Clark's nonlitigation goals include the following aims:

1. Have things go back to where they were before Miller took over (Garden of Eden).

2. Keep his job and be happy in it.

3. Keep his job and not be hassled.

4. Be respected.

5. Not be shunted aside as useless.

6. Keep his job, at almost any cost.

7. Preserve his status and reputation.

8. Preserve his quality of life.

9. Preserve retirement benefits, and so forth.

10. Keep the consulting activity.

11. If he has to leave, do it on his terms.

12. If he has to leave and is treated badly, get even with Miller!

Think about how best to proceed to achieve one or more of Clark's goals. If you wait until Clark's dismissal is a *fait accompli,* you haven't done your job. The strategist doesn't necessarily jump in with all guns blazing away. As we saw with both Sun Tzu and Musashi, strategy is often quite subtle rather than the clashing of crude and powerful forces. There are times to use a hammer and times to be as soft as silk. You must initially approach such a situation as this with a gentle, problem-solving spirit because a contact with Miller may itself trigger the very thing you seek to avoid. Even a cooperative posture may not be enough, however. Unless you have good ammunition in support of Clark's claim, Miller may be the type who will blow up and use what he could consider to be an act of disloyalty as the final nail in Clark's coffin.

On the other hand, you could decide that the only chance to achieve Clark's nonlitigation goals may involve early intervention. There is a risk, but it may be justifiable. You could meet with Miller and say, "You'd better not terminate him because we're convinced you are illegally discriminating against older workers and are vindictive. It will cost you more time and money than it's worth to you. So why don't we try to work it out before the situation explodes?"

The approach the United States used in Cambodia was anticipatory preventive reaction, a strategy much the same as Musashi urged in controlling the enemy by anticipating and forestalling the initial moves. The Vietcong and North Vietnamese were using Cambodia as a sanctuary where they could regroup and mobilize resources for attack, so we bombed the hell out of everybody and everything near the Cambodian border. The premise of this tactic is to hit your enemies in their sanctuaries; hit them early, repeatedly, and hard with preemptive strikes. This strategy anticipates problems and preempts them by taking stern and effective action that attempts to remove the threat or prevent the opponent from "coming out." The SLAPP-suit strategy reflects such a preemptive approach.

Strategic problem-solving need not inevitably involve "nuking" the opponent, however. A reasonable and even gentle early intervention has the potential to defuse many situations. It is almost always advisable to see if strategic diplomacy can prevent war—whether military or its legal equivalent. Sun Tzu emphasized that battles should be fought only if necessary, and that the excellent *commander* engages the enemy only after positioning forces in ways that ensure the battle has already been won. Musashi tells us to project the most useful strategic spirit and in this instance that spirit may be one of cooperative problem-solving among professionals and senior executives.

In the Clark situation, for example, you should try to become involved in the developing conflict at a point at which there is a chance to settle with the least cost to your client, and where the lines of conflict and ego aren't drawn as rigidly as they will be after Clark is fired. Once Clark is fired, he no longer will have much income. After the lines are irrevocably drawn and the conflict joined, he will have to spend several years trying to win the case. This quite possibly will involve a radically changed lifestyle for Clark and his family—significant stress, depression, possible marital problems, health effects, the probability of greatly reduced earnings, and dwindling savings—exactly the kinds of consequences Louis Clark is trying to avoid. These consequences are better avoided if possible, both because it is almost certainly in Clark's interest if the controversy can be resolved without his being fired, and because there is greater dignity for most of us in being able to work and be productive. He could try to find another job, but it is almost impossible for a 55-year-old man to find a senior position equivalent to the vice-presidency he now holds. Once fired, he is tainted goods. The United States is filled with former mid-range executives who cannot find jobs years after being "downsized" by their companies.

A significant part of the lawyer's job is obtaining valid information. This is a recurring theme with both Sun Tzu and Musashi. Part of your responsibility as Clark's lawyer is not to take what he tells you as gospel and immediately begin attacking Miller and Mega. You need to understand what really is happening, see the problem accurately, and try to help solve it, rather than make it worse. It is almost always better for clients if "client wars" are prevented, or resolved quickly and early. Wars are expensive. Wars hurt. Clients and combatants both tend to lose something in a war—legal or otherwise—even if they ultimately win the struggle.

It is almost impossible to put a realistic monetary value on Clark's emotional well-being and continued employment. As long as there is a chance to achieve Clark's nonlitigation goals, it is important for his lawyer not to define the value of the case primarily in terms of potential litigation outcomes. Until the employment situation is resolved one way or another—while there is a relationship between the potential litigation outcome and the ability to achieve Clark's nonlitigation goals—the litigation path of action should be kept in the background. At this preliminary stage, the implicit threat of litigation exists to generate the subtle pressure required to increase the likelihood that Mega will be willing to engage in good-faith bargaining rather than a precipitous dismissal of your client.

Because your client has identified his primary goals as keeping his job until normal retirement and not being seen as useless, heavy-handed threats directed toward Miller may not be the best way to help achieve these goals. Assume that you, Clark, and Miller arrange a meeting to talk about what is occurring. As Sun Tzu remarks, there is no substitute for direct observation and intelligence gathering. You might attempt to function primarily as a mediator between Miller and Clark to see if their problems can be resolved. This approach could result in defusing a potentially explosive situation. The best course of action, however, might be for you to stay completely behind the scenes and prepare Clark to approach Miller in an effort to resolve their problems. It's a tough call, but if Clark brings in an outside lawyer it could be seen as an act of disloyalty that causes his immediate termination. In part, it depends on whether Miller is willing to meet with Clark at all. Even if Clark is fired, it doesn't mean Miller can't reverse his decision, but the intensity of the conflict—and the stakes—get higher. After Miller takes the action to fire Clark, Miller's ego, judgment, control, and reputation are on the line. That makes it more difficult for him to back down under pressure. Even if he does change his decision, the work climate for Clark will most likely be altered radically.

You may find that Miller does not seem a vicious ogre, but comes across as a reasonable man who is willing to talk things out and get on with the job. Or you may find that he is a complete jerk and everything Clark has said about him is true. You can still try to work it out so that the situation doesn't explode, but it may be that you will end up talking about Clark serving Mega in a different capacity, or taking early retirement, or moving into an independent consultant role in which he provides services to Mega for a specified period of years at a guaranteed income level. These are possible intermediate solutions. There is, however, a real chance of Clark being fired and the dispute taken to the litigation level.

Suppose Miller doesn't want to talk with a lawyer for Clark, but instead refers you to his own lawyer. You find out the lawyer works for a law firm that is on a substantial retainer from Mega and handles most of its outside legal work. You meet the lawyer in her office, and she tells you Mega is fed up with Clark and is about to cut him loose. You talk for thirty minutes about how that would be an expensive mistake, and suggest some other approach would be in everybody's interest. The opponent responds that Clark is an at-will employee, so Mega can terminate him anytime it wants. But then she asks what you have in mind. You propose that Clark be shifted to another senior position—one in which he wouldn't be in Miller's way.

First of all, as a legal strategist, it is important to recognize that it is very unlikely an outside attorney would be able to reach an agreement on creating a position for the corporation without going back and discussing it with the key people in the corporation. If you thought Mega's outside counsel would have the authority to make such an agreement, you would be making a serious misjudgment. No corporation would give an outsider that kind of authority, particularly when the discussions are only at an exploratory stage, and the specific proposal is being raised for the first time.

Contrast that scenario with a situation in which you are dealing with Mega's general counsel instead of an outside firm. General counsel is a significant position in many corporations. You should try to discover the scope of the general counsel's authority before the negotiation begins. The general counsel is part of the corporate hierarchy and understands the corporation. This includes knowing where the proposed special position might fit, and whether it could work. The general counsel knows the personalities of the executives and the inner workings of the company.

What if you want to talk about possible solutions, but Mega's outside counsel communicates subtly there are no solutions short of Clark's discharge? The implicit message you may be receiving from Mega, underneath all the surface talk, is, "There really aren't any solutions. We aren't going to spend a long time discussing this because it's just a waste of time. Mega is going to find something seriously wrong with anything you suggest." This can undermine your cooperative spirit, but it may not be a real or honest statement of their position. They may be using it to intimidate you and your client. You are familiar with Sun Tzu and Musashi, and know that deception, fear, and misdirection are all basic parts of strategy.

The opposing lawyer, for example, may have just spoken with Miller and agreed on a negotiation strategy designed to soften you up and see how intent you are on pushing this case forward. Hypothetically, she and Miller may have said:

Mega's Lawyer: "Jim, I need to know if there is anything to Clark's position. Is Mega exposed in any way?"

Miller: "Don't worry, Jane. We're covered. But I'm tired of dealing with that old corporate hack. I need to get a younger guy in here who I can work with. Do you understand?"

Lawyer: "Uh, Jim, I should tell you not to refer to Clark as old, or his possible replacement as young."

Miller: "Why the hell not?"

Lawyer: "Well, there's a law against age discrimination. Tell me, have you let anyone else go lately for the same reason?"

Miller: "What do you mean?"

Lawyer: "You know—because they were older than who you like to work with?"

Miller: "Only two or three. Is that a problem?"

Lawyer: "Could be. Look, it's your decision. But I think maybe you'd better think about figuring out how you can keep Clark at Mega for awhile."

Miller: "If you think that's best, I'll do what you say. But see if there's any way we can cut a deal with him and buy him out. If you can't, then I'll probably keep him on. But be tough on him. Make him squirm a little and work for it."

As Clark's lawyer, you don't know what they are really thinking, so for the moment assume you believe what they are signaling, that is, the unwillingness to have Clark stay at Mega in any capacity. If your interpretation of a negotiation interaction is that your opponent is not interested in anything you have to say, how should you respond? The problem you have to deal with is that deception, probes, feints, and trial balloons are all part of strategy. But if you decide you are perceiving their real intention you have to ask yourself whether the particular interaction is worth continuing. You could simply call your opponent on it by getting up and leaving. Your interest in achieving a settlement is one of the primary levers by which an opponent is able to manipulate you. As Musashi warns, a skilled strategist can *"lead you around"* by controlling you through their accurate perception of your true goals. If you keep on talking in an effort to convince an opponent to settle, you will eventually reveal something that helps the opponent. If you think the professed unwillingness to settle represents your opponent's real attitude, then you need to consider how much energy you want to invest in this particular discussion and whether you can gain anything from continuing it. Remember, Musashi also tells us that a strategist suppresses an enemy's useful actions while allowing or encouraging useless ones. If you decide you can't change their minds, don't give anything away.

What you are trying to determine is whether their attitude is just a tactic, or is real, even though you personally might consider it stupid. You have to allow for the fact that opponents often do dumb things, and sometimes do things that seem dumb at the time, but really aren't. The strategist must decide what an opponent is doing and, if he or she is making a miscalculation, discern whether the opponent is educable. You have to take action that tests the opponent's true intent. In the Clark situation you may test their attitude by saying, "I get this funny feeling you aren't interested in a serious settlement discussion. Am I right?" Working to achieve solutions requires that both sides are willing to participate and cooperate. It "takes two to tango," and both sides to settle—unless you are surrendering unconditionally. If you sense that your opponent is not interested in settling, you can say, "The reason I'm raising this, Jane, is that I have this funny feeling but I can't quite put my finger on it. But I sense you don't really think there is any way we can resolve this. If that's true, there is no reason for us to be here with each other, or even to meet with a mediator. This is just not going to work out short of litigation. Am I right or wrong?"

She could have been playing games with you without any intention of letting the situation explode into full-blown nasty litigation. Given what happened in her preparatory discussion with Miller, we know this to be the case. If she believes you are about to leave, and possibly file a lawsuit as your next step, this approach may help cut through the smokescreen.

You can go on and say, "I am not trying to push you, but I need to know if there are avenues you see to make this exchange a real process worth going through? If we have a chance to work something out, I am willing to explore it. But if we can't, and in your judgment you have already determined that to be so, then we might as well stop here. You think that we can discuss this situation reasonably?"

She might respond by saying, "We may not need to jump right into litigation. What kinds of things do you think might be in the ballpark as to the types of settlement you are interested in?"

You could answer, "The same as we mentioned the last time we got together. Some kind of redefinition of Clark's job with existing pay and benefits, and a guarantee of decent treatment and no retaliation."

The opposing lawyer should have already done the thinking necessary to recognize the consequences of various courses of action, although too frequently this basic analysis hasn't been done. You have to take the risk of educating your opponent.

Mega's Lawyer: "We mentioned during the prior discussion that we might be willing to talk about perhaps creating a position."

Clark's Lawyer: "Creating a position. Tell me what that might be like from your perspective of what the company could do? The position would have to be something Miller is comfortable with, right?"

Mega: "Exactly. But as outside counsel, you know I can't commit to something specific. It will have to go back to Miller."

Clark: "Well, certainly because we already talked about it during our initial discussion, and you said at that time you were going back to Mega and talk to Miller, you must have at least explored the idea with him. You don't have to tell me everything. Just give me a sense of what you're actually willing to do."

At some point in this settlement process you must find out whether your opponent has authority to commit. There are places in the interaction where you have to bend, or the interchange breaks down. If, for example, it is a morning negotiation in which the other lawyer has the rest of the day to investigate, you could, ask, "Can you call Miller as soon as we leave here to set up a meeting and get a firm read on what he is willing to do?"

Mega: "I can't, because he is out of town today, but I will try to contact him first thing tomorrow morning."

Clark: "Then he will be back tonight, or be available tomorrow?"

Mega: "He's scheduled to be back tomorrow morning."

After you leave, she telephones Miller and reports on the discussion.

Miller: "I don't like this, Jane. Clark is a pain in the ass, and I don't like being pushed like this."

Mega's Lawyer: "It's up to you, Jim. All I can say is that the age-discrimination thing will make you a little vulnerable if you fire him. And, I have to tell you that Clark's lawyer raised a few questions about how you are supposedly handling Mega's pension fund. We need to talk about it."

Miller: "Never mind that. There's nothing wrong. Look, keep talking with him. I want to know what they think they know. Tell them I'm thinking about how we can resolve this. Until I decide, say Clark can stay on the job."

Mega's Lawyer: "Are you actually going to keep him on?"

Miller: "I don't know yet, but I really don't want to. Talk to Bob Brown about whether he has any ideas about how to use the old bastard."

Mega's Lawyer: "Jim, I told you. Don't refer to Clark as old."

Assume that after all is said, the opposing lawyer comes back and tells you that Miller's answer is that it is very unlikely Clark can stay at Mega, but that he hasn't made up his mind yet. If the relationship between Clark and Mega does not appear salvageable, you should think about whether this conclusion is true and work in terms of a different kind of negotiated settlement that doesn't involve Clark's continued employment with Mega. But you still don't know the reality at this point, although the dispute may move to a litigation posture in which lines are drawn more clearly, and costs and tension escalate. Even if you file suit on Clark's behalf you can still negotiate, but it will take on a different character and have different goals.

Clark is concerned not only about his salary but with his pension benefits, health-care, and retirement security. He also wants to ensure he would be entitled to at least full retirement benefits under any agreement that was reached. He wants as much salary or severance pay as he can get. His reputation is also involved, so one of his goals includes an agreement that preserves his status and reputation. This could include a confidentiality agreement, a guarantee of positive job recommendations, consulting business from Mega, use of an office or letterhead, and perhaps some kind of job title that reflects a continued connection to the company.

If you are trying to either save Clark's job or negotiate a severance package with a graceful exit from Mega without having to spend years in protracted and expensive litigation, where do you start? What if Mega eventually makes a buyout offer of a lump-sum payment of $350,000 to resolve all Clark's potential claims and for him to leave the company? If you respond to Mega's offer of $350,000 with a demand for $750,000—plus pension and benefits—Mega's lawyer could say, "How the hell can you possibly say Louis Clark should get $750,000 cash plus benefits from this case? I can understand it if you went to trial and were somehow able to sell liability to a jury, but how can you possibly say that he actually deserves $750,000? You aren't going to be able to win on liability, and even if you did, the damages would be much lower."

There are several ways to look at the terms of a negotiated victory when you are trying to resolve the conditions of ending Clark's employment with Mega. You may seek an agreement that involves such terms as $750,000, payable over seven years, to compensate Clark for his lost earnings from what you consider a wrongful discharge. If successful, you could decide to maximize the return by taking the whole payment in a lump sum now. If you take all the money up front, your client could earn interest on the principal over that period of time. The approach depends on a determination of what is best for your client. Clark might prefer to have the settlement paid out in installments as a regular annual income, rather than a lump sum that he might be tempted to spend too quickly. He could decide he can use the money more productively by investing the entire amount himself rather than relying on Mega. Clark then wouldn't have to bother with Mega other than to make sure they're paying into his pension fund, and Mega wouldn't have to deal with him.

Why would Mega be willing to pay Clark any money, much less a package worth almost $1 million? At this intermediate level of potential settlement, between Clark remaining employed and the situation returning to normal, and a full-blown process of public, embarrassing, and expensive litigation, each side must be able to see that a settlement might be in its best interests. The considerations that come into play at this point include such factors as what legal rules apply to the situation, whether there are factual uncertainties that can cut either way, the expense of intense conflict, the loss of focus and waste of energy by the parties that could be better spent on more productive pursuits, whether either side has "skeletons" they really don't want made public, and the probability of ultimately prevailing if the case is litigated.

The potential age-discrimination claim Clark has against Mega, based on evidence that three other senior executives were also terminated and replaced by younger people since Miller took over, might have some merit. At least Mega Corporation may fear it does, given the rapidly expanding area of employment-discrimination law and wrongful discharge. A pattern of action is critical in such litigation and is one of the first things for which lawyers on either side should look. As Clark's lawyer, you can't be certain until you have done a substantial amount of research, investigation, and discovery. Preliminary research and investigation might reveal enough to allow you to file a complaint, but formal discovery is almost certainly needed before you can gather enough information to prove the claim or understand how strong or weak it is. It is a very difficult claim to evaluate early in the process. This illustrates Musashi's idea of the appropriate cycles of timing and rhythm that are intrinsic to any strategic situation, particularly the consideration of what he calls *background timing*.

Assume that at least two of the men who were forced out by Miller, and replaced by younger people, felt it was because of their age. The third individual isn't certain, but "suspects" it might be true. That is at least something to go on. Similarly, there is the possibility that Miller has been dipping into the employee pension fund in unjustifiable ways and this could cause embarrassment and legal problems if brought out in a lawsuit. There is also the significant expense and "hassle" factor involved in any lawsuit. These considerations may make Miller willing to deal—at least to some extent. What if the following discussion took place between Miller and his lawyer before any final decision was made about Clark?

Mega's Lawyer: "Jim, I know you want to get rid of Clark, but this could cause some real problems and cost you a lot of money."

Miller: "What kinds of problems?"

Lawyer: "First of all, he will raise the pension-fund issue."

Miller: "Don't worry. My house counsel has looked at it and says he doesn't think there's anything really wrong with what I've done. He said I could skim the surplus in the fund, and also borrow against it."

Lawyer: "That's not my area so I can't tell you. But I always have the impression Bernie tells you whatever you want to hear."

Miller: "Never mind. What else?"

Lawyer: "The age discrimination. I have to tell you I think you are exposed on it. I see a pattern, plus the way you talk about older executives shows your motivation."

Miller: "I said it to you, and what I tell you is confidential, right?"

Lawyer: "Yes it is. But my bet is you've said such things to other people. And if it comes out, you'll lose."

Miller: "I'll take my chances. Bottom line is I want him out. Negotiate some kind of buyout deal with a release of all claims or I'll fire him next week."

Lawyer: "Okay, but I wish you'd reconsider. Anyway, how much are you willing to pay?"

Miller: "Maybe up to $500,000, complete, based on what you told me last week when you said I'd end up paying you lawyers almost that much if we don't make a deal."

What if Mega's lawyer then comes back and offers Clark $450,000 to leave the company plus his pension and health benefits? What fee arrangement exists between Clark and his lawyer? How is the pension to be valued in the settlement for purposes of computing the lawyer's fee? The fee contract should take into account such factors as what happens if you settle, as well as when you settle. It should consider whether there are applicable statutory attorney-fee provisions, or claims that represent exceptions to the American rule against litigants recovering attorney fees from their opponents and consequently allow a prevailing plaintiff an award of attorney fees. If so, what are the standards, the hourly rate, the records needed to justify the fee claim to the court, and how much of the decision is discretionary with the judge? If the case is settled and there is a valid age-discrimination claim, you need to negotiate with Mega to have the company pay at least part of your attorney fees as an element of the settlement.

Mega's attorneys are (or should be) making similar expense and outcome calculations. They should be thinking in terms of, "It is going to cost Clark at least $50,000 to bring this to court. If we go ahead and fire him, he doesn't have a job now, and he must factor that into his case evaluation. If we fire him now and then string it out long enough, he'll never get to trial. When we get reasonably near the trial, we can offer him an incrementally larger amount and because he will be low on money he'll probably take it. Perhaps the whole process can be made so nasty and stressful that he'll give up to relieve the pressure—or maybe we'll get really lucky and he'll die."

Mega's lawyers should be sitting in their offices making such calculations, which suggests how nasty the strategic process can be. It is a ruthless and ultimately Machiavellian process that, as I said earlier, involves estimations and decisions that aren't very nice—particularly if you are good at it.

This case will take between two and four years to reach trial in most courts. Mega's lawyers should determine how much it will cost Mega to defend against Clark's wrongful-discharge lawsuit, and any collateral consequences to the corporation, even if Mega wins the legal battle. Statutorily provided attorney's fees for Clark if he prevails—ones that the defendant would be potentially obligated to pay—could easily reach $150,000 to $300,000, with an additional $50,000 in litigation expenses. Mega's own legal fees and expenses could well exceed $500,000 if it goes through trial, even if Clark loses. Mega's lawyers also need to think about the net potential outcome package that might result from a jury verdict in Clark's favor, including the award of attorney fees by the judge.

Defining Victory: Louis Clark's Litigation Goals

In the end, nothing was resolved and Miller fired Clark outright. Obviously, the conflict is moving inexorably toward a state of "legal war," with the potential for the final battle being a jury trial. Now we follow Sun Tzu's advice regarding strategic excellence and enter a phase of more extensive intelligence gathering, maneuvering, and positioning of forces. If the battle must be fought we will know that we have done everything possible to position our forces in ways that, if not making victory inevitable, will significantly increase its probability, as well as the opponent's sense of the validity or "weight" of our case.

What are Clark's options and goals at this point? Go back to the facts. In his nineteen years at Mega, Clark had a good record and was promoted numerous times. He spent the last five years as vice-president for personnel and human relations, and during that time senior management promoted him, gave him raises, and paid Clark substantial executive bonuses. Investigation and discovery should document that he did a good job, although Mega may attempt to rewrite or downplay his employment history. Before he was fired, Clark should have acquired copies of his records. Then, if Mega does subsequently doctor the files, you will be able to catch them on it.

From the standpoint of your jury presentation, why is it important that Clark was promoted? It is important because, if he really were an unproductive troublemaker, Mega would have removed him long before this situation arose. We may then convert these facts and assumptions into the argument that Clark gave a substantial and productive part of his professional life to Mega, was a valuable employee, and that Miller fired Clark because Miller wants to be free to "play games" with Mega's personnel policies and its pension fund. Clark resisted him, and was in Miller's way. This conflict happened because Clark wanted to ensure things were done properly and legally, and to protect the integrity of Mega's pensions. Miller didn't want Clark looking over his shoulder. At least that is what the jury will be told.

Remember how Frank Galvin scored his *coup de grace* in *The Verdict* by showing the altered hospital admission record? People really do destroy, "lose," and tamper with evidence. I was recently talking with a lawyer who was handling a case in which the defendants claimed during discovery that pertinent records had somehow been destroyed in a hurricane. Unfortunately for the defendants, the only records "accidentally" lost in the hurricane were those relevant to the plaintiff's claim. Clumsy? Absolutely. But evidence is destroyed many times without the perpetrators being caught or sanctioned. What people do and say in an attempt to cover up or to look good for higher-ups in the short term often puts their lawyers on the spot later. Clients frequently engage in such conduct and tell their lawyer only after the damage has been done. Something that could and should have been dealt with at an early point becomes a knife in your back because of your client's duplicity or your failure to face reality.

It wouldn't even be surprising to have the following conversation between Miller and his lawyer:

Miller: "Jane, I've been thinking about the deposition I have to give tomorrow, and there's something I should probably tell you beforehand."

Mega's Lawyer: "Jim, we've prepared you thoroughly. I think you'll be fine, at least on most of it. From the beginning I worried about the age-discrimination thing, but the way you handled the sexual harassment complaint against Clark as the basis for his discharge makes me think there's a real chance a jury will buy it. Unless, of course, there's something you haven't told me."

Miller: "Well, to tell the truth, there are a couple of things we should probably talk about. First of all, I'm supposed to bring all the records and memos on the pension stuff, and some of it doesn't look all that good when you're reading it. I went over it with Bernie today and he was actually pretty upset."

Lawyer: "Wait a minute. You told me Bernie cleared all the pension shifting you've been doing."

Miller: "I sort of exaggerated. He really didn't know much about it, and now that we've actually talked, he told me it wasn't a very good idea."

Lawyer: "Jesus Christ, Jim! Why did you lie to me? Our whole approach was based on what you said. What else have you been hiding?"

Miller: "Come on, Jane. I'm still paying you a lot of money to take care of this. So I played it wrong. I didn't think it would go this far. I always thought we'd be able to settle for the $750,000 they were asking for before I fired Clark. How was I to know he'd turn around and insist on $2 million after they sued. I mean, this is why I told you to offer $1 million last week. I never thought Clark would turn down $1 million."

Lawyer: "Smooth move, Jim. Now I get to look like an idiot!"

While this is going on behind the scenes, Miller may have already given several specific reasons for why he fired Clark. Miller may claim a conflict of interest because of Clark's outside employment. He may allege expense account violations by Clark, cite the sexual-harassment complaint, or reiterate the charge that Clark failed to work hard enough. Other people in Miller's management group have said Clark isn't part of the team. But what does it mean to be part of the team when his job is in personnel and human relations? Clark's job is to make sure the corporation acts in a way that benefits both the employees and the corporation. His job is to be a watchdog because if he doesn't insist that Mega's management treat its employees fairly, there will be serious labor problems, or potentially costly violations of federal labor laws and regulations. That is why positions such as Clark's are created.

Many of the regulations Clark attempted to ensure Mega followed are issues of gender and age discrimination, race discrimination, employment discrimination, and labor conditions. They relate to situations involving work conditions and how companies treat their employees. Increasingly, corporations have had to create this type of position as a check against their own tendencies to abuse power and to take unfair advantage of employees. If they employ someone such as Clark to ensure they are following the rules, then they are less likely to have to worry about going to court or having serious management-labor problems. But that doesn't mean corporations enjoy doing this.

This line of reasoning is an important part of the plaintiff's strategic analysis because the strategist must always consider who will be the most sympathetic person if the case goes to a jury. The jury will tend to identify with the everyday person, the person they see as being wronged, or who is most like them. The vice-president of such a big company as Mega would ordinarily not be a sympathetic person from a jury's perspective. Who cares when powerful and privileged people fight? More often than not, a jury would probably like to see both Clark and Miller lose. A strategist, however, must be able to take such considerations into account and develop approaches that shift the perspectives of the relevant decision-makers, whether jury or opponent. After he is fired, for example, Clark can be portrayed to a jury as a good man who has been treated badly by Miller because Clark was doing his job and trying to protect other people. Jurors can understand someone being treated in that way and become angry about it. You can almost see part of the plaintiff's closing argument: "Louis Clark is a man who dedicated his life to helping the workers of the Mega Corporation. His job, one he loved and did well, involved protecting the ordinary employees. He made sure their complaints were heard, their health and safety benefits provided, and their pensions protected. Louis gave many years to Mega and then made two mistakes. He was "old" in the eyes of his new boss, and he tried to protect the workers' pensions from an arrogant and greedy man who was looting the pension fund."

It is important to think about how to present a case even at a point considerably before trial. Knowing how a case "feels" is an essential part of negotiation because it helps keep you focused and on track. Since Miller has terminated Clark, Clark's goals have changed character. Miller just discovered this when Clark rejected his $1 million offer, one that would have been snapped up prior to termination if Miller had allowed Clark to leave with dignity. While the fact that he has been terminated does not mean that Clark could not be rehired as part of a negotiated or litigated outcome, after he has been fired there should be a basic shift in dynamics in which our dispute moves from the prelitigation, problem-solving, and conciliatory phases to the litigation mode. Once they enter the litigation mode, disputes have a tendency to get nastier, more drawn out, and expensive.

Now Clark's goals are defined in relation to the rules and outcome potential and probability of various paths within the litigation process, including litigation-referenced negotiation, possible mediation, consensual arbitration, and trial. As is discussed in the final section of this book, each path has a different outcome potential, both net and gross. Sometimes the disputants' calculations of outcome potentials and competing assessments of outcome probabilities are so far apart that a litigant has little choice but to take a chance on a riskier path (i.e., trial or arbitration) in which the payout or cost is far greater, but less certain.

Think about the negotiation ranges and options that were discussed by Miller and Clark prior to termination. At that point, the resolutions were relatively inexpensive and had the potential to be designed in such a way that meant neither party had to be embarrassed or subjected to costly and stressful conditions. There was even the potential for working out a possible "win-win" solution if each side showed wisdom and maturity. The termination ended this possibility. Now there is no turning back—at least not to the original conditions—and not without going through an expensive and time-consuming set of processes.

Tables 1 and 2 show what the radical shift in perspective and process between prelitigation negotiation and litigation-referenced negotiation has done to the case and the positions of the disputants. Although the tables are in no way exhaustive and offer only approximate figures, they present some of the factors both sides must take into account in trying to figure out what to do. Assume for the moment that you feel Clark will be able to convince a jury he was wrongfully discharged and is entitled to recover damages for lost wages and benefits, as well as have the judge assess attorney fees. What is the gross value of Clark's potential recovery?

How probable is it that a jury would find liability and award damages at the levels reflected in Tables 1 and 2? How realistic is it? On what assumptions are the lawyer's evaluations based? How can the lawyer explain these considerations to Clark? How does the lawyer use strategy to increase the probability of achieving a realistic outcome that is toward the upper end of the case's outcome potential scale?

The point of the exchange is the need to project the appropriate strategic *spirit*. Musashi focuses much of his work on the control, generation, and projection of strategic *spirit*. *Spirit* can be communicated, but if the *spirit* the strategist projects isn't believed, or lacks supporting substance and principled justification, the attempt can backfire. This means it is essential for a legal strategist to determine reasons why a client is entitled to whatever amount is being requested, or conversely, why the client is not liable for what the opponent is demanding. This requires a process of agenda creation, development of principled reasons for demands, and the design of multitiered packages that allow for necessary tradeoffs. This is discussed in more detail in subsequent chapters.

After deciding on the goals to be achieved, an advocate creates strategies, generates themes and theories, and selects and interprets facts to implement those strategies and themes in ways designed to increase the probability of achieving the client's desired outcomes. What if, after looking closely at the facts Clark has provided and taking steps to verify those facts and others relevant to the case, you decide Clark's claim has a gross potential maximum value of $3.63 million? For the lawyer, gross potential maximum value is only one consideration. How confident should Clark's lawyer be that at trial he will be able to recover $3.63 million in damages, plus attorney's fees? How likely is it that such an amount will actually be recovered in a trial? What is the likelihood of being able to negotiate a settlement in that general range? What if mediation or binding arbitration is suggested? Each of these strategic paths has distinct outcome-generation potentials. Trial usually offers the highest outcome potential for seriously harmed plaintiffs, but also tends to be a more uncertain and risky strategic path.

$3.63 million sounds like a great deal of money, but is it unrealistic in this case? First, we need to ask how that figure was reached and identify the best principles, doctrines, facts, and arguments to support it convincingly both in negotiation and trial. The most obvious place to start is Clark's salary and benefits, projected over his remaining years of work if he had not been discharged. This is a major part of the figure and calculations included in Tables 1 and 2. Clark is 55 years old. Assume for the moment that Mega discriminated on the basis of age, and it can be proved in a way that is compelling to a jury. He would have worked until he was 62, but because he has been fired, he will find it virtually impossible to be hired into an equivalent position. An examination of Mega's retirement policies may reveal they have several retirement options. Clark has made $135,000 this year—including consulting—and has received raises during each of the nineteen years he has worked with Mega. His lawyer must investigate what similarly situated executives have received, how the economy is performing, and determine whether raises have been received by some executives in spite of company performance. Mega has apparently been doing well recently and earnings are up. This may mean that at trial Mega must admit the company's productivity has increased

Table 1. Louis Clark's Total Loss (5%)

Year	Salary/Bonus (7 yrs.)	Stock Options (7 yrs.)	Benefits (7 yrs.)	Pension/Salary (15 yrs.)	Pension/Benefits (15 yrs.)	
1	$135,000	$12,500	$7,000	$120,000	$7,000	
2	$142,000	$12,500	$7,000			
3	$149,000	$12,500	$7,000	[15 yrs. at 3%]		
4	$157,000	$12,500	$7,000	[annual increase]		
5	$165,000	$12,500	$7,000			
6	$174,000	$12,500	$7,000			
7	$182,000	$12,500	$7,000			
TOTAL	$1,104,000	$87,500	$49,000	$2,250,000	$140,000	$3,630,500

Table 2. Louis Clark's Total Loss (10%)

Year	Salary/Bonus (7 yrs.)	Stock Options (7 yrs.)	Benefits (7 yrs.)	Pension/Salary (15 yrs.)	Pension/Benefits (15 yrs.)	
1	$135,000	$12,500	$7,000	$144,000	$7,000	
2	$148,000	$12,500	$7,000			
3	$163,000	$12,500	$7,000	[15 yrs. at 3%]		
4	$179,000	$12,500	$7,000	[annual increase]		
5	$197,000	$12,500	$7,000			
6	$217,000	$12,500	$7,000			
7	$239,000	$12,500	$7,000			
TOTAL	$1,278,000	$87,500	$49,000	$2,687,000	$140,000	$4,241,500

in the past few years. This makes it difficult for Mega to claim Clark has been hurting the company. This also requires that you find out why Mega's earnings are up, and be certain it is not due to a one-time-only accounting aberration.

There could also be possible bonuses and stock options that would contribute to Clark's potential damage figure, along with annual raises averaging somewhere between 5 (Table 1) and 10 percent (Table 2). Assuming a 5 percent annual increase in salary over the next seven years, Clark's salary at the end of that period would be approximately $182,000. This means the 5 percent annual increase would result in a final average salary (based on the average of the last three years) of $174,000, and a pension of $116,000 per year.

At first, calculations based on entirely reasonable growth assumptions seem to involve only small differentials. Over a period of only seven years, however, the assumptions quite quickly generate surprisingly large numbers. It is very important that the assumptions made about the increases are reasonable and wholly justifiable, including assumptions about economic trends, future rates of inflation, and interest rates. To show how relatively small differences can end up with large amounts of money, Table 2 assumes that Clark receives a 10 percent raise each year, rather than the 5 percent used as the basis in Table 1. Four years from now his salary would be approximately $179,000, in five years $197,000, in six years almost $217,000, and in the seventh year $239,000. Using the 10 percent raise figures, if he worked the next seven years at Mega, Clark's total salary over that period would be $1,278,500, and the final average salary (FAS) for purposes of computing his pension would be $217,000. At a pension rate of 63 percent of FAS, this would result in a pension of $144,000 per year.

The 10 percent growth assumption is obviously preferable to Clark because it results in gross, prediscounted damages of $4,241,500. But your claim to it must be justified by such specific and reasonable criteria as how that industry or specific company has been doing and the probable trends for the future. If the figure selected is 5 percent, 6 percent, or 7 percent, then convincing an opponent or a jury that the figure is reasonable is relatively easy. The skilled litigator will not hesitate to bring those figures in from the beginning of the trial, using common sense demonstrations of the impacts of the financial situation, building the claim through charts, graphs, and the testimony of expert economists to show with clarity why Louis Clark has been damaged in the requested amount. After this is done through three careful economic scenarios, even the opponent is subconsciously conditioned to accept the intermediate figures.

If 5 percent is used as the baseline growth assumption for Clark's annual salary increases rather than 10 percent, his final three-year average salary drops significantly, but the number still remains large. With a 5 percent rate of increase, seven years of lost salary equals a gross pay of $1.104 million plus the value of stock options and benefits. That amount represents just the sum of his total base salary for seven years. Dollars received now, representing payments that would normally be received in the future, must be discounted to their present value. There are formulas and tables to help do that, geared to assumptions about interest rates and cost of living. The key to reducing a future-payment obligation to present value is not in the computations themselves, because they are reasonably straightforward. The results are dependent on the assumptions and numbers plugged into the formula and how well you justify your choices.

But salary is only the most obvious part of Clark's losses. What else can Clark legitimately claim as damages? Pension benefits and stock options should be on the list, as well as health-care and insurance costs, and various other fringe benefits. If Clark has to begin paying for health-care coverage, then, given the skyrocketing price of health insurance, he could add $5,000 to $8,000 per year to his damages figure; $7,000 per year is used here without making any assumptions about rising costs. This figure could escalate if health-care prices continue to rise. If discharged, Clark would be forced to purchase an individual policy in which the premiums are higher and he is more vulnerable to cancellation. When such costs are factored into Clark's outcome potential, his total damage figure at the 5 percent level exceeds $3.63 million.

The calculations presented in Tables 1 and 2 reflect just an initial, crude approximation of the "hard" damages, lost salary, benefits, pension, and so forth. Clark will also be arguing bad faith and age discrimination by Mega. In some jurisdictions, the bad faith or punitive damages allegation may allow Clark to seek damages for negligent, reckless, or intentional infliction of emotional distress, create the possibility of an award of statutory attorney fees (if he prevails on the age-discrimination claim), and even allow for punitive damages. It must also be determined whether his pension is fully vested or if Mega stands to save a great deal of money by disposing of its older executives. If it can be reasonably argued that his discharge was retaliation against him for raising concerns about the pension fund, that may open up another category of damages, and the right to attorney fees, if Clark prevails on his claim.

Table 3 is offered to demonstrate that no outcome is cost free. It is also offered to emphasize that, although almost everything has a cost attached to it, some of the costs cannot be converted to money, others are too difficult on which to calculate a realistic monetary value, and some are risky and/or unrecoverable. Values have been inserted into Table 3, but they are merely illustrative. Key to interpreting Table 3 is recognition of several fundamental points of consequence to legal strategists and their clients. The left-hand column, for example, presents five of the basic strategic paths through which such disputes can be resolved. These paths are discussed at length in the next chapter. One, pretermination negotiation, was attempted but was unsuccessful. Once that failed, the dispute changed to a litigation mode in which the paths of strategy still include negotiation, but it is a litigation-referenced negotiation conducted according to a different set of considerations, rules, and sources of leverage than were in existence prior to Clark's termination. Litigation negotiation operates under the looming specter of resort to formal rules, mandatory discovery procedures, judicial power, legal standards, and the inevitability of either the judge or jury as ultimate decision-maker if the parties can't resolve the dispute. The litigation paths used by the strategist all operate according to such characteristics.

An important aspect of Table 3 reflects that each strategic path imposes consequences of various sorts, including important nonmonetary effects. Both Miller and Clark, for example, should realize the emotional costs of litigation, the amount of time they will have to put into the process, and the period over which the dispute will stretch. These effects are not assigned a monetary value but are quite real.

At this point, the lawyers and clients are poised to make decisions about appropriate action. They need to determine which path of strategy is the best avenue through which to attempt a resolution of this case given their goals and resources. As Tables 1 through 3 reveal, this is not an easy decision. There is a great deal of uncertainty concerning what actually happened, whether liability can be proved by Clark, what happened between Clark and the young woman, as well

Table 3. Clark's Potential Net Litigation Value

Strategic Path	Gross Revenue From Path	Expenses	Legal Fees	Downtime	Diverted System Costs	Emotional & Psychic Costs	Collateral Costs & Consequences	Collect-ability	Net Gain or Loss to Clark
Pretermination Negotiation	$650,000	$1,000	$5,000	Slight	Small	Reasonably Slight	Small	100%	$644,000
Litigation Negotiation	$1.2 M	$40,000	$400,000	Substantial	Substantial	Substantial	Substantial	100%	$760,000
Trial	$3.0 M	$75,000	$1.2 M	Great	High	High	High	100%	$1.725 M
Post-Trial Negotiation	$2.0 M	$75,000	$800,000	Great	High	High	High	100%	$1.125 M
Appeal	$3.6 M	$100,000	$1.2 M	Great	High	High	High	100%	$2.3 M

as how the episode will be perceived by a jury (if the case goes that far), what damages exist and how a jury will see them if they find liability, and much more. The reasons a strategist chooses one path over another are explored in the next several chapters. As part of this process, the consideration of *Clark v. Mega* is continued in the contexts of negotiation and trial.

Part IV
The Paths of Legal Strategy: Negotiation and Mediation, Trial and Arbitration

Nine
The Paths of Legal Strategy

"In war . . . let your great object be victory, not lengthy campaigns."
Sun Tzu, *The Art of War.*

The Paths of Strategy and Relevant Characteristics

How does the legal strategist know whether to take the "war" to trial or settle the dispute through negotiation? Does mediation offer the best solution or should arbitration be used? The concept of the paths of legal strategy is a construct that symbolizes the primary environments through which legal strategists work. They provide what Sun Tzu would call the terrain of strategic interaction, its structure, and its sources of power and leverage; he would refer to these characteristics as a combination of *earth* and *heaven*. His use of a narrow pass to bottleneck an enemy's forces during a storm or Musashi's attack when the sun is in an opponent's eyes are examples of how the strategist uses the tangible and intangible characteristics of a strategic environment to obtain greater advantage.

The strategic paths are not isolated from one another, but are dynamic and interdependent. They are parts of a coherent system that is linear while at the same time being aspects of an interacting, mutually reinforcing, multidimensional whole that involves the issues of time, evidence, people, resources, and "weight" in the forms of burdens of proof and persuasion. An important aspect of the concept of strategic paths is that while they have predictable and occasionally immutable characteristics of the kind on which Musashi reflects in his idea of the *background timing* within which a dispute or conflict moves, the paths are also open to what might be called "new construction"—high-speed lanes, bridges, speed bumps, varying speed limits, unmarked railroad crossings, blind curves, and so on—as well as sabotage and surprise created by you and your opponent.

179

The functions served by the various paths of legal strategy help the strategist determine the best choices about how to resolve disputes in the client's favor. A vital function of negotiation, for example, is not only settlement, but investigation and information acquisition. The legal strategist will often use the negotiation or mediation paths to acquire information, evaluate the case, transmit messages and impressions to the opponent, and seek to set the case up for trial by verifying information and assessing the ability, level of preparedness, commitment, thematic approaches, and positions of an opponent. It can also be used to shape and control the opponent's approaches, timing, and actions. This is similar to Sun Tzu's observation made in connection with how to gain information from an opponent: *"Rouse him, and learn the principle of his activity or inactivity. Force him to reveal himself, so as to find out his vulnerable spots."*

This litigation-referenced approach to dispute resolution is tied to the concept of the jury as decision-maker and other decision-makers of last resort over whom the lawyers have no direct control and increasingly little indirect power. Most of the litigation process is spent with an eye to avoiding the ultimate submission of the dispute to decision-makers who possess great discretion and only slight accountability to the parties and their lawyers. The specter of the jury—and increasingly that of a panel of arbitrators whose decision is binding—drives the dispute-resolution process more than any other single factor except, perhaps, the ability to pay for the legal services required to bring the dispute to those decision-makers in the first place. Assuming the disputing parties overcome that hurdle, the strategist looks to the jury and its decisions for guidance. The jury is the critical decision-maker that drives and defines the processes of litigation, including negotiation. The decisions of juries create the benchmarks for settlement negotiations as the lawyers and parties seek standards by which to establish the value of their particular dispute.

One of the most important aspects of the jury system is that it tends to represent the values of ordinary people, a consideration of importance in our democracy. It is important to realize that the ordinary, decent people of the kind who make up juries have often been subjected to the obstinacy, callousness, and cruelty of other people and groups of people in their own lives. This makes them more willing to punish such behavior when they have the opportunity. The importance of this fact is that if you are the plaintiff's lawyer, you should look for aspects of your case that fit such criteria because it will mesh with the decision-makers' (the jurors') frames of reference and values. Because the defendant company in Example 3 refused to listen to warnings about a defective pressure-release valve, one of its former workers has only one hand and the other's face is disfigured.

This suggests why the emotional aspects and themes of a case are so critical, and why a jury trial has such potential. The plaintiff-oriented lawyer understands quite well that the jury is a populist voice capable of high levels of indignation. As Example 3 indicates, if there is behavior on the part of a business that reflects sound economic principles but represents detestable human insensitivity, juries will often be punitive in their verdicts—even though the damages technically fall into other categories. "Bean counters" who justify saving a company $10 or $20 million in design, manufacturing, or recall and retrofit costs, even if there is a significant probability lives will be lost or ruined, are trading human lives for profit. Although this kind of decision-making is often justified by economists and corporate executives, juries tend to be unforgiving when they discover this deliberate choice has been made and are able to put faces on the unsuspecting victims. Many businesses and professionals don't seem to understand or care that the values and methods of economics and institutional decision-making for profit operate within different frames of reference than those that characterize the more humanistic values according to which jurors decide.

When defendants are willing to monetize helpless victims, they shouldn't protest too loudly when the juries monetize them in return. This is why so many jury verdicts have been escalating when juries believe such choices have been made. It isn't the plaintiffs' greed or unrestrained litigiousness, as insurance companies, doctors, and businesses complain, but it is a protest by the ordinary, disempowered people who serve on juries. Jurors are responding to the dehumanization and devaluation of human beings who are much the same as themselves. Members of juries are saying, "People like us count, and you better believe it!" What many of the interest groups who are trying to short-circuit the tort system don't care about, because they are trying to force the system to use economic rather than humane values, is that much litigation is caused by their clients' irresponsible anti-humane behavior and desire to escape accountability rather than by the supposed greed of "dishonest" plaintiffs. Any lawyer who fails to take such considerations into account when evaluating a case is doing a disservice to the client.

If you are the defense attorney in such a case, it is vital that you determine how your client behaved, discover the skills and strategies of your adversary, take depositions to see how the plaintiffs and their witnesses come across, and factor such considerations into your evaluation of both the settlement and trial values of the case. A part of this process also means, as was illustrated earlier, that you must discover your own clients' secrets. This isn't as easy or obvious as it sounds. As did the defendant doctors in *The Verdict*, clients often are trying to hide the reality of their behavior from you. Jim Miller in *Clark v. Mega*, is another example of this behavior. He may only tell the truth when the process is heating up and he is afraid of being exposed. The lawyer is then supposed to clean up the mess.

Each approach—negotiation, mediation, arbitration, and trial—generates a unique *ground* within which the action occurs, and creates its own field of energy, spirit, leverage, and power. The legal strategist must understand these differences, both in general terms and in their application to individual cases, clients, and opponents. The strategist must carefully identify and use the strategic path that offers the best outcome potential and probability, while still allowing the strategist to manage and minimize unreasonable risk.

The characteristics and goals of the parties, and those of the decision-makers help dictate the choice of the most effective path. These strategic paths and their characteristics are outlined in Figure 1. One path may be preferable for resolving a particular kind of legal dispute while being counterproductive for another. Or a path that is useful at one time may lose its appropriateness as a dispute unfolds and changes its nature and characteristics. This obviously applies to the *Clark v. Mega* situation. Up until the point that Jim Miller fired Clark, Miller was able to unilaterally exercise his legal power to terminate Clark. But by actually doing so, he transformed the dispute into a different kind of process over which he has considerably less control.

In Figure 1, various characteristics listed with the strategic paths represent a range of considerations varying in intensity and applicability as a dispute shifts from one context to another, or moves along the timing and pressure continuum of a particular path. As it suggests, each path possesses distinct rhythms, internal and external timing features, differing decision-makers, more or less intense cost and re-source requirements, and distinct outcome potentials and probabil-ities.

Figure 1. The Strategic Paths and Their Relevant Characteristics

Strategic Paths	Range of issues
	Opportunity for alternatives
Nonlitigation negotiation	Formality
Mediation	Privacy
Prelitigation negotiation	Ease or difficulty of
Pretrial negotiation	implementation
Court-ordered arbitration	Nature of disagreement
Binding arbitration	Intensity of disagreement
Summary adjudication	
Eve-of-trial negotiation	**Decision-Making Characteristics**
Trial negotiation	
Trial	Internal decision-makers
Post-verdict negotiation	External decision-makers
Post-trial motions	Subjective decision-makers
Appeal	Objective decision-makers
	Control over decision
Timing Characteristics	Burdens of proof and legal
	presumptions
Background timings	Private v. public
Inside timings	Thematic potential
Internal rhythms	
Cycles of pressure	**Resource and Cost Characteristics**
Bottlenecks	
Collectability	Resource intensivity
Time to final payment	Resource availability
Degree of risk	Resource timing
Value of benefit	Direct costs
	Indirect costs
Miscellaneous Characteristics	Recoverable costs
	Nonrecoverable costs
Suitability to client's goals	Outcome potential
Flexibility	Outcome probability

The Outcome Potential of Each Path

When looking at Figure 1, an important reason for choosing a particular path over another is understanding the outcome potential achievable for the kind of dispute with which you are involved. Different kinds of outcomes, as well as different degrees and certainties of outcomes, are achievable for each strategic path. Each path has the potential for a type of outcome that is not only monetary but—often at least as important—allows for greater or lesser flexibility and the ability to reach agreement on a wide variety of nonmonetary concerns and solutions.

In looking at the strategic paths and their characteristics, how would you advise Louis Clark if you were his lawyer? Visualize the following conversation between Clark and his lawyer:

Clark's Lawyer: "Louis, I talked with Mega's lawyer and I have some good news."

Clark: "Great! What's the good news?"

Lawyer: "Well, you're fired. They changed the locks and put all the stuff from your office in a box."

Clark: "What are you talking about? You said it was good news. Is this a joke?"

Lawyer: "No, really. Look Louis, now they really screwed up, and I'm pretty sure we can get them for age discrimination and a lot more."

Clark: "But I told you I wanted to keep working at Mega. That was what I really wanted."

Lawyer: "Sure, but Miller didn't see it that way and cut you loose. Don't worry, I'm sure you'll be able to find a job at McDonald's to hold you over and keep busy. Did you ever see the morning shift? A lot of older guys work there. And if you can't find work, that will just push up the damages."

Clark: "My God! I should have just gone to Miller directly and tried to work it out. Now I've lost everything. My career, my office, my salary. Nobody is going to hire me now that I have been fired."

Lawyer: "Come on! You're looking at this all wrong. I've already started drafting the complaint. We'll sue for millions."

Clark: "Are you certain we'll win? How long will it take?"

Lawyer: "Well, of course I can't guarantee anything, but it looks good. We'll probably have to settle near trial or do the trial, so it'll take about three years. Oh yeah, by the way, I'll need another $10,000 if you want me to go ahead with this."

Clark is not feeling very good about his lawyer right now. While this dialogue is obviously tongue-in-cheek because no responsible lawyer would be so insensitive as to break the news of his termination to a client in such a callous manner, it is a reminder that a client and lawyer will often see disputes in quite different terms. For Clark, his nonlitigation goals of continuing work, retaining his dignity, not suffering from continued stress, and protecting his reputation have not been achieved. Clark is out on the street, in emotional turmoil, has no real job prospects after devoting a significant part of his life to Mega, is facing a period of despondency and possible depression, in addition to finding himself with a lawyer who can't tell him anything concrete and wants more money. The lawyer apparently needs remedial work in client relations and in nonconfrontational approaches to dispute resolution. Clark is understandably upset, but he is an experienced professional and refuses to be put off by vague generalities. Rather than writing out a check for $10,000 he asks questions.

Clark: "I need to know how we are going to proceed. What is really going to happen, how long will it take, what will it cost, and how much can I expect to win?"

Clark's Lawyer: "It's like I said. There are a lot of variables and it's not easy to pin things down at this point. There's still a great deal of information I have to find out through discovery, and I can't do that until after we file and they answer."

Clark: "Look, I understand all that. I'm not stupid. I'm asking for your best judgment about what this case is worth, how much it will cost me, how long it will take, and when I can expect to get some money from it. I also want to know if there is any chance things can be patched up with Miller, and I can get my job back."

Lawyer: "OK, here are some potential figures on damages we can ask for (shows Clark Tables 1 and 2 from pages 170 and 171). You can see this case is potentially worth a lot of money if it goes all the way through trial. It has substantial settlement value even if we don't actually try it. All I'm asking is for you to bear with me on this. I'm trying to help you."

Clark: "You really think a jury is going to give me over $3 million?"

Lawyer: "It could happen if everything falls into place, but I can't be certain until I do discovery."

The discussion between Clark and the lawyer is very preliminary and unsatisfactory on several levels. First is the insensitivity with which the termination news was given to the client. This is so obvious that little else needs to be said about it. Clients come to lawyers to help them achieve outcomes they are unable to attain themselves, and to some extent for their knowledge and a little "handholding" to reduce the stress of legal disputes. Lawyers aren't therapists, but they have the responsibility to be aware of the difficult conditions under which their clients are operating, and should strive to support them and reinforce their basic human dignity.

The irony reflected in the above dialogue is that it is Clark—rather than the lawyer—who has identified some of the most critical considerations that go into the estimation of a case's outcome potential. Look at the questions with which Clark is concerned: How will the case proceed, how long will it last, what will the case cost, how much can he expect to win, and what is the probability of achieving the various outcomes?

How do you explain the outcome potential to a client in terms that are useful? Assume the following discussion between Clark and his lawyer:

Clark's Lawyer: "Louis, I'm sorry to telephone you at home. I know it's late, but I thought you needed to hear this. Miller made his decision today, and his lawyer just called me."

Clark: "From your tone it doesn't sound all that good. Am I right?"

Lawyer: "I'm afraid so. I tried, but you were right, he is an insufferable bastard. And to not even be man enough to deal with you directly after you gave so much to Mega. Are you okay? I know this is a blow."

Clark: "Actually, I feel pretty good. I'm surprised. I suppose it will hit me in the morning, but the way they have been treating me made it almost inevitable this was what was likely to happen. In some ways it is a relief. But what happens now?"

Lawyer: "We get right to work on our litigation strategy. I need to see you first thing in the morning to go over the options and decide where we go from here. Can you make it down to my office at 9:30?"

Clark: "I don't have too much on my calendar so that shouldn't be a problem. I do want to run by my office and pack it up sometime, though."

Lawyer: "From what they told me that won't be necessary. Everything was thrown into boxes and will be delivered to you."

There is a substantial difference between this interaction and the initial dialogue. Here the lawyer shows support and concern for the client. The empathy to which someone in Clark's position is entitled as a matter of both professionalism and human decency is now present when before it was absent. But even so, Clark still needs to know what is going to happen in this dispute. Assume it is 9:30 the next morning and Clark comes to the lawyer's office.

Lawyer: "Louis, I'm glad you could make it. How are you feeling?"

Clark: "Angry. I stopped at Mega this morning and tried to get into my office to make sure they didn't lose or break something, but they wouldn't even let me in the building. Twenty years of my life and I can't even get into a place where the general public can enter. I want to pay Miller back for this. I felt like some useless fool. I really need to know what we can do."

Lawyer: "Good. I've been thinking about this and I feel that Miller is vulnerable on several fronts. We are going to go after him for wrongful discharge based on age discrimination and for retaliatory firing related to your questioning him about the pension-fund violations."

Clark: "How strong do you think those claims are?"

Lawyer: "It depends on what we can pin down when we get deeper into Mega's records, do some depositions, and talk to the other executives who Miller has forced out one way or another since he became CEO. Based on the records you have already shown me and the conversations you reported, I think the age-discrimination case will only get better as we go on. The retaliatory claim will have to wait for discovery. I have a feeling that it's our ace in the hole. If you're right and Miller has been doing some stupid stuff with the company's pension fund there's a real chance he won't want it to come out. I think that it gives us some negotiation leverage."

Clark: "Then you feel there's still a chance to settle this?"

Lawyer: "Almost all cases settle. There's no reason to think some kind of settlement won't happen, but we're involved in a different kind of situation than existed before Miller cut you loose."

Clark: "That's really what I need to know. What happens from here? What can I expect?"

Lawyer: "That depends in part on what you want out of this. What I do and how I proceed is all about what you want."

Clark: "Before this happened, all I wanted was to keep my job until I retired and be treated decently. I did my work, and I was good at it. I just wanted to be able to keep at it. Now I have to focus on what I want now that I've been fired, and I have to be realistic about it."

Lawyer: "And?"

Clark: "First, I want to make sure about our financial security. There's the pension issue and what happens with that. The pension's vested and while I still feel like a young man, who knows what will happen? I don't want to end up poor in my retirement, or leave my wife without adequate income if something happens to me. I really need to know what's going to happen with that and if there's any way it can be protected and even increased. I don't deserve what happened, and I don't feel the pension I would have received at retirement in seven years should be cut. Second, I don't know why I'm saying this, but I'd like you to explore the idea of Miller letting me come back to work. I don't really expect you can do much with that, but if things can be smoothed over it seems that we might all come out ahead. If you can't do that, then I want to hit Miller with everything. I want you to get every dollar you can from him because of what he did. What do you think?"

Lawyer: "I think we can get a lot of money from him before it's done, but if you really want me to try to smooth this thing over and convince Miller to rehire you then the path of action we initially take has to be reasonably conciliatory. I have drafted a complaint, but if I file it there probably won't be much chance of a negotiated or mediated settlement that results in him letting you go back to Mega. But I see what you want, and it's my job to help you get it. So what I'm going to do is redo this complaint a little and then send it over to him."

Clark: "But I thought you just said that will make getting my job back almost impossible?"

Lawyer: "No. Filing the complaint with the court and making all this public would most likely have that effect. What I'm talking about is sending it over to Miller so he sees what could happen if he doesn't start being more cooperative. I don't think he has had any real idea up to this point of the potential consequences to both him and Mega, and I want to bring this out to him."

Clark: "But I thought you said this to him already?"

Lawyer: "Words don't come across with the same impact that they do when you see them down in a complaint. Plus we were trying to keep things as nonconfrontational and low key as possible during negotiations. Remember?"

Clark: "I do. Okay, I trust you. So do what makes sense, and keep me posted. By the way, can you give me an idea of what this is going to cost me?"

Lawyer: "Well, right now that's easy enough. I think you are up-to-date except maybe for two hours of my time. I see no more than three or four more hours involved in my dealing with Miller about possibly working things out instead of going full bore into litigation. That's at $150 per hour, so we're talking about a range of $450 to $600 if we're lucky, and I can shake him up enough for him to realize it isn't worth his time and energy to keep playing hardball."

Clark: "And if that doesn't work?"

Lawyer: "It's like my law school professor always told me, the stakes keep getting higher, and the solution costs everybody more. If we have to go all-out on litigation, it will be more expensive, but we are going to try to avoid that. In any event, let me try this approach first, and if it works you're home free. If it doesn't, then we need to sit down again and talk about a retainer as an advance against fees and expenses. There we are talking about $10,000 up front, but after that it could go to another $20,000 to $40,000 if we have to go all the way. That won't be for lawyer fees, because as we discussed in the beginning, if discovery bears out what you told me I'll be handling the bulk of any claim we litigate on a contingent fee basis, and there is a chance I might be able to get an award of statutory attorney fees if we prevail."

Clark: "So you're saying this could cost me up to $50,000 if we have to try the case?"

Lawyer: "You're a consultant, Louis. You know what experts cost, and we'll need an economist and several others, as well as paying for depositions at over $1,000 a pop. Litigation isn't cheap, and I'm going to be taking pretty close to an all-or-nothing risk on this. Very little of the money you pay is going to me. You know that."

Clark: "I know. But laying out that kind of money without any guarantees of return is scary, particularly since I've just lost my job."

Lawyer: "No question about it. Let's just hope Miller will see reason. After I send this over I'm going to call him and see if he'll agree to a mediator. If I can get him to do that, it can create a way for him to save face and be reasonable."

What Clark and his lawyer are doing is determining the client's goals now that he has been fired and discussing the most effective ways to achieve the goals. They need to do this because each path represents a different outcome potential that is dependent on the type of case, the specific characteristics of the individual case, or the strategic situation. Each law case is simultaneously unique and similar to cases of that general type.

Mediation is a variation on negotiation, with many of the same considerations. It is considered in the next chapter along with negotiation. Because mediators can't compel decisions, mediation may not help the disputants reach a satisfactory outcome. A mediator may, however, be able to show litigants reasons why their expectations are reasonable or unreasonable, help deescalate tensions, and facilitate the identification of alternative solutions. But mediation tends to be most useful for resolving problems that involve continuing relationships rather than for maximizing damages. In many ways, the Clark/Mega situation appears to be a perfect vehicle for a mediated approach, particularly prior to his termination, but even during the period when litigation is pending. It is a useful strategic path because the litigation downside is significant for both parties. As long as there is a chance to resolve the conflict amicably and to either dampen the fires of the conflict or to deescalate its intensity, mediation is by far the most humane, intelligent, and cost-effective approach to use. Even after suit has been filed, mediation can allow people to gain a sense of the validity or inadequacy of their positions at a point before the litigation expenses of a case become catastrophic. Such insights can lead to earlier settlements in many civil cases.

While mediation may be of substantial assistance to Clark in his attempt to repair a badly deteriorated employment situation, it is not useful in all types of cases. A totally different kind of case, for example, one that involves personal injury, suggests the need to follow other paths. What outcome potential would a lawyer whose client was burned by a fire caused by an allegedly defective toaster expect if he or she decided to participate in a mass arbitration process? How would that outcome potential change if the case were pursued through negotiation of the individual claim or trial?

To answer a question such as this, the strategist needs to be able to take all the cost variables and potential benefits of each strategic path into consideration. If a particular burned client has unique or tragically serious injuries, in a situation in which there are numerous plaintiffs with injuries of widely varying severity, the lawyer may want to be certain that case is personalized and individualized. This tends to favor opting out of any class action, and going it alone. Otherwise there is a substantial risk that your client's more severe injuries may be submerged into a general pool of injured claimants in which the client receives only a small part of what a jury would be likely to award. This is a particular problem for seriously injured plaintiffs in mass-tort cases.

Another factor to keep in mind when choosing the best strategic path involves knowing the nature of the decision-makers who will either accept or reject offers or claims in each path. Negotiation, for example, may often not be the best strategic path for a plaintiff to reach an outcome that awards the highest amount of damages, particularly if the damages are "soft" and will have to be driven upward by jury sentiment, indignation, or outrage. This has obviously been the situation in cases discussed previously involving leaking silicone breast implants and asbestos. In such situations, trial may offer the highest outcome potential for the most severely harmed individuals, but the unpredictability and the all-or-nothing risk that many trials represent are limiting factors that we can think of as outcome probability contrasted with outcome potential. While the two concepts are similar in many ways, it is helpful to think of outcome potential as coming closer to the terms of a best-case scenario, while outcome probability involves the lawyer's best and most pragmatic estimation of what is likely to actually happen. Each aspect is practical but the probability modifies the potential of a case. This consideration is important because probability and risk must be considered in determining a case's most realistic and concrete value.

The lawyer's estimation of the value of any case should be discounted in a responsible assessment of the risk factors associated with taking the case all the way through a trial verdict, and subsequent appeal. On the other hand, one way a plaintiff's lawyer can hedge the bet for the client is to sue multiple defendants when appropriate, and settle with some of them prior to trial. In that situation, the plaintiff already has a guaranteed win, and can afford to go for broke against the remaining defendants. In an Illinois suit against Owens Corning, the estate of one asbestos plaintiff who died of mesothelioma sued twelve defendants. The plaintiff settled with nine defendants before trial, another was dismissed, one settled during trial, which left Owens Corning as the sole remaining defendant. The jury then returned a plaintiff's verdict of $12.5 million, all of which represented compensatory damages. The plaintiff's trial risk was controlled, the trial became more focused, and the plaintiff already had a guaranteed monetary win because of the prior settlements.

There are two essentially distinct arbitration paths—court-ordered and contractual. Court-ordered arbitration, as opposed to contractually-binding arbitration, often fails to produce a final outcome. Although there will be a decision reached by the arbitrators, the participants can choose to accept or reject it. If they determine it realistically reflects a figure close to what a jury is likely to award, why go to the time and expense involved in a full-blown trial? Conversely, if the decision is considered badly skewed by one of the parties, then why should it be accepted unless the transaction costs of going further are prohibitive, or the probability of achieving the better outcome is not very good? On a positive note, the arbitration process does pull the two sides into a dialogue, requires that some thought and preparation be given to the case, produces a decision that can provide a frame of reference for more specific settlement discussions, and can help resolve the dispute at an intermediate level of compromise.

Contractually-binding arbitration is a path you can rarely avoid if there is a preexisting agreement to submit disputes to arbitration. Mandatory binding arbitration is likely to involve lower damage potential for claimants because most arbitrators are lawyers, and most lawyer-arbitrators aren't going to be emotionally oriented to maximizing awards. The arbitration agreement may put a cap on damages or limit the kinds of damages that can be recovered. Additionally, courts have ruled consistently that people who have agreed to arbitration procedures are "stuck" with the process and the outcome. This judicial trend will continue because many judges are resorting to ADR (alternative dispute resolution) methods whenever possible to reduce pressures on the courts, and the Federal Arbitration Act also favors ADR.

The desire of judges to use ADR approaches, or other methods of resolving disputes rather than a complete trial, can paradoxically increase the opportunity to deal intelligently with disputes in less costly and more reasonable ways, while heightening the risk of injustice for many individual plaintiffs. Numerous plaintiffs are choosing to opt out of class-action settlements to pursue their claims individually. Women who were members of the class-action suit involving the proposed silicone-implant settlement, for example, found that the $4.25 billion fund originally agreed to by the defendant companies and plaintiffs' lawyers was grossly inadequate. By June 1995, 440,000 claims had been filed by women who had breast implants. This meant that many members of the class action could expect final awards as low as $5,000, or only 5 percent of what had been expected when the settlement was first negotiated. Compare that amount to the $5.2 million jury award to a Texas woman for a leaking silicone implant. Another woman with a silicone-implant claim was awarded $3.9 million compensatories and $10 million punitives by a Nevada jury.

In many class actions a significant number of plaintiffs are being betrayed by the process, while others receive settlements they don't deserve. This is because there is an inherent tendency to blur the subclasses of injured parties and treat different cases as if the harm to the people was identical. Large classes of claimants are falling victim to the economics of the situation in which the court system uses the class-action vehicle and settlements to reduce its own stresses, costs, and overloads; the defendant companies use the settlement to control costs and convert their liability to a known factor, which means they can continue doing business without being concerned with the specter of a vast contingent liability; and the plaintiffs' lawyers receive an enormous amount of money relatively early in the process. This is a regular result of the recent flood of mass-tort litigation. Most of the class members become bystanders, while the lawyers on both sides profit. A 1995 $31 million Remington settlement, for example, was estimated to pay only a few dollars to each person who had bought a shotgun from the company over the past thirty years. The lawyers for the plaintiff class, on the other hand, received millions of dollars in attorney fees. The pharmaceutical company in Example 2 is quite likely to try to buy its way out of its difficulty by offering a class-action settlement pool and even a medical monitoring fund. If successful, it may win by bribing the plaintiffs' lawyers with an offer that provides the lawyers (in essence) with millions of up-front dollars at the expense of their clients and the impairment of future claims.

Outcome Probability:
Risk/Benefit and Collectability

Part of knowing how you should proceed with a strategic path depends on the amount of risk the client is willing or able to accept. If a client with a legal problem were dealing with an investment counselor rather than a lawyer, the prospective investor should expect to be asked how much return is wanted or needed, and what degree of protection or safety the individual desires in the investment program. The investment options would range from the most highly speculative and leveraged investments, which would bring very significant returns if everything turned out right, to bank certificates of deposit (CDs) insured by the federal government. There would be little risk of loss with the CDs, but the investment return would be relatively low. With the most speculative investments there is the risk of losing the entire investment, plus—if the investments are heavily leveraged—the investor might face disaster if forced to cover the losses. The upside is a big win, but the downside can be catastrophic.

The same kinds of considerations apply to legal strategy, but too many lawyers are not very good at identifying the risks, benefits, costs, and options for their clients. Of course, there are different variables involved in many law cases, but civil cases can be looked at as investment vehicles with identifiable risks, characteristics, and costs of doing business. As lawyers, we need to explain these factors better to our clients. An example of risk and opportunity assessment is provided by the previously described jury verdict against Owens Corning, in which three plaintiffs sued for the consequences of disease caused by their long-term workplace exposure to asbestos. Two of the plaintiffs had already died from mesothelioma, and one was very ill at the time of trial. Two separate juries were used, one to determine compensatory damages and the other to determine liability and punitive damages. The jury deciding on compensatory damages came back with individual verdicts for the three plaintiffs of $1.35 million, $1.145 million, and $875,000. But as we already know, that wasn't even the bad news for Owens Corning.

While the compensatory awards of over $3 million were substantial, that was just the beginning. The jury determining liability and the propriety of punitive damages returned a verdict against Owens Corning that found it was between 15 to 23 percent responsible for the plaintiffs' illnesses (several other defendants had already settled prior to trial). A week later, the same jury, after hearing evidence directed to the applicability of punitive damages against Owens Corning, returned verdicts of $18.2 million in favor of each of the plaintiffs, a total in punitives of $54.6 million. A spokesperson for Owens Corning said: "It was a ridiculous way to award punitive damages." This individual obviously doesn't understand what happens when companies treat innocent human lives as just another cost of doing business. As noted before, corporate monetization of human life leads to jury outrage, and the jury, as representatives of the community of ordinary human beings, then says, "Now we will make you pay for what you did."

The problem with such a case as Owens Corning and its liability in the asbestos lawsuits is that it is virtually impossible to completely resolve the dispute short of trial. The competing estimations of settlement value and each party's corresponding settlement range are simply so far apart there is no overlapping. Each side is taking an enormous speculative risk. A complicating factor for Owens Corning—and a simplifying one for the plaintiffs—is that after other defendants settled with the plaintiffs for substantial damages it became easier for the plaintiffs to take the risk against Owens Corning. Once the trial was stripped down to only one defendant it became more likely the jury would focus on that defendant as the particularly bad actor. The plaintiffs and Owens Corning may well have been close to settling at some point, but the settlements agreed to by the other defendants shortly before trial left Owens Corning extremely exposed and vulnerable. This suggests the inherent danger of alliances which, after all, are nothing more than marriages of convenience, and also points to the shifting and adaptive nature of strategy.

At trial, the plaintiffs had to hope the jury will buy into the "18 = life" standard when making its decision. Owens Corning simply wasn't able to deal in those terms, or couldn't believe a jury was likely to return such an enormous punitive verdict. Additionally, defense lawyers won't believe in that kind of possibility until it has happened several times and has also been upheld on appeal. In late 1995, Ford was stunned by a $62 million jury verdict for rollover defects in its Bronco II vehicles, which led to a plaintiff's death. Such a judgment can be expected to affect Ford's evaluation of its potential exposure in pending cases, as well as those of other plaintiffs in similar situations. This is because each side now has a different perspective on what is realistic and possible. But until a pattern becomes clear, the outcome potentials and probabilities can be seen by both sides as being so radically different that a pretrial settlement is very unlikely. In such situations, resort to the trial path is almost inevitable.

A lawyer is responsible for evaluating the case for the client in terms of its legal and financial viability, and the unavoidable costs that must be paid by the client. This is part of the information Louis Clark is seeking from his lawyer. These costs, and the realistic outcome probability, nearly always reduce the "face value" or apparent worth of the case. If, for example, there is only a 10 percent chance of winning a $50,000 case, but the lawyer will generate $10,000 to $13,000 dollars worth of billable hours and the client must pay an additional $7,000 in expenses, then the client deserves to be told the case is not worth pursuing unless he or she can afford the expense or it is a matter of principle for which the client is willing to pay. For calculating probable outcome, the equation the client needs to see is:

$$(.10 \times \$50,000 = \$5,000) - \$13,000 - \$7,000 = -\$15,000$$

Provided with this negative outcome information, most clients would choose to not pursue their claim. As the probability of recovery increases to a 60 or 70 percent level, the calculation shifts. Similarly, so does the probability of a lower, but less expensive, outcome through settlement. There are significant differences between the outcome potential of a negotiated settlement of a litigation-referenced dispute and the outcome potential of rejecting settlement and taking the case through trial. For a negotiator, the problem is how to keep the opponent uncertain concerning the low outcome probability of the plaintiff's case at trial, so that they will be willing to pay your client $20,000 to settle the case. This is why so much of legal strategy is about creating false impressions, reinforcing an opponent's expectations, and concealing the weaknesses of your case.

The considerations also shift if you are handling the case on a contingent-fee basis because, for the client at least, this reduces the amount they have to pay in attorney fees unless the case is successful. In this particular example, if the $10,000 to $13,000 in fees is converted to one-third of whatever is actually recovered, then the cost to the plaintiff may or may not shift in absolute terms. The obligation to pay, however, is contingent and is generally more acceptable to the client while, as the case drags on, it becomes less so for the plaintiff's lawyer who will set limits on how much time and energy can be diverted to the case given the magnitude of the case and probability of the potential return.

Fees and expenses are a critical part of evaluating the realistic outcome potential of a case, as opposed to the abstract possibilities of what might be obtained under a best-case scenario if everything happens to break the right way. The expense reality of litigation should be explained to clients in clear and down-to-earth language, but a serious problem is that lawyers who are attempting to convince a client to sign a representation agreement understandably don't want to scare off clients who represent thousands of dollars in billable hours or potentially lucrative contingent fees. Many lawyers, therefore, have a tendency to be vague or misleading about the real costs of their services or the probability of a favorable outcome.

The other deceptive part of the sales pitch is that the lawyer's ability to help may be subtly overstated to hook the client into buying legal services from the lawyer. In a situation where a client has money to pay fees, or if it is highly probable that some money will be forthcoming from the case because of insurance or some other source of revenue, lawyers have an unconscious incentive to overstate the beneficial outcomes that they can achieve for their clients because there is a guaranteed source for their fee.

Divorce cases are among the worst examples of client abuse by lawyers who string out the cases interminably to maximize fees. Months after retaining a lawyer, clients can be overwhelmed when the legal fees in their divorce proceeding have somehow escalated to $20,000 or $30,000, in addition to rapidly ballooning expenses. Too many divorce lawyers fight viciously until there are no assets left. Then it is time to settle or to sue the clients for unpaid fees incurred "on their behalf." Most lawyers do not behave this way, but too many do. One of the most frustrating aspects of law practice that allows this to happen is that the "negotiation dance" always takes two to do it right. Even if you are trying to settle a case in good faith, when you find yourself opposed by a lawyer who is churning the case to run up fees, there is virtually nothing you can do because the opposing lawyer is working in his or her own interest—not the client's. This is a strong reason to follow the lead of such states as Colorado where the courts require referral to a mediation process in domestic-relations cases. This can help to dampen the inevitable hostilities that characterize many marital breakups, and which make it easy for lawyers to foment antagonistic states of mind in their clients.

Although there are serious abuses by some lawyers—committed consciously or without deliberate intent—most lawyers are trying to perform well for their clients. One of the problems is with perception, however, because a lawyer costs a considerable amount of money and much of a lawyer's most effective work is invisible. Few clients understand how much time good lawyers spend on research, investigation, depositions, and other forms of discovery, case preparation, and so forth, in the effort to help solve their clients' problems and disputes. Sometimes, however, there is no avoiding client resentment, even when the lawyer has been completely honest and specific at all stages. People who themselves have no difficulty charging significant sums for their own services—mechanics, plumbers, doctors, contractors, businesspeople—somehow feel entitled to extremely low-cost legal representation. Knowing the likelihood of client resentment of legal fees and expenses, a lawyer should take care to send clients regular updates of activities, charges, and expenses— even if operating pursuant to a contingent-fee contract. Most lawyers now do this, having learned their lesson from a series of unpleasant disputes with clients over fees and expenses.

The full costs of representation—including inevitable and unavoidable costs, the most probable costs, and the contingent costs that depend on how the opponent proceeds and which path of strategy is successful—should be specified to the extent possible at the beginning, or as soon as they become reasonably obvious. Otherwise, a lawyer can expect client complaints to bar associations and grievance committees, as well as loss of word-of-mouth recommendations and referrals that can be provided by satisfied former clients.

There is a mutual distrust between lawyers and clients concerning whose interest the lawyer is working for. This is a particular problem when lawyers are handling a significant number of reasonably similar clients, in effect creating a better economy of scale for both the lawyer and clients up to a point, and for the plaintiffs' attorneys in class-action suits and mass-tort cases. Go back to the hypothetical toaster example. If the client's injuries from the defective toaster are relatively minimal, the lawyer may want to take advantage of a pool of damages made available to the plaintiff class. In the process, the plaintiff will be attempting to "piggyback" on more seriously injured plaintiffs. The lawyer takes advantage of economies of scale created by the class-action or mass-tort approach. The defense strategist faced with almost certain liability, thousands of potential claimants, and uncertain prospects with juries may want to create a substantial pool of money for class-action damages. The defendants have the court approve the settlement pool and then step back from the fray while the plaintiffs and their mobs of lawyers fight among themselves over how the money should be allocated.

Increasingly, this is the defense choice in mass-tort litigation when liability is clear, the class or number of consolidated cases large, and the damages significant. We have seen this with Johns-Manville and other asbestos defendants, Agent Orange, the Bhopal disaster, and the silicone-implant cases. The advantage to the defendant is finality of outcome, avoidance of protracted litigation and its enormous costs, and elimination of massive contingent liabilities that affect the value of a company's stock and (more cynically), the value of its key executives' stock options and existing holdings. In the Bhopal disaster, Union Carbide gained an enormous advantage by agreeing to a fairly quick settlement involving the establishment of a fund of several hundred million dollars. Union Carbide preempted many of the cases by working through the Indian government and brought a reasonably quick end to its legal obligations.

Plaintiffs have a limit to how hard they can fight defendants in mass-tort situations because the defendants in such cases have the strategic option of a tactical bankruptcy filing and reorganization if the plaintiffs are not reasonably cooperative. When a defendant uses this bankruptcy option, inevitably the plantiffs receive less than the reasonable face value of their claim and have to fight even harder. Whether defendants—who engaged in a knowing or reckless course of conduct or concealed information from vulnerable people—should be discharged in bankruptcy is a different ethical matter. But it is a viable strategic option.

In the cases of Agent Orange, silicone implants, Bhopal, and asbestos, the seemingly enormous funds have turned out to be inadequate to realistically compensate all the victims. This is almost inevitable in such cases. The rising costs of medical care, cost of living, and the slow manifestation and long latency periods of the diseases caused by the defendants' misconduct make it likely that many people will receive only a small portion of the value of their claim. Some will receive nothing because the funds are exhausted. This is why there should be medical-monitoring provisions in such settlements, controls on the levels of contingent fees that the plaintiffs' attorneys can receive, and, within a reasonable amount of time, the ability to reopen the settlement if it is found to be grossly inadequate.

Outcome probability can't be rationally estimated without knowing the decision-maker in the case. Sun Tzu emphasized the importance of knowing the opponent and self. That remains vital for the legal strategist, but it is also critical to know the decision-maker who will determine the outcome. One of the most important aspects of case evaluation and risk assessment is understanding the shifting nature of the decision-makers who choose the outcomes for each strategic path. Each strategic path alters the identity and characteristics of the decision-makers. It changes the degree of their objectivity and motivation, and transforms the kinds of factors, motives, and evidence that persuade them to agree to a resolution or lead to the allocation of responsibility.

Lawyers develop the themes, legal arguments, facts, and human aspects of a case to make opponents and other critical decision-makers—including the opposing client—view the situation within the same frame of reference most likely to be used by the ultimate decision-makers. In negotiation, this means educating opposing clients about what will probably happen if there is no settlement. If binding arbitration is the vehicle, the ultimate decision-makers are the arbitrators. Because most arbitrators are lawyers, law professors, or former judges, their unique characteristics, experience and training, as well as past decision patterns, should be taken into account. If trial is the end result, the judge and jury must be evaluated both generally (i.e., this is what many judges and many juries have been doing in these cases) and individually (i.e., this is what this particular judge does, and what these particular jurors are likely to do).

Advantages and Disadvantages of the Strategic Paths

Just as Sun Tzu emphasizes the importance of understanding the special characteristics of strategic terrain and environment (i.e., *heaven* and *earth)*, the lawyer must understand what is allowed or precluded in each path of strategy and what are the special advantages and disadvantages of each path. A tactic that works well in one strategic path may not work as well—or at all—in another. This awareness influences what the lawyer should reveal in negotiation and mediation or in presenting the case to a panel of arbitrators. If you feel almost certain you are going to end up in court anyway, don't give away the best parts of your case strategy before trial. As a strategist, you should ask, "Do I reveal the real theory or theme of my case, the one that will knock out a jury, or do I hold back?" The answer to that question should be, "I'm not going to lay everything out before trial because that will educate my opponents and give them time to anticipate, react, and develop a strategy to undermine and/or counter my best arguments."

As stated earlier, surprise is important in strategy. There are risks involved in providing a strong opponent with a clear picture of your strategic approach. Giving the opponent such insights can cause you to lose the battle if the dispute can't be settled through negotiation. Being careful to not reveal your underlying strategy reminds us of Sun Tzu's warning, *"All men can see those tactics whereby I conquer, but what none can see is the strategy out of which victory is evolved."* Think about Frank Galvin and his surprise rebuttal witness, Caitlin Costello Price. If Galvin had done his investigation earlier, discovered what the doctor had done to the admitting nurse, and brought out the doctor's threats and record-changing during negotiations, Ed Concannon would probably have been able to concoct a defense or have his pet judge rule the document inadmissible before trial. Even at trial, the judge could have ruled that Price's testimony should have been brought out during plaintiff's case-in-chief, rather than rebuttal, or that she couldn't testify because notice hadn't been given to the defendants. Another example is also found in the Owens Corning case in which it might have been useful during negotiations to expose the defendants to the "18=life" theme designed to appeal for punitive damages and create juror outrage, but should the plaintiffs' lawyers have revealed their specific approach that could have risked some kind of objection and/or given the opponents a better chance to develop a response?

Part of the decision about what to do depends on your estimation of the opponent's level of preparedness, frame of reference, and capability. It also involves judgment on your part about how much the theme will influence the opponent's decision-making and whether there is a realistic chance to close a significant settlement gap. Discovery rules, pretrial conferences, exchanges of exhibits and expert testimony, witness lists, trial and issue memoranda, and settlement proposals are intended to prevent surprise and enhance the chance of settlement by forcing lawyers to better understand their own case, as well as the opponent's. One of the main functions of these processes is to prevent surprises about critical aspects of the case and to encourage realistic settlement evaluations and dialogue. In *Clark v. Mega,* for example, consider the effect of the following interchange during the final pretrial conference:

Mega's Lawyer: "We aren't going to pay any more than $555,000. There is absolutely no way I will go higher."

Clark's Lawyer: "You know, I meant to mention this earlier but I didn't quite know how to handle it with the judge, so I haven't told her yet. Louis was going through some more of his materials the night before last and found a tape recording he made about a month before he was fired."

Mega: "You're kidding me, right? What is this, Perry Mason? If it has anything to do with this case then you should have already produced it. You'll never get it past the judge at this point."

Clark: "Does that mean you don't want to hear it?"

Mega: "What's on it?"

Clark: "Jim Miller calling Clark an old, washed-up has-been, who is finished at Mega. There are also threats by Miller to get even with Clark if he says anything else about the pension-fund matter."

Even with all the rules of discovery, this still happens. At this point, the Mega lawyer has to decide what to do, but if she has been playing games with the settlement figures, the surprise itself can be enough to cause her to increase the offer and try to get out from under this case.

Procedural Formality

Procedures become increasingly formal and driven by more explicit rules as a case moves from negotiation into mediation, arbitration, and trial. The rules define how and what evidence can be used and the kinds of arguments that can be presented. Trials reduce and limit the factual and legal arguments. In trial, for example, such considerations as relevance, the substantive laws applicable to the particular case, and more rigorous rules of evidence and procedure combine to limit and alter the issues that can be presented, the evidence that can be introduced, and the type of relief that can be granted. Arbitration has many of the characteristics of trial, although the rules of evidence and procedure generally are looser. Negotiation and mediation are much more open-ended. As the processes become more formal, they generally also become more expensive, time-consuming, and constrained.

Privacy

Privacy is another important factor to consider when determining which strategic path to follow. Most forms of negotiation are private. Privacy and secrecy are often particularly integral to mediation. Contractually based arbitration tends to be somewhat more public—although it depends on the parties and the contract—and could be entirely private. Court-ordered arbitration is public in theory, although few people other than those directly involved bother observing court-ordered arbitration hearings. Trials are far more public. Given American society's current fascination with trials as part of a human melodrama, anyone who is involved in a case with seamy allegations or sensationalist charges can expect little privacy. Consider, for example, if either Louis Clark or Jim Miller would want to have their dispute aired in court.

Timing, Speed, Rhythm, and Pressure

Musashi urged the strategist to become aware of the *background timing* of a strategic interaction. This applies with full force to analysis of the strategic paths. Each process moves at different speeds and rhythms. Does the lawyer want a quick resolution or a lengthy delay? Speed stands not only for the quickness, but the slowness, of case resolution. Negotiation can resolve a case in moments, or can take years even if done in good faith. Arbitration has its own pace and rhythm, which is more compressed and accelerated than is found in trials. If a mediator is brought in early in a dispute when the parties say, "We have a problem and are hitting each other over the head without getting anywhere. Let's involve a mediator and see if we can resolve it," the situation could be concluded quickly, or this strategy may not work at all. On the other hand, good-faith negotiation and mediation can be considered successful if parties learn important issues about the case—including whether settlement is likely. A successful negotiation does not necessarily require a settlement.

A quick resolution may be important to both parties. It can mean that clients don't have to pay nearly as much money to expensive lawyers. People in California and several other states are agreeing to "rent-a-judge" procedures, and are using both advisory and binding mini-trials to resolve conflicts. These alternative processes are being created because in major urban jurisdictions any civil case of consequence takes a minimum of 18 months from start to finish. It often takes more than two to three years for a case to reach trial, and can take even more. The first appellate stage of a case after the trial verdict can easily take another two years. It is not at all unusual for six or seven years to elapse between initial intake and the final resolution of a case. Even then, a plaintiff has to have made certain the defendant is collectable, and is not exhausting, concealing, or transferring assets while the process goes forward. If the opponents declare bankruptcy when faced with a substantial verdict, or exhaust their tangible assets by the time you "win" a verdict against them, your apparent victory can turn sour.

Corporate executives are using mini-trials to make informed judgments at relatively earlier points about whether the probable outcome is worth the expense of litigation. In the private mini-trial, only one party participates while lawyers on the same team present the best of the opponent's case. This allows for a test of the case on people similar to those who will serve as jurors in the actual trial. This can help a lawyer prepare for trial more effectively by seeing what works and what offends these rented jurors. It can also allow the lawyer to find out whether the case will likely be lost and, if so, how much the loss might be. Lawyers can better identify the flaws in their themes and evidence, talk to jurors about how their witnesses come across, and adjust their strategies when informed with this knowledge. Many well-funded lawyers have tried their cases several times to rented juries before they walk into the courtroom for the real trial.

Lawyers tend to assume control and "legalize" disputes that clients might be able to resolve if they better understood the issues, stakes, probable outcomes, and costs. For corporations involved in disputes with other corporations, the size of legal fees in a bitter and protracted dispute can be enormous. In many instances, if the client-principals on both sides are given the chance to sit down and say, "How do we resolve this?" rather than, "How do I beat you?" a large amount of money can be saved that would have been spent on legal fees, litigation expenses, and wasted employee time and energy.

This is, or should be, a significant consideration in a case such as *Clark v. Mega*. Both Clark and Miller can save themselves significant expense and energy if they can resolve their problems and put aside their dispute. Once the work dispute becomes legalistic, however, it tends to become more expensive, emotionally debilitating, and negative for everyone involved. Lawyers who really have their clients' best interests in mind must continually remember that, while it is often necessary, there are many occasions when conflict does the client a severe disservice.

A mini-trial can also help sophisticated clients look more closely at their case and decide whether there are strong reasons to go back to negotiation to try to resolve the dispute. A mini-trial can also be extremely helpful for corporate decision-makers to see and hear what the case is about through their own eyes rather than being entirely dependent on their attorneys' judgments. Lawyers like to control their cases, and many like to act as conjurers and magicians in regard to their "secret" professional knowledge. The clients who are most affected by the outcome may not, however, have a realistic sense of what the case is about.

If the speed of a strategic path represents an important consideration, so do the rhythms and pressures characteristic of each path, and the rhythms and pressures generated by the interaction of the paths. Law cases have predictable cycles and characteristics, and there are identifiable rhythms for each path. The rhythms are not necessarily inevitable because they can be varied and will take on a distinct flavor depending on the type of dispute, but the underlying rhythm, Musashi's *background timing*, remains. The existence of a rhythm means that each path requires a specific set of behaviors as it unfolds. For example, if you don't settle a dispute quickly, a different settlement rhythm takes hold. If a plaintiff files pleadings, then negotiation still takes place, but it is a different kind of negotiation. Litigation negotiation becomes part of, and is responsive to, the formal rhythms and timing schedules imposed by litigation rules and judicial practices. It is therefore distinct from nonlitigation and prelitigation negotiation. The parties will become part of the timing patterns dictated by the rules rather than being in control of their own timing. When litigation occurs, the process itself is more in control of what is happening, and of the pressure-cycles at which settlement is most likely, than are the litigants and their attorneys.

Each strategic path has its own internal mechanisms for generating pressure. There are channels within cases designed by the systems of informal and formal dispute resolution that allow for the steady building of pressure on the disputing parties as they approach the deadlines and tasks demanded by the rules of litigation. As you proceed, the channels through which you act become increasingly narrow. Bottlenecks develop that intensify the case's pressure as they approach, and then decompress the process if the parties don't settle. The pressure may be high at initial stages, low for a significant period afterward, and then build again as the lawyers perform the intermediate tasks of case preparation and exploratory negotiation against the backdrop of a process that is moving steadily toward trial or binding arbitration if the parties can't agree. These rhythms and pressures are built into the process, and are enhanced by the costs of litigation and the various deadlines.

Finality

Finality of result is important. Which strategic path is conclusively final in the specific case? What is the path's timing? What quality of result can be realistically achieved? Court decisions are final, but the finality is in the hands of others. Working through the trial process also requires a long time. Appeal can delay the final outcome for years, while increasing the costs to each party. Contractual arbitration, which typically has extremely limited opportunities for subsequent review by a court, generally ends the dispute, but the arbitrators will be the decision-makers, not the parties. Conversely, the parties can control the certainty of the decision by specifying the terms of the settlement agreement through mediation or negotiation. A negotiated agreement allows the parties to retain the power to make the conditions of the settlement certain and the resolution final. But even in this type of dispute resolution, much depends on the nature of the case and how the lawyers write the settlement agreements. Lawyers may think they have reached an agreement, only to be surprised when they attempt to put it in concrete and detailed terms and find the other side balking, or discover that critical items were left unresolved.

A settlement agreement is a contract, and like the drafting of any contract, the lawyer and client need to think about the real terms, ambiguities, the ease or difficulty of enforcement, the various parties' ability and willingness to follow through on their commitments, and the agreement's clarity. If, for example, in the future there is a dispute about whether the terms are being honored, how will it be resolved? At whose cost? Even if all persons involved are acting in good faith, an agreement in principle can fall apart on unanticipated details and specific implementing steps. The settlement agreement should be seen as the means by which the parties bring closure to their dispute, and if it fails in that purpose by being difficult to implement then the lawyers haven't done their task.

Control Over Terms and Result

Lawyers surrender the ability to control the outcome of a dispute when they allow it to be decided by people over whom they have no direct control. This distinction is critical. You, as a lawyer, control what is in a settlement agreement. You can't control a judge's or jury's decision. You have very limited control over the amount of damages awarded, except in contract cases or the like. At least in contract cases, you generally have an upper limit on your potential liability or recovery. Arbitration involves the same kinds of considerations. Lawyers retain the power of persuasion and the power of procedure during trial and arbitration. But they surrender control over what these other people (i.e., judges, juries, arbitrators) ultimately decide.

Just as no chain is stronger than its weakest link, no case submitted for final resolution to an arbitrator, judge, or jury is better than the quality, values, and interests of the people serving in those roles. Their interests and perspectives are unlikely to be the same as yours or your opponents. On the other hand, the most critical lever in negotiation is that a dispute can be turned over to a decision-maker not under the control of either side. This fact increases the risk, stakes, and degree of uncertainty. To avoid this, most litigants settle.

Cost

Another critical factor is cost. Which path of strategic action is more expensive and what do we mean by expense? There are various ways to look at the expense of a strategic path. How do you measure real cost versus apparent cost? Generally, the expense of taking a case to trial is much greater in terms of money expended, and the time and energy consumed in the process, than are the other strategic paths. The higher expenses are produced both by the added thoroughness and intensity of the preparatory phases required to try a case, and the effort involved in the trial and appeal.

Negotiation and mediation are almost inevitably less costly than trial in terms of direct expense, attorney time, and litigation costs. When determining the true costs of a case, however, we need to visualize a balance sheet, revenues on one side and expenses on the other. This requires identifying the path of strategic action that creates the greatest outcome potential, as well as considering the risks involved in achieving that potential. Think back to the *Clark v. Mega* situation, specifically Table 3, in which the net value of the case was presented.

Taking a case through trial may, for example, be twice as expensive as negotiation. But what if you feel there is a 90 percent probability you can achieve a $300,000 verdict at trial and that you have essentially reached the limit of the defendant's willingness to pay much more than their offer of $100,000 made only a week before trial? Although the defense may increase the offer to $125,000 at trial, the most desirable strategic path is likely to be to try the case because of the differential between your expectation of $300,000 and the defendant's probable offer of $125,000. Part of the decision turns on the quality of your evaluation of a 90 percent probability of a $300,000 verdict, collectability, the likelihood of appeal, and the significant gap between your expectation and the defendant's offer.

Questions you need to ask include: How much can your client afford to pay? How much can your opponent afford to pay? What are the ways to reduce your costs by following Sun Tzu's recommendation of "foraging on the enemy"? Is the opponent's lawyer obtaining his money up front? If so, what will be left for you and your client after a long and hotly contested struggle? If the opposing lawyers aren't receiving all their money up front, and it is a noncontingency defense case without a deep-pocket client, if you impose significant costs by forcing the action early and the defendant's attorney is a *"hand-to-mouth"* general practitioner, how long will the opposing lawyers be able to carry that client? As the bills for legal fees and expenses mount, when will the case's "sticker shock" hit the opposing client?

Collectability is certainly one of the most basic questions. Determining the paper value of a case, such as was done in Tables 1 through 3 of the *Clark v. Mega* fact pattern example, is only a preliminary step. The effective strategist seeks to understand the real resource conditions under which opposing clients are operating in order to know not only how hard and long they can afford to fight, but what resources exist to satisfy judgments. If you can't collect the money, the paper value is little more than symbolic. Such questions are presented much more explicitly in the following chapters entitled *The Negotiation and Mediation Paths* and *The Trial and Arbitration Paths.*

Ten
The Negotiation and Mediation Paths

*"Deal with a thing while it is still nothing; Keep a thing
in order before disorder sets in."*
Lao Tzu, *Tao Te Ching.*

*"One who excels as a warrior does not appear formidable [while] [h]e
who is fearless in being bold will meet with his death."*
Lao Tzu, *Tao Te Ching.*

"He will win who knows when to fight and when not to fight."
Sun Tzu, *The Art of War.*

The Purposes and Functions of Negotiation and Mediation

If trial is the legal system's equivalent of war, negotiation and mediation are the legal forms of diplomacy, which involve the staging of a campaign designed to put a strategist in a situation to win by maneuvering, planning, spying, discussion, compromise, alliances, and positioning. Like a military campaign, negotiation and its mediation subset are complex processes with many different functions and purposes. We collect these processes under an all-encompassing heading called negotiation, but this single term collapses negotiation into an overly simplified concept. Negotiation is a strategic campaign, not an event. As set out in the previous chapter, there are a variety of types of negotiation, including nonlitigation negotiation. To some extent all the various kinds of negotiation reflect a linear set of processes, but each also operates according to its own rules, dynamics, and functions.

The types of negotiation include:

• prelitigation negotiation

211

(margin note: Types of negotiation)

- nonlitigation negotiation
- post-filing/pretrial negotiation
- "eve-of-trial" negotiation
- trial negotiation
- post-verdict negotiation
- negotiation during the appellate stages of a case.

In *Clark v. Mega*, we have already seen efforts to resolve the emerging dispute before Louis Clark was terminated. Those types of attempts will be explored at greater length in this chapter. Many of the forms of negotiation depend on the intensity of the conflict and its outcome potential for one or both sides. As we will see, it is easy for powerful people operating within the context they dominate to lose sight of what might happen when the dispute shifts to one in which their power is diluted and is subject to others' decision-making discretion and evaluation.

Mediation can be an element at any point, although it is more likely to be used in the earlier stages of dispute. Each negotiation form differs in terms of function and concreteness, at least as measured by the likelihood of being able to actually resolve the dispute. The complexity of the negotiation process is revealed in Figure 2, which sets out the purposes and functions of negotiation and mediation.

Think about some of these factors in relation to *Clark v. Mega*. Remember the planning that went on before Clark's lawyer ever dealt with Mega's lawyer. When a lawyer is in the early stages of a case much of the information and approach is little more than a hypothesis. Interviews with clients and potential witnesses, and investigation are important parts of the process, but at some point direct knowledge must be gained about the opposing lawyer and client. This goal and such others as acquiring and transmitting information through the negotiation or mediation interactions are among the purposes achieved through the dialogue.

Consider, for example, if you decided Mega's lawyer was probably unaware of the seriousness of Miller's dipping into Mega's pension fund. You feel that this pension abuse is one of your strongest negotiation levers and that, regardless of what the lawyer says, it has to have a significant effect on Mega's willingness to negotiate. One of the decisions you should make is how to find out what she knows. You

(margin note: Finding out what opposing atty knows)

Figure 2. The Purposes and Functions of Negotiation and Mediation

---

Preparation, Assessment, and Planning

Assessing your opponent
Assessing the opposing client
Obtaining strategic information
Setting the tone for the next interaction

Clarifying, Generating Certainty and Uncertainty

Educating your opponent
Planting seeds in your opponent's mind
Assessing the opponent's general willingness to deal
Causing your opponent to reevaluate his or her position
Reevaluating your position
Uncertainty enhancement for the opponent
Agreeing to disagree
Proving your settlement case

Information Acquisition and Transmission

Information acquisition regarding general matters
Information acquisition regarding trial needs
Information acquisition regarding your evidence

Information acquisition regarding questioned information
Transmitting impressions about your case
Communicating your spirit
Controlling the timing of the process

Adaptation, Alternatives, and Solutions

Inventing and testing alternatives and solutions
Creating specific settlement resolutions
Reaching concrete proposals
Clarifying the terms of overlapping proposals
Closing the deal
Collecting or complying
Implementing the agreement

Proposing and Bargaining

Proposing, bargaining, compromising, trading off
Exploring common ground
Exploring areas of apparent disagreement
Exploring areas of real disagreement
Sending and receiving signals about general possibilities
Sending and receiving signals about specific possibilities

---

also must judge whether it even matters what she says because as long as you make sure she is aware of Miller's pension abuses and the fact you know about them, it should have the desired settlement-enhancing effect in Clark's favor.

When figuring out how to achieve this goal, you are combining a variety of the functions listed in the outline. First of all, you may be trying to obtain strategic information about your opponent's level of knowledge. You also want to educate your opponent concerning the pension abuse and the extent of your knowledge of it. By doing so you are planting seeds of doubt, creating uncertainty about the strength of Mega's position, causing Mega to reevaluate its position, and "proving" your settlement case. You may hold this information back until you feel it is of greatest weight for enhancing the probability and value of your settlement.

Assume, for example, that Clark hasn't yet been fired and you are trying to achieve a settlement of $800,000, use of an office at Mega for two years, full pension at age 60, a positive recommendation from Miller, no bad-mouthing by either side, and consulting business from Mega. Mega has responded by agreeing to everything, but is only offering $500,000. You may choose to bring out the information about the pension abuse at this point.

Mega's Lawyer: "Miller really won't go higher. We discussed it at length before you arrived, and he feels he's being extremely generous already."

Clark's Lawyer: "You know as well as I do that Clark could do a lot better at trial. You and I have tried to be reasonable about this, and I appreciate the way you've dealt with this situation. Both of us want to work this out without Clark being fired and Miller and Mega looking bad."

Mega: "You've hinted at that before. But Clark is an at-will employee. Miller can fire him if he wants. Plus, I don't really want to bring this up, but there is that allegation of sexual harassment. That's not going to help Clark's image if it comes out."

Clark: "We can deal with that, but you've been straight with me, and I don't want to see you sandbagged by your own client on this pension-fund issue. I mentioned it once before and didn't really want to bring it up, but. . . ."

Mega: "I talked with Miller about that, and he says it's all legal. He even cleared it with Mega's general counsel, so I don't really consider it an issue."

Clark: "You should talk with him again. I discussed it with Louis yesterday, and he showed me that what Miller did is a clear violation of ERISA. Clark's an expert on this and is very convincing. He sold me. And I probably shouldn't tell you this, but I found out from somebody who knows that Miller wasn't fully honest with you about what the general counsel told him, or even if they talked. You ought to ask him, because the $500,000 just won't do it. The point is, I want to settle but Louis really needs the $800,000. If he can't get it then all bets are off and we file. Then the pension-fund stuff is going to be the basis for a retaliatory discharge and we go for broke. You saw my damage analysis and what I'll be asking for. All Louis wants at this point is that $800,000 and the pension and office guarantees. After you talk with Miller, I think he'll probably agree."

It can be seen that negotiation and mediation are primary vehicles for the application of strategic planning, assessment, manipulating the opponent, and implementation and adaptation of your strategy. Even if you never settle the case—and you almost always will—negotiation is a critical way to learn about the opponent's position, transmit messages about your own, and gauge whether a resolution close to your strategic goal is possible short of trial, binding arbitration, or appeal. To do this, you need to think about how you can persuade an opponent to do something he or she does not want to do. This is explored in the concept of the burden of proof in the settlement process.

The Burden of Proof in the Settlement Process

There is a "burden of proof" in the settlement process, just as there is in trial. At trial, depending on the nature of the claim, you must be able to prove your claims, counterclaims, or defenses by such standards as preponderance of the evidence, clear and convincing evidence, or proof beyond a reasonable doubt. What these burdens really mean depends on the facts and people involved in the case. Other standards apply to review of administrative decisions on both the state and federal levels, to appellate review, and to affirmative defenses.

Being an effective lawyer involves selling yourself to your opponents. The sale includes conveying an impression of your skills, intellectual and perceptual capabilities, insightfulness, and the abilities to organize, persuade, listen, visualize, talk, and communicate. To do this, lawyers must first design a marketing package on behalf of their clients. Then they have to sell it effectively. Your opponents need to understand you are capable of selling the persuasive package to the jury or other decision-maker if the situation reaches that point. It is useful to help your opponents understand how the decision-makers in a strategic path over whom they have increasingly limited control will view the situation. When your opponents respect your persuasive and analytic abilities, the probability of a satisfactory settlement is enhanced significantly and is probably closer to what you estimate could be realistically won.

The ability to sell or effectively communicate your vision to an opponent often hinges on whether you have dealt with the person before, what kind of reputation you have in the relevant legal community, your experience, and the quality and preparedness of the opponent. If you haven't dealt with this opponent before, the thoroughness of your preparation, as reflected in the pretrial discovery process and case management conferences, can have a significant role in convincing the other side that you are competent, professional, and capable.

The nature of the settlement burden of proof varies depending on the type of case, the decision-maker's identity and degree of subjectivity, how much is at stake, the extent of risk, pending and already imposed transaction costs, interest in the outcome, and the values and characteristics of the specific decision-makers. In *Clark v. Mega*, even if each lawyer is advising the client at the peak of his or her professional skill, knowledge, and insight, there is still significant uncertainty and unavoidable risk. The question becomes that of how a lawyer and client obtain valid information, estimate risk accurately, and decide about acceptable resolutions. Think about *Clark v. Mega*, and how either side might be persuaded to accept a settlement. If, for example, Miller was reasonably certain he would lose $3.5 million at trial, spend an additional $500,000 on his own attorney fees and expenses, and also be responsible for Clark's attorney fees of $350,000, then from an economic perspective he would be crazy to go through the trial process, as opposed to either keeping Clark on in some mutually acceptable capacity or paying him a substantial amount in settlement.

If Clark, on the other hand, were certain he would lose at trial, pay $100,000 in attorney fees and expenses, and be without $150,000 per year in salary and benefits, it is difficult to conceive of him turning down a $350,000 to $400,000 settlement offer. In each situation, we are assuming the existence of a rational decision-maker armed with at least relatively complete and accurate knowledge. This assumption, of course, is the flaw. Just as is the case with economic models that are premised on full knowledge on the part of the economically rational decision-maker, the settle or litigate model operates on considerably less than full information.

The importance of the burden of proof for settlement is the recognition that to sell or prove a case to an opponent for purposes of settlement, you must design a communication and evidentiary presentation strategy, much as you are required to do to win at trial. Negotiations can be usefully seen as a kind of diffuse trial in themselves in which you are trying the case, not to a reasonably impartial jury or judge, but to extremely interested and subjective opponents who stand to gain or lose by their own decisions. How does Clark's lawyer decide on what will persuade Miller to agree on a particular settlement? Similarly, how does Mega's lawyer decide what matters most to Clark and which risks he considers acceptable? Depending on how much is being sought, the burden may be insurmountable, or it may be slight. Settlement burdens of proof aren't set out anywhere in rules and statutes, but nonetheless, they operate to determine when and whether to settle, and the terms and conditions of the settlements.

Even though the threat of trial drives the settlement process, you don't need to have the evidence and witnesses that would be required to prove the case to a judge or jury to win your settlement "verdict." Nor must your opponent. Trials involve decision-making under uncertainty, and within the constraints of formal rules. Negotiations often operate under even greater uncertainty, contain a wider range of interests and possible solutions, and work according to a different set of rules. The negotiation rules are much more tenuous, imprecise, and slippery than those of trial. The decision-makers in negotiations are themselves highly subjective and interested in the outcome. This means it can actually be much harder to convince an opponent in many negotiations, particularly when you seek to maximize your outcome at the opponent's expense.

The negotiation burdens of proof vary with the types of clients, lawyers, resources, and cases. A critical part of negotiation is the inherent mystery of a dispute and uncertainty about how much your opponent knows. Opponents may fear you will be able to piece together enough to win the case if it is tried, or they may be hiding something they don't want to reveal that doesn't have much relevance with this single controversy, but which they fear has larger implications. In *Clark v. Mega,* for example, Mega may be concerned that during discovery you will gain access to internal memoranda that would allow you to convincingly argue a case of age discrimination, not only for Clark, but several other terminated executives. Clark may not know this, but it still will affect Mega's timing and willingness to deal.

Victory Through Compromise

Negotiation is about compromise. A lawyer's willingness to compromise depends upon the outcome he or she realistically believes could be obtained through another strategic path. For example, if you seriously think a million dollars can be won if all goes well in trial, you must also be aware of how much it will cost to obtain that result, how long it will take, the element of risk at trial, and the collectability of the judgment. It also takes into account what will be lost in a litigation process characterized by hostility rather than the spirit of amicable dispute resolution.

The idea of real compromise has to be approached carefully, because an aggressive opponent can decide it reflects weakness. One defense lawyer who has criticized companies who have decided to settle disputes because of rising legal costs, suggests it is a short-sighted approach that ultimately costs the companies more. He warns that such defendant companies are developing reputations as easy targets, and that, "Word gets around quickly in the plaintiffs' bar because settlements are widely reported in legal publications (and) identify the companies that will pay handsomely on almost any kind of case rather than go to court." Given the nature of many plaintiff-oriented lawyers, this is like bloody meat thrown into a school of sharks.

The need to be seen as a strong rather than vulnerable opponent is one obstacle to compromise. It often means the opposing lawyers don't know when the time has come to shift from this macho posture to a more cooperative, settlement-enhancing approach. Or one lawyer may do so with a different timing than the opponent and find his or her overtures ignored or rejected.

Another obstacle to compromise is that different perceptions exist on each side concerning the potential and probable outcomes of a dispute. The opinions are likely to be different even if each side is acting in complete good faith and are highly skilled diagnosticians. When one or both sides fail to do the work needed to diagnose the case properly or fail to communicate their position effectively, there is an inevitable breakdown in communication that makes fair compromise more difficult. Consider the following situation: Assume you are the plaintiff's lawyer in a contract dispute and there is virtually no question that you will be able to win a trial verdict on a claim of $1 million based on breach of a contract between you and defendant. Your opponent has no real defense, but has created a smokescreen that you feel completely capable of dissipating. Preliminary efforts to resolve the dispute are unsuccessful, there is no binding arbitration clause in the contract, mediation was unsuccessful, and you filed suit. Two months before trial is scheduled, you demand $1 million and they counter with a $500,000 offer. How do you figure out what to do? If you decide to settle for less than $1 million, why do it and how much less should you accept?

The first step is to recognize that no matter how certain you are of your ability to win at trial and obtain a specific amount, your certainty can never be 100 percent. Regardless of your strength, ability, and confidence in your case and skills, whenever a jury is involved there is always some chance of losing outright, or of winning considerably less than you think is likely. Your settlement figure will almost inevitably represent a discounted value related to various risks and the probability of achieving your desired outcome at trial, as well as the unrecoverable transaction costs. If you put your chances of winning an award of $1 million at 85 percent; $950,000 at 90 percent; $900,000 at 95 percent, and so on, you can begin to factor in the inevitable uncertainty of the trial outcome.

There are unrecoverable costs even if you win a trial verdict of $1 million. Unless there is a provision in the contract for payment of attorney fees by the breaching party, the successful plaintiff will spend a great deal of money pursuing the case to completion. Assume, for example, that a prelitigation settlement could be had for $450,000, with no real litigation expenses, and thirty hours of legal work at $150 per hour. For an outlay of perhaps $5,000, the aggrieved plaintiff might net $445,000.

But assume your client is unwilling to settle at that level and demands at least $750,000. The defendant refuses and you file a lawsuit for breach of contract for the entire $1 million. The defendant answers, denying breach, claiming misleading representations by the plaintiff, that the plaintiff should have taken steps to mitigate damages, and, in the alternative, that plaintiff breached the contract and is liable to defendant in the amount of $500,000. In one recent case, a plaintiff suing for breach of contract faced such a response, which ended with a verdict against the plaintiff on the defendant's counterclaim for $7.2 million. Nothing is guaranteed.

In our hypothetical situation, assume that you, as the plaintiff's attorney, initially scoff at the defendant's answer and counterclaim, but then you begin to question the client about her expectations, about any factual representations she might have made to the defendant, and whether reasonable mitigating steps might have been possible. A few problems are discovered, but nothing that seems very damaging. The controversy heats up, and within the next three months you begin discovery, receive reports from several expert witnesses, and spend an average of twelve hours per week on the case. The litigation expenses are $12,000 at the end of the three months, and at an average of $1,800 per week over thirteen weeks, the attorney fees are $23,400. Along with the initial $5,000, the combined prelitigation and litigation expenses plus attorney fees are now at $40,400. At this point, the defendant raises his offer to $500,000, telling you that he is doing so only because it is time to decide whether to begin to gear up for trial. Following an acrimonious case-management conference, the judge sets the trial seven months from now.

The plaintiff looks at the offer of $500,000, and realizes that if she had accepted the $450,000 offer three months ago, she could have avoided the additional $35,400 in fees and expenses and even earned interest on the money. But now she has spent the additional money on fees and expenses and wants it back. She discusses the matter with you and you tell her that she will probably get an offer of $600,000 if you take the case near trial, and a verdict of between $800,000 and $900,000 if you try it. You say, "Of course, nothing is guaranteed," but that it is a reasonable ballpark figure. The plaintiff tells you, "Go ahead."

Over the next seven months, you complete the investigation and discovery. Six weeks before trial you begin to prepare witnesses, exhibits, experts, and so forth, as if you are actually going to try the case. You put in 15 hours per week for the first two months (120), 18 hours per week for the next 13 weeks (234), 20 hours per week for the next two weeks (40), 30 hours per week for the next month

(120), and 45 hours per week for the two weeks immediately preceding trial (90). The total period is 30 weeks, and the number of billable hours is 604. At $150 per hour, this adds up to $90,600 in additional attorney fees, plus perhaps another $10,000 in expenses. Assume the total added expense for plaintiff is $100,600 over this seven-month period. On the eve-of-trial, the plaintiff has already incurred $141,000 in total fees and expenses.

Assume that when the defendant shows up on the day of trial, the defense attorney raises the offer to $600,000, proving that you have been correct in your prediction. You communicate the offer to your client, who either accepts or decides she wants more. She is a bit miffed as she realizes for the first time that, even if she now accepted the defendant's new offer, she has lost at least $600 plus any interest she could have earned if she had accepted the defendant's initial $450,000 settlement offer seven months earlier.

If your client takes the offer the case is over, depending on the specific terms and whether the check clears. But assume she wants to recoup all her fees and expenses by winning at trial. After all, you said it was likely to be a favorable verdict of at least $800,000. Your client decides that because you have gone this far, "Why not just play it out?" She instructs you to reject the offer and go to trial.

The trial is only moderately complicated and is over in a week and a half. You bill at $2,000 per day for trial work. On the weekend, you review transcripts and other materials involved in the trial. The total is ten days of trial, $20,000 in attorney fees, plus $12,000 in added expenses, including expert witness fees for economists and technical experts to testify that it was all the defendant's fault. This total added expense is $32,000. By the end of the trial, the plaintiff has incurred $173,000 in attorney fees and litigation expenses.

The jury takes a day to return a verdict for the plaintiff of $575,000, agreeing with the defendant that your client failed to take all reasonable steps to mitigate damages, and also agreeing with the defendant's experts that the issue about who was at fault wasn't quite as obvious as the plaintiff claimed. You then tell the defendant you are thinking of appealing. Defendant says, "Fine, go ahead. I think I will too." Two years later, after vigorous briefing and argument by both sides, the appellate court upholds the verdict. You bill your client for an additional 250 hours of time ($37,500) plus expenses ($5,000) and congratulate yourself on a job well done. As your client writes the check for $42,500, she mentally adds it to the $173,000 she already spent and comes up with $215,500 in attorney fees and litigation expenses. When your client receives the defendant's check for $575,000 plus $35,000 in post-judgment interest ($610,000), she thinks back to the defendant's first offer to settle at $450,000, from which she would have netted $445,000. A quick computation shows that $610,000, minus $215,500, comes to a net of $394,500. Plaintiff keeps working with the figures but they come out the same each time. She decides she needs a new lawyer. "Somebody made a lot of money from this," she thinks. "But it sure as hell wasn't me. If the defendant paid as much to his lawyers as I did, then he laid out over $800,000 in total. We're both a couple of idiots to have let these lawyers take over $400,000 of our money."

In our hypothetical example, we were discussing a contract-based claim, rather than a dispute involving "soft" or such quasi-speculative damages as are found in personal injury, wrongful death, emotional distress, discrimination, or similar claims characterized by substantial elements of more discretionary and less predictable damages. The uncertainties increase in cases involving disputed-fact situations, conflicting witnesses, counterclaims, and the softer categories of damages. Even if you are able to prove liability, it is impossible to be truly precise in your estimations of damage awards that a jury might return either for or against you. The question of basic liability can be reasonably certain, or it may be seriously questioned, reflecting a judgment call that could go either way once the decision-making power is put in the hands of a jury.

Consider Example 3 from Chapter Three, which involved the injured workers. The defense took the risk of rejecting the plaintiffs' $500,000 pretrial settlement demand and lost a $4.3 million trial verdict. Liability can be clear, or even admitted, but the amount of damages highly controverted. Similarly, there is always a question about how your witnesses and your opponent's witnesses will be received by the specific jury impaneled to hear the case.

Jury decision-making is a very human process, with most of our best points and some of our worst tendencies coming into play. Juries are decent "judges" who can look at people and figure them out. Sometimes this works in your favor, and other times your clients or key witnesses are recognized as the slimeballs they really are—or at least seem to be. Jurors react instinctively to witnesses and parties based on the experiences of their own lives. We all tend to project onto other people the biases, favoritism, and prejudices we associate with people we know. Jurors may not even be aware they believe someone is telling the truth primarily because the person reminds them of someone they respect or trust. Jurors may feel as though they are dealing with a beloved brother, but it's really Jeffrey Dahmer, or they may think they are listening to a sainted grandmother, but it's really Ma Barker.

This type of inaccurate perception could just as easily work in the opposite direction. A juror may disbelieve, dislike, or suspect an honest person because of past associations the juror has had with someone who seems similar. You can win or lose a case due to unfathomable juror experiences and feelings of which they may not even be aware, and over which neither you nor they have control. This realization is an important part of a lawyer's decision about whether to settle or try a case. Some of the problems with how your witnesses will appeal to a jury can be identified before trial, but each jury is unique. In many instances, a lawyer can't make an informed judgment until the actual jury is chosen. This is why some settlements occur during trial.

A by-product of the fact that such a high proportion of cases settle, but tend to do so late in the process, is that many lawyers inevitably cut corners in their trial preparation. They do this because they either lack the resources and time to fully prepare a case, or they decide to risk what they consider to be a remote chance of actually trying the case because they still expect to settle on the verge of trial. This dynamic leads to substandard preparation by one or both sides if the case is ultimately tried. Substandard preparation generates a willingness on the part of many lawyers to settle at the time of trial because they know they haven't done the thorough preparation needed to try the case well. Although this sounds unprofessional, few clients can afford to pay for a thoroughly prepared case. When it is a plaintiff in a contingent-fee situation, the plaintiff can easily be shortchanged because many plaintiffs' lawyers have not spent the time or money required to prepare the case adequately. On the other hand, I know very ethical personal injury attorneys who "eat" the development expenses in cases that they ultimately don't pursue when the experts' reports demonstrate the claim isn't valid.

Agenda Design and Mutually Beneficial Outcomes

Given that few lawyers are actually fully prepared to try cases even on the brink of trial, it becomes very important that they become sophisticated negotiators. Agenda design and identification of mutually beneficial outcomes are critical elements of effective negotiation. Part of the reality of agenda design is that lawyers should begin their settlement demands at a point that holds enough in reserve so that they can offer concessions in the process of compromise, or at least appear to be compromising. This is also why it is useful to develop different kinds of demands or damage claims, rather than one claim in a massive lump of damages. If you are representing Louis Clark and feel there is a 60 to 70 percent probability that you can prevail at trial on liability and an 80 percent probability of winning $3 million after the jury buys into liability, where do you begin your settlement demands and how do you design your demand agenda?

You can rarely afford to begin at your desired goal (or even very close to it) because everyone expects negotiation to involve compromise. This emphasizes the importance of designing your agenda with the realization you will need to concede some of your allegedly desired points. Design your initial negotiation agenda with the knowledge that you will have to abandon something that allows you to seem to compromise. But, in reality, you will be compromising without giving away too much.

What if you go through an honest series of calculations that involve your best assessment of outcome potential and outcome probability, and decide, based on your estimations of a jury's most likely decision, that a fair, discounted figure that Clark deserves to receive is $1.5 million? If this is your target where do you set your initial demands and how do you justify or carry the settlement burden of proof to the opponent? If you start Clark's demands at the target point, you will almost always achieve considerably less—if for no other reason than that negotiators are expected to compromise. "Take it or leave it" strategies don't work that well in achieving settlements.

The ability to seem to compromise, and having issues to concede that don't require exhaustion of your negotiation capital, is essential to most of the negotiations in which lawyers engage. It is important to be able to project the attitude of compromise and concession, while, at the same time, appearing to give or demand a *quid pro quo* in a relationship of exchange with the opponent. But to make it seem that you are ready to compromise about an issue that matters, you must have principled reasons for justifying why you are starting at a significantly different point than your objective.

Conversely, you need to identify the points of principle in your case that enable you to convince an opponent you can't compromise on a particular point, or if you do they will have to give you something significant in return. Lawyers continually look for sticking points, which involve arguments of fairness, reasonableness, and similar value-laden terms designed to signal their unwillingness to go any higher or lower, or to accept or reject a particular term in a contract. Remember Sun Tzu's idea of the *moral law*. It represents the recognition of points of principle that are likely to be accepted as real by an opponent. Musashi's concept of deciding on the strategic spirit you need to project to an opponent contains the same insight. A principle or specific strategic spirit is much more effective if it has the ring of truth. It gains this substance by being consistent with how someone ought to think or feel in the situation.

Think again of *Clark v. Mega*. Clark could use principles of hard work and reward, fairness, damage to quality of life, indignation over bad treatment, and so forth, to create benchmarks that justify his demands. Mega can respond with a claim of lack of loyalty to the company, the impropriety of Clark's conduct, and the poisoning of relationships with co-workers. Each approach creates a principled position, and the power of principle is derived from our willingness to believe an opponent if he or she is successful in convincing us that a valued principle is, or at least could be, involved.

Another approach is discovering ways to implicitly communicate the message, "Look, I'm a reasonable person, but I've got this problem with my client. It's my client's agenda, not mine. I have to do it. I'd like to work things out with you if the two of us can come up with something I can sell to my client. Let's form a relationship based on professional pride and cooperation. We're two lawyers trying to settle this case, but my client (or your client) is taking a hard line." This is a kind of "false allies" overture of the kind used by the Archdiocese in the initial settlement discussion in Example 1. The insurance company lawyers presented Frank Galvin with a settlement check for $210,000 which, he noted, was divisible by three, the typical one-third contingency percentage. In that case, it backfired because it was too obvious and, ironically, was an attack on Galvin's principles.

As Sun Tzu emphasizes, strategy is an almost continual process of deception and illusion. You need to see through the smokescreens. How do we know an opponent's approach is likely to be a professional "lie," or at least not truly reflective of the real situation? As a legal strategist, the first point is to remember that considerably more than 90 percent of cases are settled. If people didn't want or need to settle the cases, they wouldn't be settled. But negotiators use illusions and threats, and even though we know they are often false, overstated, or that there is little chance the threats will be carried out, the illusions and threats still have an effect on us because of the uncertainty involved in the legal process, and the fact that roughly 5 percent of cases aren't settled. This means there is always the lurking possibility that the "fool" on the other side really means it when he or she threatens to take the case all the way through trial. It may also mean that the opponent knows something you don't about the trial probabilities of the case. Putting aside the questions of discovery, if Frank Galvin had been able to call his missing medical expert to the stand in *The Verdict*, and know in advance of the defendant's alteration of the plaintiff's admission record, then the pathetic negotiation exchange with the insurance company would have had a very different tone. Galvin would have been stronger, the insurance company less smug and more uncertain. Concannon did not know of the medical expert until his spy informed him. Nor did he know one of his clients had falsified the plaintiff's admission record. If you know such facts about your opponent, and he or she is ignorant of the point of vulnerability, then you have significant leverage.

The ability to obtain a beneficial outcome is influenced by how you design your case agenda. What you include, and the reasons you develop to demonstrate why you are entitled to what you are asking, are particularly critical because they define the terms of engagement. This is why you create your demands, claims for relief, definition of the nature of the dispute itself, justifications, principled positions, defenses and counterclaims, cross-claims, human issues, and so forth, in such a way as to threaten something you know your opponent holds dear, and/or offer a solution your adversary can recognize as being in his or her best interest. This reflects Sun Tzu's observations that you gain victory by accommodating yourself to the enemy's purposes, by seizing or threatening something he holds dear, and by foraging on the opponent's resources.

It is also why you create an agenda with multiple elements rather than crafting a single all-or-nothing claim. Having multiple claims and proposed solutions or demands not only helps define the agenda for negotiation, but enables you to have more things to "trade." There is little room for maneuvering with a single claim, regardless of how large it is. For this reason, Louis Clark's litigation negotiation agenda is likely to include claims for past wages, future earnings, the lost value of benefits, damage to his consulting opportunities, emotional distress, possible defamation, loss in the value of his pension, damages for a retaliatory discharge, so on. This diverse damage agenda gives his negotiator the freedom and ability to deal.

Your claims, defenses, principles, and demands are the variety of trade goods you set out on the blanket to swap with your opponent. Negotiation is a type of barter, and you have to be sure to bring enough different goods to the fair. Otherwise, you will be seen as a "store" that has only one product on its shelves. If people want it, you will probably do alright—at least while the item is in demand. But having a variety of products gives you a much better chance to be able to appeal to their consumer interests.

In a negotiation, it is useful to view your opponent and the opposing client as consumers. You do "market research" to figure out what the opposition wants most that you can provide, or that which they are at least willing to buy. In the previously mentioned Microsoft/ STAC situation, for example, in which Microsoft was found to be infringing STAC's disk-compression technology, it was probably much easier to "sell" Microsoft on investment in STAC, and a future license for STAC's technology, than on paying "damages." The most acceptable solution is often in the packaging. If one of the items is of particular importance for your opponent, but of no use to you other than as a bargaining chip, this still makes it of substantial value in an exchange. Part of your strategic task, therefore, is to try to put something of value to your opponent into the negotiation equation.

Part of Mega's agenda design, for example, prior to the point of Clark being fired, may well be the importance to Clark of his reputation and preservation of status for the purpose of future consulting work. These are basically of no value to Mega, except that they can be potential items of damages if the case is litigated and Clark wins. But they have high "privacy" value to Clark when they can still be protected. At the point in which the privacy can still be preserved, Mega has leverage afforded by the value Clark has for avoiding the embarrassment and the potential lost consulting earnings that may result. On the other hand, after the matter becomes public and Clark has suffered the consequences of dismissal, then their value is considerably less. Mega's CEO discovered this when Clark rejected a $1 million offer after he was fired.

A situation in which what you want from your opponents is something they can easily concede because it has nothing to do with what they want, is ideal. In a criminal case, for example, a prosecutor may be primarily concerned with obtaining a conviction with the least expenditure of time and effort, while the defense attorney is seeking the most lenient sentence for the client. This doesn't apply to notorious cases that receive significant publicity because both prosecutors' and defense lawyers' careers are made in such cases. When these cases happen, the rules of negotiation change. In the run-of-the-mill criminal case, however, the prosecutor and defense attorney are often operating from within different frames of reference. For a prosecutor, this is likely to be just one of many cases to be disposed of, while to the defense attorney his client's case is (I hope) the most important case in the world. In such a situation, assuming the defendant would most likely be convicted if the case were tried, each side can obtain that which they consider most important through plea bargaining. Mass production of cases is not only the province of prosecutors. Many public defenders, as well as court-appointed counsel in criminal cases who receive only minimal fees from the state, tend to function in much the same way and depersonalize their clients. The results of their labors are seldom equivalent to the best that should have been reasonably achieved for their clients by a top-level professional committed to zealous and effective representation of the client.

To determine which path to use, when to settle, and when to go to trial or to binding arbitration, requires a comprehensive evaluation of the case. A critical factor in evaluating a case is knowing what the specific court in which you will try the case (and similarly situated courts) has done with equivalent cases in the recent past. As with everything else in this world of accelerating change, you must be aware of the trends of jury decisions and settlements in similar cases.

Judges are increasingly putting both formal and informal pressure on litigants to pursue viable settlements. Increased judicial insistence that civil litigants explore reasonable possibilities of settlement, and have the authority to settle on realistic grounds, raises the probability that serious offers will be made at points in cases in which critical decisions tend to occur. Courts are showing greater willingness to impose sanctions when they do not feel good-faith efforts have been made by one of the litigants, as reflected in the actual jury verdict. Recent verdicts in two Philadelphia product-liability cases have demonstrated how this can be taken to a new level. Philadelphia-area courts are applying a new rule that provides "delay" damages that take the form of awards of prejudgment interest. The rule is invoked when the defendant has not made a settlement offer prior to trial that is at least 80 percent of the jury's actual verdict. Two plaintiffs' verdicts were enhanced by judicial awards of delay damages in excess of $1.3 million dollars. In those two cases, approximately seven years had elapsed between filing and verdict, and this resulted in substantial judicial enhancements. As might be expected, this new rule is reported to be producing more settlements. Whether such an enhancement is completely fair, given the inherent uncertainty involved in predicting the size of jury verdicts, is a different issue. But it is certainly a new factor that both defense and plaintiff strategists must take into account when deciding how to proceed and in evaluating the trial and settlement values of cases. Of course, part of the assessment depends on how clear the evidence of defendant's liability is in a particular case, and how untenable the defendant's denial of liability turns out to be.

Acquiring Strategic Information

What was a good settlement in a case two years ago may be entirely inadequate today. The irony is that, given the protracted delays in taking a civil case to trial, the advice you gave to a client about the worth of a case in the early stages of intake and development may be irrelevant two or three years later when the case actually goes to trial. If the changes cut in your favor everything is fine, but the trend can be against you. A friend in Colorado who engages in representing plaintiffs in personal-injury litigation recently described how a downward trend in the size of jury verdicts was affecting his valuation of clients' cases. A good lawyer keeps track of such things. Monitoring shifts and trends in verdicts and settlements is an obvious and important part of the strategic process for both plaintiff and defense strategists. This constantly updated knowledge helps you decide whether to engage in trial or attempt to resolve the case through an alternative path.

This updated knowledge should include such issues as whether plaintiffs or defendants are winning or losing particular types of cases when they go to trial. If plaintiffs are losing, is it because of a new legal ruling, the absence of a particularly important kind of evidence, a claim for damages that rings false but only came up in a specific case, an atypical judge or jury that doesn't represent the trend, or are there some other important considerations? If plaintiffs are winning verdicts, how often and in what amounts? Are the verdicts high enough or frequent enough to justify the costs of taking a case to trial? Are the plaintiffs' lawyers creating a base of professional knowledge by working on the early cases so that much of the investigation, discovery, expert analysis, strategic assessment, and trial strategy is a capital investment? These lawyers can be learning from their mistakes and this makes subsequent cases of the same type easier and less time-consuming as the attorneys become specialists in this particular area of litigation.

With the rapid expansion of computer capabilities, many software applications and informational resources have been created that provide a lawyer with ammunition to support one side of a case or weaken the other. To justify a $750,000 or $1 million settlement demand in a wrongful-discharge case based on age discrimination, such as is involved in *Clark v. Mega*, for example, the lawyers need to know what juries have been doing in similar cases. One partner in a New York investment firm recently won a $3.7 million verdict in a wrongful-discharge case based on age discrimination. What implications does this fact have for both Clark's and Mega's lawyers as they advise their clients about potential trial outcomes if their dispute is not resolved? How similar is Clark's situation to those in which wrongfully discharged plaintiffs have received substantial damage awards? A lawyer seeking to understand the relationship between her case and others needs to ask questions such as:

- What counts as a "similar" case?

- How many such cases have been filed?

- What have been the settlement outcomes?

- What percentage of the cases are tried?

- What have been the trial outcomes?

- What kind of financial gap exists between the negotiated settlements and any cases that have actually been tried to a jury?

- What are the critical characteristics of the cases that have gone to trial as opposed to those settled?

- How many trials have resulted in favorable verdicts for the plaintiffs, or for the defendants?

- How many have produced only nominal damages, even if the plaintiff wins?

A Louisiana jury, in a wrongful-death case based on cigarette smoking, found the cigarette company liable but awarded no damages to the plaintiff. Each lawyer interpreted this as a victory. The specific plaintiff in the case might not regard this as a win, although the plaintiffs' bar and pending plaintiffs are likely to look at the situation differently, because it helps them know how to better structure the presentation of their future cases.

One useful by-product of the proliferation of computerized databases is that a wide and deep array of detailed information on the results of fully litigated cases, as well as settlement, is readily available. It is now possible to detect, structure, and create patterns in ways that were previously unattainable. The lawyers are provided with important information when analysis reveals that, for example, most cases in a particular category have been settled or arbitrated at an average value of $100,000, and there are 2,000 total cases of the relevant type in the last five years. These cases have an average monetary resolution of $100,000, but only ten have been tried to a jury, with five of those plaintiffs' verdicts between $60,000 and $250,000. This type of knowledge helps provide a frame of reference within which both sides can maneuver. It makes inherently ambiguous situations more concrete. The lawyers have to decide how to take advantage of favorable trends in their settlements or trial strategies, or how to undercut the trends and past decisions by showing why their cases are different. But, at least a frame of reference for settlement dialogue has been produced, which allows the lawyers to develop justifications for their positions. Of course, it doesn't always work because of such factors as perceived differences in cases, disagreement between the opposing lawyers, lawyers who haven't done the work, data being from different jurisdictions, or shifting outcome patterns that haven't settled down yet.

One important decisional benchmark is that certain kinds of injuries can be identified as drawing particularly strong and sympathetic responses from juries. If, for example, a plaintiff has been paralyzed or has lost the use of a body part, damage awards tend to escalate rapidly once liability is determined. Significant damages are likely if an amputation has occurred. If there has been some kind of brain damage, even if difficult to establish at times and reasonably minor, juries tend to return large verdicts. This, for example, has much to do with the final outcome in *The Verdict*.

Nor is this type of jury sympathy limited to physical injuries. If a trust relationship existed between the plaintiff and defendant, and the jury feels the plaintiff has been encouraged to put health and life in the hands of a company, person, or entity who has a duty to provide high-quality services, for example, a doctor, hospital, or an airline, damages for a breach of that trust relationship can escalate quickly. Jurors can easily see themselves as being dependent on the same kinds of services and have little mercy for those who breach trust in such situations.

One of the ways lawyers put a dollar value on a case is to see what juries are doing in roughly similar cases, or they look at the amounts for which such cases are being settled. This information doesn't give all the needed data but, whether you are a plaintiff or defendant, it helps create expectations and justifications for what you are either seeking or resisting. Consider, for example, the following verdicts and settlements for several 1994 cases:

- Personal injury, Columbus, Ohio. A man was injured in a traffic accident when he was rear-ended by the defendant's truck. He suffered mild, but permanent, brain damage. The jury awarded him $1.55 million and gave his wife $250,000 for loss of consortium.

- Personal injury, Cleveland, Ohio. A jury awarded $1.4 million to a survivor of the 1993 USAir crash in New York. He had a badly fractured leg.

- Personal injury, wrongful death, Cleveland, Ohio. A jury awarded $8.1 million to the surviving spouse for the death of her husband and her own injuries sustained in the N.Y. USAir crash.

- Personal injury, Oregon. A jury awarded $7.1 million against the Boy Scouts of America for injuries to the plaintiff because the Boy Scouts inadequately supervised a touch football game that turned into tackle. This included $2.14 million noneconomic damages and the plaintiff was found to be 32.5 percent at fault.

- Personal injury, a N.Y. car rental firm was ordered to pay $4 million to a woman who was hit by a driver while she was jogging. She suffered leg, pelvic, and skull fractures, along with minor brain damage. She is now back working full-time.

If juries are awarding millions of dollars in personal-injury and wrongful-death cases, this suggests the settlement value of a wrongful death case in which liability is reasonably straightforward begins at a point well into the millions. Again, the information about what juries are doing provides a sort of "market value" to which the plaintiff's lawyer can point and use as justification for settlement demands. The burden then subtly shifts to the defendant to show why the plaintiff's figure is inappropriate, why liability doesn't exist at all, why there is substantial comparative negligence, why the plaintiff's assumptions are all wrong, or why a jury wouldn't give anything even close to what is being requested.

The quality of information is obviously critical. A single source should rarely be sufficient to enable you to feel confident. Sun Tzu's general is constantly using spies, scouting parties, probes, and other techniques to acquire "real" information. Musashi's techniques include seeking to force the opponent to respond to a gambit so the strategist can identify strengths, weaknesses, tendencies, and priorities. The strategist is continually acquiring and cross-checking information to discover nuances and to discern an opponent's intentions. As a strategist, you are identifying patterns you can rely on, and ones that provide insight on how best to attack. You are seeing if there is a thread that unravels an otherwise beautiful, but deceptive, tapestry. You are also trying to discover what your opponent knows, senses, or feels about your case. You want to know before trial if your opponent has discovered your weaknesses. You also want to discover your weaknesses so that they can be factored into your strategy. Many of these aims are involved in the questions outlined in the next section. These questions are part of a methodological construct which, as in Sun Tzu's *five constant factors* and *seven considerations for victory*, tell you what you need to know about your situation and your opponent.

Questions to Consider Before Talking With an Opponent

Settlement discussions don't necessarily take place during formally structured negotiation sessions "around a table." Formal sessions occur in many cases, but they are usually facilitated by other kinds of interactions that are equally necessary and integral to the

Not all Negot. is formal (handwritten margin note)

negotiation process. Cases are settled or are moved toward settlement through telephone conversations, chance meetings in courtrooms, during or after scheduled meetings on the specific case or on another case, during or after pretrial exchanges mandated by court procedures, and through informal but significant pressures put on the lawyers and parties by judges, the rules, and the outcomes of discovery and investigation. Many times, lawyers settle cases in hallways, over coffee or lunch, and offer ideas and suggestions for possible solutions in a very fluid process. These are the strategic *terrain* on which negotiation campaigns are conducted. Many problems can be solved, or solutions first proposed, through informal, off-the-record contacts. Raised informally, and by persons without obvious authority, ideas and suggestions can be floated and responded to without the need for final agreement. Just as in diplomacy, deniable intermediaries don't commit the principals, and are an extremely useful negotiating tool.

All this means that it is important to develop a realistic sense of what is actually happening within a specific negotiation discussion, what seems to be happening, and what is realistically possible at that point within the rhythm, timing, and flow of a case. It is very important throughout the process to keep track of the *background timing* because this keeps you anchored to an intuitive awareness of what is likely and unlikely at a particular point. As a set of varied processes within an overall strategic campaign, negotiation moves according to largely predictable and identifiable rhythms and patterns—each possessing specific timing realities and limits that are very difficult for lawyers to change. It is important to ask yourself each time you deal with your opponent, "What are the possibilities to be achieved by this specific interaction?" You must approach contact with an opponent or the opponent's agent very differently each time, depending on what you think can be realistically accomplished. It is useful to approach an interaction by considering the applicability of the questions listed in Figure 3.

As you read through the questions, think about how you would answer them if you were representing either Louis Clark or the Mega Corporation and were approaching:

- your initial interaction with opposing counsel

- your second or third meeting after a previous exchange of positions and ideas

- an interaction in which the Clark attorney felt it likely Clark might be fired

- after the complaint is filed

- a pretrial conference
- the day before trial
- the first day of trial
- during trial when the case seems to be going well for your opponent
- after verdict when you are representing Clark and the jury has rendered a $3.5 million judgment in your favor; a $2.0 million verdict; a $1.0 million verdict; a $250,000 verdict; or a $50,000 verdict
- you are representing Mega and are faced by any of the above verdicts
- you are representing Mega and the verdict is in your favor, but you feel there was substantial error by the trial judge that substantially prejudiced Clark's case.

In each of these different scenarios your needs and goals (and your client's) can vary radically. Just as Sun Tzu and Musashi emphasize strategic rhythm and timing, these distinct negotiation "events" call for a different approach.

Depending on the answers to the questions listed in Figure 3, a lawyer can know whether it is desirable or even possible to settle a case in a specific negotiation interaction. It is important to think this through in advance because strategists use their opponent's desire to settle as one of the major tools for manipulating them to obtain information and test and evaluate how their adversaries are responding to their probes. If a lawyer feels, for example, that he or she is in the final stages of a negotiation in which it is possible to work out an agreement, and the opponent is sending out signals consistent with settlement but then at a certain point says, "Gee, that's good. We've had a useful discussion, but now I'll have to go back to my client and talk about it," the other lawyer will sit there thinking, "What just happened? What did I do wrong?"

Figure 3. Critical Negotiation Questions

Victory and Goals

What outcome do I really want?
What are my purposes for this specific session?
What are my opponent's purposes likely to be?
What outcome does the opponent want?

What Is Known and Needs to be Known

What do I actually know for sure?
Where are the critical uncertainties?
What do I need to find out?
Who has the authority to settle for them?
Have all the right questions been asked and answered?
Are the answers satisfactory?

My Opponent's Strengths and Weaknesses

How good is my opponent's ammunition?
Does my opponent have skeletons?
Can my opponent deal with his skeletons?

My Strengths and Weaknesses

How good is my ammunition?
Can I conceal my skeletons?
Can I deal with my skeletons if they come out?

Impression Management and Deception

What impression do I want to project?
How do I project that impression?
Are they playing games?
Are we playing games?

Cost and Resource Considerations

How much has it cost to get my case to this point?
How much has it cost my opponent?
How much more will it cost after today if we don't settle?
When is the next big cost escalator for my opponent?
When is the next big cost escalator for me?
When will the costs be irreversible?
Can I afford to go on?
Can my opponent afford to go on?

Timing Considerations

What has already occurred?
Is the timing right for settlement?
Where did we leave off in our last contact?
How close are we to an agreement?
If the timing isn't yet right or "ripe" for resolution, what is the most probable resolution timing?
Are we ready to close?
Can they lock up a deal or are they just playing for time while doing something else?
When would a settlement be likely in this type of case?

Figure 3. Critical Negotiation Questions (cont'd)	
Settlement or Trial	Consequences of Not Settling
Do I want to try the case? Do they want to try the case? What do we save by settling now? Why do they want to settle? Why don't they want to settle? What are the probabilities I will win if we try the case?	What are the consequences if we don't settle today? If we don't settle now, what is most likely to happen? Can my opponent collect from me if I don't settle? Can I collect from the opponent if I don't settle? Is bankruptcy an option for me? Is bankruptcy an option for my opponent?

The Strategies and Tactics of Negotiation

Assume you have done a great deal of strategic planning and have identified and answered as many of the critical questions as possible. You have prepared to negotiate, and are now in a position to do so. Sun Tzu and Musashi are not concerned with strategic planning as an intellectual art form, but as an important part of taking effective action. Now it is time to convert planning to action in the form of a strategic negotiation campaign.

The methods of negotiation are extensive. Many of them are deceptive. Each must be examined closely because they almost all have the ability to be turned around and used against you. As suggested at the beginning of this chapter, negotiations are part of a strategic campaign very similar to military planning, information acquisition, positioning and maneuvering of forces; and major and minor engagements designed to probe and test an opponent, create uncertainty and willingness to avoid further conflict, convince the opponents it is in their interest to negotiate a peaceful outcome, or create turmoil and confusion. The overall process of designing and conducting a negotiation campaign can be even more complex in some ways than a military or martial arts struggle because in physical combat there can be an overwhelming initial onslaught that concludes the matter through death or total dominance of the opponent. A negotiation campaign rarely allows for such an early outcome unless the matter is relatively trivial or the opponent is totally inept.

Negotiation campaigns are nearly always conducted over time, with skirmishes, exploratory probes, maneuvering of forces, and intelligence gathering to determine the opponent's real strengths and weaknesses. In litigation-oriented negotiation campaigns—and even in high-stakes negotiations of other kinds—a powerful surge at the beginning is unlikely to resolve the matter. It may initially set opponents back on their heels, but it is also likely to convince them of the need to put up their guard at an earlier point and build stronger defenses. Intensity and aggressiveness during negotiations can therefore be counterproductive by forewarning or alienating the opponent. Early aggressiveness may also reveal too much about the attacker and/ or exhaust too many resources.

Due to the need to acquire information, and the necessity to discover the intentions of the opponent, the early stages of negotiation campaigns are often a careful probing process more than an all-out attack. Exploration, rethinking and evaluation, "scoping out" of relative positions and claims, and gaining impressions about opponents and their interests characterize the initial evaluation phases of negotiations. The probing, for example, may even help determine whether there is a real need to fight or if the burgeoning conflict can be defused and resolved without further harm to the disputants. The complexity and importance of the process of acquiring information, planning, and strategic action are reflected in Figure 4.

Figure 4. The Skills and Tactics of Negotiation	
Diagnosis	**Cooperative Action and Spirit**
Goal recognition	Cooperating
Goal justification	Tone
	Sharing
Acquiring and Transmitting Information	Playing to the decision-maker
	Revealing
	Compromising
Educating	False compromise
Probing	Revealing your weaknesses
Establishing standards	Confirming
False impressions	Common ground
Certainty enhancement	Releasing
Exploring	Interest
Uncertainty enhancement	Mutual victory
Revealing	Friendship
Detailing	Allies
Demonstrating your strengths	Treaties

Figure 4. The Skills and Tactics of Negotiation (cont'd)	
Problem-Solving and Reassessment	**Combative Action and Spirit**
	Pricking
Rethinking	Punching
Specifying	Counterpunching
Releasing	Challenging
	Denial
Fundamental Skills of Perception	Threatening
	Attacking
Listening	Pressuring
Watching	Defending
Verbal Communication	Deadlocking
Nonverbal communication	Tone
Patience	Feinting
Silence	Arguing
	Playing to the decision-maker
Setting up the Negotiation	Confirming
	Contradicting
Agenda setting	Indignation
Agenda substitution	Competing
Agenda buy-in	
Agenda preemption	**Offering, Closing, Implementing**
Setting-up	
	Proposing
Deception	Responding
	Suggesting
Feigning	Satisfaction
Pretending	Closing
False compromise	Writing the agreement
Revealing your weaknesses	Alternatives
Bluffing	Agreeing to the agreement
False Allies	

Think about the approaches listed in Figure 4 in the context of *Clark v. Mega*. In the first part of that dispute—whether you were representing Clark or Mega—you were learning from the client what goals were priorities, developing a sense of possibilities and obstacles, and acquiring background information. You were also establishing a preliminary set of strategies designed to test whether you could achieve your client's goals, whether alternative approaches and solutions exist, along with transmitting strategic impressions to the opponent, and attempting to evaluate the opponent's true intent. The strategies and tactics set out above are ways to achieve these goals.

Remember, for example, the early discussion between Mega's lawyer and her client concerning how to approach the initial negotiation session. They agreed she would project the impression that there was no solution acceptable to Miller short of Clark's discharge, even though that decision was still up in the air. This was a false impression designed to put pressure on the opponent and draw a response. The particular response was basically, "Then I'm out of here," but that also was little more than a gambit by the plaintiff's attorney. The response could just as easily have been, "Look, Clark really wants to stay at Mega and work, so please help figure out how to keep him on."

Either response transmits information, but the information is of a radically different character. Another approach could be for Clark to demonstrate strength by laying clear evidence of other age-related discharges on the table, including statements from co-workers repeating remarks Miller made about "old" workers and how he "hated people over 50." This can presumably have an effect on how Mega's lawyer will evaluate the risks in the case.

Uncertainty Creation and Certainty Enhancement

Uncertainty creation and certainty enhancement are important aspects of the negotiation process. You are seeking to gain greater certainty about your opponent's case and to discover what the opponent knows about your case. Lawyers should always go into a negotiation with the thought that they are going to learn something about their own case that they didn't already know. That's why you don't generally want to settle a case until you have had the opportunity to deal with your opponent several times. After the contacts, you need to step back to reevaluate your case and talk with your clients and witnesses about what you have discovered from the opponent. If you are representing Clark and have just talked with Miller about whether he is going to reinstate Clark, you need to step back and examine the meaning of what he has said or done. Then you discuss it with Clark and decide where to go from this point. After you do this, you will be prepared to go back to negotiating again and be much closer to a mutually agreeable reality in your judgments and goals.

Providing opponents with reasons why their case is substantially more uncertain than yours—or at least less certain than they think—can be an important part of a settlement approach. You may, for example, let your opponent know you are aware of obstacles in their case they either can't get around or that will be extraordinarily troublesome. During settlement discussions, lawyers often deliberately reveal knowledge about the strengths and weaknesses of their own cases, about what they have in mind if it goes to trial, and about their knowledge of the weaknesses in an opponent's case. Revealing the weaknesses of your own case, especially when they are of a kind the opponent likely knows, can send a signal that you feel able to cope with them if you have to try the case. Clark's lawyer waited until a critical moment before revealing to Mega's lawyer the seriousness of Miller's pension-fund abuses and the extent of Clark's knowledge about it. The risk of revelations that educate your opponents is that this new knowledge can help them better prepare for trial. Sometimes the opponent will not be aware of their weaknesses at all, or be unaware they are as severe as you are able to demonstrate. If you haven't revealed the extent of their weakness, and instead bring it out for the first time at trial, the surprise might improve the outcome you can obtain from a jury.

On the other hand, revealing knowledge that results in educating an opponent is a calculated risk that often must be taken in negotiating, or you will never get anything settled. Negotiation is about accurate diagnosis and proving your case to opponents with sufficient weight and clarity that it will shift their diagnosis more toward your position. The reverse is also true. As noted before, a negotiation campaign is a process of proof. To do this, you must be willing to offer evidence sufficient to carry your "burden" in the specific type of case.

Until confronted directly with certain evidence, themes, issues, characterizations, and law, an opponent may not have realized the significance of what you are revealing, or hoped that you weren't aware. Perhaps the opponent didn't know how effectively you could communicate. Even if an opponent pretends your demonstration of strength doesn't influence his or her judgment, or even if he or she consciously thinks it has not, it is still likely to have an effect and increase the willingness to settle. Being willing to reveal strengths and weaknesses also communicates you are a confident and capable lawyer.

Cooperation is sometimes impossible. Negotiation is very often an extended process of playing "chicken" to see who quits or weakens first as the ante is upped. The person who is being most reasonable or intelligent about the worth of a case may be the one who sees all the reasons why he or she should "blink." Some negotiators achieve better outcomes than rational analysis and case diagnosis suggests they should, because, given the inherent uncertainty of predicting a case's outcome, their willingness to play the game longer than the opponent gives them the critical psychological edge.

This is where Musashi's concept of *spirit* comes into greatest play. In negotiation, just as in any other competitive process in which humans engage, the winner is often that person or team best able to focus, control, and project the competitive spirit most effectively. Where more intelligent and rational analysis says, "Quit, settle, that's enough, I'm tired, and so on," those who are toughest and most relentless keep on and persevere. In the end they may gain outcomes their more cautious and rational counterparts can never achieve. A good negotiator always has the intrinsic toughness needed to persevere and accomplish more.

Negotiation strategy has many of the strategic attributes of a game of chess, in which you set up subtle patterns and gambits early on that are aimed at determining the outcome much later. It is also like poker, in which you must decide whether to ante at all, risk a little or a great deal, call, raise the stakes, cut your losses, or fold during the process. As a well-known country western song tells us, "You got to know when to hold them, know when to fold them, know when to walk away, and know when to run. You never count your money, when you're sittin' at the table. There'll be time enough for countin' when the dealing's done." Before the gambler gave this wise advice "his face lost all expression," so his true spirit and intention would be hidden from his opponents.

Your approach to certain actions will be looked at closely by skilled opponents trying to identify patterns that give them insight into how you are likely to behave in similar situations, in this or subsequent games. If they detect a pattern, they won't tell you what they have discovered, because possessing your secret provides an advantage. They file the information away to use against you at the time when it matters most. This is why Sun Tzu and Musashi repeatedly emphasize varying your tactics and acting in unpredictable ways. Otherwise, an opponent is able to see your rhythm clearly, know where you are going, and take advantage at a critical moment.

In negotiations, much the same as in poker, you have to decide whether to "call" an opponent, raise the stakes, or "fold." If you call or raise, you risk the entire bet. You may win because the opponent may have absolutely nothing and be bluffing totally, or may have an average hand, while your cards are very good. But in poker it doesn't matter how good your hand is if you aren't willing to pay the price to stay in the game. Even if you could win if you "call" the other player—if you don't take the risk, you lose. What makes it interesting is the risk factor. You also may lose if you do call the bet, and your opponent has a better hand.

How do you know when to fight and when not to fight ("when to hold them, and when to fold them")? First of all, don't be fooled into fighting reckless battles. When lawyers use anger and hostility, they must always be used as tools, not because they are actually succumbing to emotion. Musashi's *middle attitude* of balance and constancy keeps your true spirit from showing, while allowing you to move quickly in response to an opponent's moves. Legal strategists can only afford to become angry when they want to project that emotion to their opponents or to someone else involved in the case. Regardless of the strategic spirit they decide to project, strategists must always be objective. Much of the strategist's clarity, perception, and strength comes from the ability to maintain that balanced *spirit*, one that also links the master strategist to the natural power and insights of what Musashi calls the *void*. The strategist must always keep a critical part of self at a distance from the conflict, observing the events from outside the arena. A significant part of the strategist's choice of true spirit centers on calmness, balance, focus, and poise.

Releasing From a Deadlocked Spirit

Musashi emphasized the need to be flexible and overcome deadlock, using the term *to release four hands*. This advice applies when you and your enemy are contending with the same *spirit*, equally matched—balancing and resisting each other. In negotiation, this equality of *spirit* tends to produce deadlock. When you and your opponent are strategically balanced, and both seem unwilling to back off or concede, you must be willing to abandon a particular spirit and seek to win through alternative approaches. Rather than just giving up and wasting time and resources when you reach a condition of deadlock, *release four hands*. When you are in a deadlocked struggle with another lawyer, step back, release, and shift. Alter your strategic approach and cause a loss of balance in the opponent. Shift from a hostile spirit to one of cooperation or, perhaps, invent new solutions.

Otherwise, you will remain unproductively entangled in a wrestling match between two titans or two midgets, in which neither has the advantage, and the power is too evenly balanced. You could struggle forever, but all you would accomplish is the expenditure of huge amounts of energy and money. You must have adaptive strategies that provide options, fallback positions, and alternative strategies to be used against the opponent if the situation requires it. Of course, either you or your opponent might have reasons to want the situation to remain deadlocked, because either could be able to profit from the delay. Deadlock involves delay and imposes a timing on the dispute. One lawyer may stretch out the process by generating what appears to be deadlock, or inability to agree. In fact, the lawyer may completely agree with the opponent, but is implementing a strategy that requires seemingly intractable disagreement. It can simply be a matter of timing and leverage.

If you want to resolve a deadlock, you should begin by determining its real causes. It could be due to poor communication. It could be that the other side doesn't understand the case well enough to deal at the level needed to resolve the matter. It could be that your opponents are using the pressure of deadlock to put you "up against the wall" in the hope of gaining a significantly enhanced deal. They may need to be educated about the case or they (the lawyers) could be attempting to maximize their fee, and the deadlock enables them to accumulate more billable hours. Additionally, each side may have legitimate arguments that must be sorted out and weighed by a judge, jury, or arbitrator. Each cause requires a different approach that needs to be part of your negotiation strategy.

In many instances, the only way you can make opponents understand you aren't bluffing is by actually walking away from significant investments or opportunities and taking the loss or risk of loss. This is what the defense team did in Example 3 in Chapter Three involving the injured workers, and it cost the client millions of dollars. This is where Musashi's *resolute acceptance of death* comes in. If the conditions on which you base a strategic decision prove to be wrong, or the conditions change, you must be able to recognize the changed circumstances and know when you are in a bad situation that is not going to improve. You don't want to throw good money after bad. You can't recover some capital costs anyway. This often includes what you or your client have already invested in a law case.

As was emphasized by Sun Tzu, it is critical for the strategist to define the pragmatic meaning of victory, but it is equally critical to understand the meaning of defeat. You must know when you have lost, or when you no longer have any realistic chance of winning. Don't make the situation any worse by fighting valiantly—but suicidally—when it is wasteful and vain to continue. Rather than attempt to hold on for too long, recognize that your investment is forfeit. Don't continue to struggle and incur higher and higher losses that end up bankrupting you or your client. Sun Tzu tells us to let our goal be victory, not lengthy campaigns, and to not bankrupt the nation's treasury. If we apply this to legal strategy it proves equally wise advice. When you have found enough information through investigation and discovery to conclude your client is in a losing situation, which will lead to financial hemorrhage or ruin even the best strategy, explain why the losses must be written off and salvage what is possible.

This cuts both ways. DuPont, for example, before winning the previously mentioned May, 1994 jury verdict in the Benlate litigation, had already paid out $500 million in settlements in similar cases around the United States. Being "nice" and cooperative simply encouraged an increase in litigation as more and more plaintiffs pursued DuPont's deep pocket. Then the company shifted to a considerably more aggressive defensive strategy. Since adopting that more aggressive strategy, it subsequently won the cases it tried, and Dupont probably wishes it had tested its aggressive strategy earlier. But this is the chance you take as a lawyer. To achieve your client's strategic goals, you must take risks. Sometimes this means you lose. DuPont ultimately realized that making deals and paying out money wasn't bringing an end to its legal problems, it just caused more people to sue as they decided the company was an easy target. So DuPont drew a line and took a significant risk. Upjohn has also taken an aggressive stance in litigation over its drug, Halcion, and has been winning. Plaintiffs' lawyers are now on notice they are in for a long, bitter, and expensive war if they choose to sue Upjohn over Halcion. The approach is much like the Israeli policy on hostages and counterterrorism, in which they refuse to negotiate and then retaliate with ruthless aggressiveness. At the very least, this type of policy makes potential adversaries think before they decide to take you on.

If you make a threat, you must be willing to implement it if action becomes necessary. This doesn't mean you constantly make threats about the most dire consequences if the opponent doesn't give you what you want. Some of the best threats are tacit rather than explicit. Others are sufficiently veiled so that the other side knows what you are saying, but maneuvering room is left to allow face-saving by you and your opponent.

While your threats must be serious, you don't always want to have to detonate a "nuclear weapon" if your threat is not responded to in accordance with your precise terms. It is important to allow for face-saving. One way to buffer the effect of a threat to which your opponent fails to respond in the desired way, is to deliberately leave the threat implicit or use ambiguous language so that your subsequent limited response is still justifiable. In representing Louis Clark, for example, you might offer the information about the recent New York $3.7 million jury verdict in an arguably similar age-discrimination situation, and say, "Isn't it amazing what some juries are doing. I sure hope we can work this out and keep Clark at Mega." Before making the threat you have already created credible fallback positions that involve the ability to recognize a change in circumstances from the conditions that existed at the time of the threat or bluff, or possibly to show that your intent was different than was assumed.

You can accept a limited or partial response from your opponent as representing a good-faith effort that justifies not carrying out the threat at this time. Or an opponent may call you on a partial bluff. Because you don't want it to have been only a bluff or empty threat, you must anticipate the need for believable fallback positions.

Developing Creative Alternatives

Although strategy requires definition of goals and desired outcomes, you must have backups to your preferred outcomes. This means determining alternative ways to achieve your client's desired goals, and having alternative, but realistic, goals to which you can shift if necessary. In most cases, there is a change from your preliminary goals as the negotiations progress. At times, the "next-best thing" may be better than what your clients originally thought they wanted while they were caught up in the early heat of a conflict. Set up your avenues of escape in advance and be prepared to retreat. Create your alternatives as you develop the case, explore its parameters, and discover more about the competing interests. Sometimes your reassessment will show that you initially undervalued the case, and therefore, you will go after a more advantageous outcome. Other times an overvaluation will be revealed, so you will shift your terms as appropriate. Avoid putting yourself into a box or placing "all your eggs in one basket." This also means not fighting a battle from which you have no escape, or one in which you have no chance to even match your opponent. Wasting yourself and your resources on hopeless conflicts makes no sense, unless you are willing to sacrifice yourself to save others or to serve a larger purpose. Horatio did this at the bridge, Roland did it when fighting the Islamic onslaught into Europe, but these unusual situations of self-sacrifice don't happen very often in law cases.

Developing alternatives for your clients includes designing mechanisms and approaches that allow realistic survival alternatives if your primary goals can't be achieved. Another way of thinking about it is to ask, "What alternative paths will lead you to your goal or what other goals are acceptable outcomes if your original desires are unattainable?" This requires knowledge of how the world works. In his nine points of strategic mastery, Musashi urged, *"Know the ways of all professions"*; *"Become acquainted with every art"*; *"Know gain and loss in worldly transactions."* Whether we are talking about martial-arts strategy or legal strategy, such knowledge provides the foundation for the ability to create workable alternatives and solutions. Without the combination of creativity and knowledge, the strategist won't be able to see the potential for alternative solutions. This isn't solely the lawyer's province. Clients also need to contribute their ideas, because in many situations they have the knowledge needed to invent the alternatives. Often, your role will be to lead them into the brainstorming dialogues through which their knowledge can help identify other satisfactory goals and ways of achieving them.

Both Clark and Miller, for example, know the corporation much better than either lawyer. If there were to be a solution—short of termination—in which they used their knowledge to design a mutually acceptable outcome, they would be a critical part of the knowledge-base needed to work it out.

Recognizing Surrender and Concession

How you deal with others, how they value you, and whether you can reach an agreement is involved in every culture. While we associate the idea of saving face with Asian cultures, it is an equally essential part of the American legal process. There is a basic characteristic of human nature that says in effect, "If you embarrass me, I'll forever do my damnedest to rip your head off or get even—no matter how long it takes. You may have the upper hand now, but situations change and one day it will be my turn."

This human characteristic means that lawyers must look for ways to give their opponents the ability to go back to their clients with their "face" intact. Saving face means many things. The most basic meaning is not embarrassing other people needlessly. It also means providing opponents with apparently legitimate paths of action and means of dispute resolution so that each person wins something—or at least seems to win. Your opponent comes out with the appearance of not having lost, and quite often even the appearance of having won something. Put yourself in the place of your opponent. As a lawyer, you don't want your clients thinking you are either an idiot or incompetent. Your law practice depends on your reputation. You don't want to have to go back to your client and explain, "Their lawyer crucified me. She was better than I was and we didn't have a chance. I'm sorry, she tricked me. She had more leverage and I blew it."

Musashi urges us to develop our intuitive knowledge, and this is an essential part of negotiation. Intuitive knowledge applies to the level of nonverbal communication and perception. But subliminal cues and nonverbal communication are not only involved in attacking and probing opponents. A special function of nonverbal communication is to signal opponents about our intentions, willingness or unwillingness to settle, and possible terms of settlement. During negotiations, we often make contingent and hypothetical representations from which we can back off if necessary. We also send out a variety of hints and cues that allow us a range of plausible deniability if they are rejected. This is necessary because after a period of fighting and posturing that often involves threats, grand proclamations of principle, and unwavering nonnegotiable stances, at some point we usually want to explore the possibility of actually resolving the dispute.

Strategists need to recognize when an opponent is really giving up, caving in, or is on the run. Because there is so much deception in strategy, it is often very difficult for lawyers to know when an opponent is actually giving up as opposed to trying something risky and devious. Musashi tells us to know collapse, but for lawyers, the collapse of an opponent is often covert and masked. Legal strategists must recognize when their opponents are trying to signal a real desire to capitulate, making important concessions, or offering a final deal. A surprising number of lawyers keep arguing about points in a case even after their adversary has given up—or has attempted to do so. They continue arguing because they aren't listening, are too focused on their own argument, too aggressive, or haven't recognized the often deliberately subtle nuances of surrender and concession.

Part of being able to know when an opponent is beginning to give you what you want depends on being able to identify your opponent's values and goals. Again, evaluation of how your opponents will define their victory and defeat is an essential part of your ability to be aware of the real meaning of their actions and statements. Look at your opponent and think, "I know that strategic maneuvering and smoke-screens are going to be involved. I know they will say things very convincingly that have little or nothing to do with what they really care about and hope to achieve. They are going to try to manipulate me." Musashi would know that his opponent was trying to identify his points of vulnerability, disrupt his rhythm, present a false appearance, and anticipate and control his movements.

This means you must study your opponents carefully, seek to understand human nature, and apply that awareness to the specific people with whom you are dealing. Part of this requires learning what motivates people, and evaluating your opponents in terms of what is likely to be motivating them. If you don't understand what motivates human beings, not only individually, but collectively as participants in institutions with rules and values, they can easily deceive you. But once you know what they are required to value, individually and collectively, regardless of what they claim to value, then you can see through the strategic clouds, feints, and illusions your opponents construct to hide their true desires from you. This awareness goes a long way toward understanding and mastering the negotiation timing of your cases.

Even if we accept the necessity of making a deal, we don't want to be abjectly defeated, or forced into unconditional surrender. A defeated party in a negotiation—or one in the obviously subordinate position—generally tries to avoid the appearance of total humiliation and collapse. We try to save face, or attempt to gain some partial advantage even in defeat. We don't want to come right out and say, "Alright, I give up. I'm stupid. You win." Because of this, we attempt to surrender partially, gradually and subtly, rather than overtly, obviously, and completely. But most lawyers have competitive and aggressive personalities, as well as substantial egos. Lawyers need to figure out how both sides can come out of the settlement process looking reasonably good. If Mega's lawyer finally convinces Miller that he is significantly exposed if he fires Clark, how can Miller's "face" be saved? Should it be? If he is willing to deal prior to putting Clark through the emotionally painful termination process, it is easier to structure the situation in a way that allows Miller to come out looking alright. Otherwise, Clark may want a few pounds of Miller's flesh. This, of course, can be a positive and negative part of the settlement negotiations. It is positive for Clark's lawyer, who will have no difficulty convincing Mega's lawyer and Miller that Clark is emotionally committed to punishing Miller, but it is a negative because Clark may reject a good settlement because he really feels that way.

Should the Client Be Present?

One general reason clients are absent during most parts of the negotiation process is that the negotiation interaction is changed by the psychological climate created by having clients present. If clients were present, lawyers would tend to grandstand to impress them. They would have the added pressure of needing to look good for their clients, and in that process, they may fight battles for the clients that could undermine their ability to achieve the clients' desired goals.

An absent client, on the other hand, is an intractable and even irrational force. An absent client is a mystery and a significant source of negotiation pressure. Think of the car salespeople with whom you have negotiated. Just when you think you have a deal, the salesperson says, "I have to have it approved by the manager." The salesperson may then come back and say "We can't go quite that low," or is unable to give you as much on your trade as they initially thought. But you take the deal anyway, because the psychological climate to buy has already been created. When this very common sales tactic has been used, you have been hooked into the emotional state of accepting a deal.

There are also times when the client's presence is necessary and helpful. An example of this came early in my legal career during a negotiation with a Colorado school board about racially discriminatory policies. Our client, a large, aggressive, and forceful black woman, sat in the meeting for fifteen minutes without speaking as her two white male lawyers discussed the problems with the white male school board. The school board provided all kinds of reasons why their behavior in regard to minority children was reasonable and legitimate. She suddenly exploded in anger and dressed the board down in absolutely clear language of a kind that would bring credit to a Marine drill instructor. She then stalked out of the room, saying she was going to organize a demonstration. The school board members were stunned at her level of anger, but we found them suddenly more cooperative. They didn't want to have to deal with her again. We got what we wanted because this wonderful woman and local civil rights leader, Elizabeth Patterson, was so unfamiliar and intimidating to our opponents that they would concede a great deal simply to negotiate with us rather than with her.

What lawyers say to each other during negotiation and what they say to clients outside the settlement dialogue is often very different. Within the negotiation between Clark's lawyer and Mega, Clark's counsel may say:

Clark's Lawyer: "I agree with you on some of this. After dealing with Clark for the last month, I've found him to be fussy on a lot of things. I swear there are times I'm ready to tell him to go away and not come back."

Mega's Lawyer: "See. That's the kind of stuff Miller can't stand."

Clark: "Yeah, but it's still age discrimination and retaliation for the pension fund. I just want you to know I know Louis can be a stickler for details when it comes to insisting that everything is being done right."

If Clark were present, the topic either wouldn't come up at all, or have a very different tone, for example:

Mega: "I'm sorry, but Jim Miller says he can't work with Mr. Clark anymore, says he's a real pain in the neck and there's a personality clash."

Clark: "Louis is easy to get along with. I know it and his co-workers will support him in this. The problem is that Miller just doesn't like older executives."

Negotiation strategies often require lawyers to say some less-than-flattering things about their clients, or to distance themselves from their clients in order to generate the kind of cooperative relationship with an opponent that can be essential for settlement. If your clients are present, you can't say certain things about them, or admit they did something stupid. At least as important is that information acquisition, your ability to deflect an opponent's probes, conceal strategic information, and be effective in your denials are all critical aspects of negotiation. Untrained clients—as well as many lawyers—may unwittingly provide a sophisticated adversary with damaging insights.

The information you or your opponent receive doesn't have to be overt or explicitly stated. It can be derived from nonverbal cues of which you may not be aware or can't do anything about. Many opposing lawyers will also try to communicate directly to your client, in an effort to drive a wedge between you and the client. Your opponent may try to cause the client to doubt the validity or strength of his or her case, question whether you know what you are doing, attempt to intimidate the client, or suggest an offer in a way that makes you seem unreasonable. This can add uncertainty to the relationship between you and the client, and alter the strategic texture of your case.

Settlement Ranges

Part of case evaluation and goal setting requires thinking of realistic settlement ranges before an offer is even mentioned to an opponent. Making, assessing, and responding to offers is difficult. How do you make an offer? When do you make an offer? What does your offer contain? How do you actually settle a dispute? How do you say what you are willing to do, when you don't know where the other side is drawing the line?

Cases can have substantial settlement value even if the underlying claim is seen as questionable. Or, for public-relations purposes, losing defendants may simply be attempting as much damage control as they can achieve, even if they know they are wrong. By agreeing to pay $31.5 million, Remington recently settled a class-action case filed to recover damages caused by shotgun barrels that could burst. A spokesman for Remington issued the statement that there were no problems with the guns but, "Rather than spend years in court, it was decided to settle this case." In antitrust, mass-tort, and product-liability settlements, defendant companies demonstrate incredible *chutzpah* in paying out millions—or even billions—of dollars in damages, while continuing to deny they did anything wrong. Just once I'd like to hear a CEO say, "Yeah, we did it. We knew people were going to die, but the money was too good, and we never really thought we would get caught. I wish I could say I was sorry, but that's life. . . ." It would be good to hear such an admission of culpability, if only one time.

Recognizing what has already been said about the deceptive nature of strategy, and the opponent's desire to keep you talking in order to gain critical information about the case, what seems to be an initial offer may be a lure by which the opposing attorneys want to make it seem that you are on the way to making a deal when they aren't even close to making an actual offer. Proposals and offers are very critical aspects of probing for information. Always be careful to resist the subtle influence of your own desire to settle, attain closure, and reduce stress. In reality, the opponents may not have actually said anything firm or substantive. All they said was they "might" be willing to settle, in essence because of the nuisance you or your client have created. This admits nothing and guarantees nothing.

Initial offers, closing out a settlement, what is contained in an offer, how to persuade other people to make an offer, how an offer is worded and how to interpret those words, when an offer should be made, bringing forth data needed to make an offer, and responses to offers from both sides, are all critical parts of strategy. No amount of formal analysis is sufficient to resolve all doubts about what is a fair, achievable settlement. A major part of the information needed to make critical settlement judgments is acquired from contact with your opponent, awareness of the needs and capabilities of the opponent and the opponent's client, and understanding how similar situations have been resolved.

Even all that information is insufficient, because much depends on the abilities of your opponent, particularly on whether he or she is sharp and sophisticated enough to play the game effectively. Otherwise, it is surprisingly easy to stumble over the clumsiness of a less-talented adversary. Often, opponents can cause you trouble, not because of their skill and insight, but their lack of it. Nothing they do fits into the right rhythm, and this can skew the timing of a skilled legal strategist. When this happens, you have to get inside their frame of reference to see how they are looking at the case. The seeming paradox is that being able to see a situation through the perspective of a mediocre or incompetent opponent is an important aspect of strategic planning, the acquisition of strategic information, and the ability to achieve favorable settlements. Too many lawyers are either incompetent or mediocre, and if you can't detect when you are in such a situation you will waste significant time, money, and energy.

The term "settlement range" means the extremes of the amount the client is willing to pay or accept in payment to resolve the case short of trial, or to close the deal if litigation is not involved. The legal strategist must establish settlement ranges, and the conditions and justifications for concession and agreement, and also try to discover the opponent's settlement range and real conditions of engagement. The settlement range should include the values placed on different claims or types of deals, as well as an understanding of the quality (i.e., strength, weakness, apparent value, true value) of each claim and an assessment of the overall claim.

The foundation for your settlement range should provide the justifications and principled reasons why something is worth what it is and why your client is committed to a position or demand. It should also include how much the opponents care about keeping something, how much the opposition wants to avoid being required to take a particular action, or how much they care about not being allowed to do something. Such information must be kept absolutely secure; the strategist can't afford to share it with anyone. This is why Sun Tzu remarks that the general doesn't even let his own officers know his true strategy, instead allowing them only the knowledge of the specific tactical decisions they will need to execute. The way to keep this critical information secure is to be the only one who knows it. Your real settlement range is one of your most critical pieces of strategic information.

The idea of a single, fixed settlement range is misleading. The process of negotiation, including how much things are worth and what you are willing to pay or accept, is dynamic and ever-changing. Some of the main functions of negotiation are to place realistic values on particular items, to find out whether something is worth more or less than you thought at the beginning, and to educate yourself and your opponent as to why a deal should be made, and at what level and with what conditions.

This means that settlement ranges will probably change as the strategic interactions occur. You may be convinced to slide to a point farther along the original range than you initially estimated the case was worth. You may even discard your original ideas, deciding instead to reformulate and infuse significantly higher or lower valuations into your settlement expectations. You may find other alternatives that work better than those with which you began, or even decide the process isn't going to get you anywhere near where you want to go, and change your estimations or strategic path entirely.

If there is no realistic and substantial overlapping of the competing parties' settlement ranges, the case is unlikely to be settled. The breach of oral contract and tortious interference case mentioned in Chapter One (i.e., the defendant offered $10,000 to settle shortly before trial and the plaintiff refused, then the jury came back with an $800,000 compensatory verdict and $32 million in punitive damages) suggests a situation in which the plaintiff's and defendant's settlement ranges didn't quite overlap. Even when there is some degree of over-lapping at the margins, the parties may decide they want to take their chances with a judge or jury and go for broke. If it is a business deal, or some other nonlitigative situation, one side may decide to go elsewhere and seek a better arrangement because they are fed up, or perhaps their egos have been offended.

If you are a plaintiff's lawyer, before you begin serious negotia-tions you should have first sat down with your client and gone through a damages-and-desired-outcome analysis, which includes eval-uation of what she wants, what she feels she must or would most like to have, what can justifiably be sought, what she thinks she can get, what she can prove with some specificity, and what she hopes to be able to convince a jury to give her if that becomes necessary. You also have to deal with the quality and clarity of the evidence, any defenses or counterclaims by the opponents, and the ease or difficulty of a jury being able to understand why and how your client is entitled to the specific levels of damages for which you are asking.

The strategist's task is not only to figure out the settlement range for his or her side, but to estimate the opponent's range, including nonmonetary factors when they are legitimate parts of the outcome. Even if you realistically examine the opponent's probable settlement range and decide it is unlikely there is any overlap, or at least no overlap close to what you reasonably feel you are likely to achieve through one of the other strategic paths, you will still spend a certain amount of time probing to verify what you suspect, although you know you will probably have to proceed through trial or arbitration.

As an example, let's look at a case in which Waste Management of Alabama (WMA) was sued by a neighbor for polluting the plaintiff's property with hazardous waste. WMA saw its pretrial offer of $90,000 rejected, and then the jury returned a plaintiff's verdict of $86,000 in compensatories, plus $5 million in punitive damages. This suggests a significant difference in pretrial settlement valuations between the lawyers for the defendant and plaintiff. When you have extremes like these, you probably aren't going to resolve the situation by pretrial or even pre-verdict negotiation. On the other hand, if there is a similar case in the future, WMA is likely to assign a greater weight to punitive damages in valuing cases and setting its settlement ranges. In cases involving big, "soft" types of damages, you probably have to experience a judgment such as this at least once before you accept the possibility as real. An inexplicable example of this is, in defending asbestos cases, attorneys for Owens Corning in both New York and Illinois apparently relied on a "state of the art" theory (i.e., their client's state of knowledge about the harmful effects of long-term exposure to asbestos) when trying the cases. The exposure of the plaintiffs in those cases started 10 to 15 years after asbestos manufacturers became aware of the dangers of asbestos. Use of such a defense is almost guaranteed to lead to very high losses because the jurors react not only to decades of coverup, but also to the untenable claim by the defendant that it "didn't know." As already discussed, the punitives awarded in the New York case ended up at $54 million.

Assuming, however, that you decide there is the potential for some significant overlap between your settlement range and the opponent's, your strategy is predicated on doing what is necessary to convince the adversary it is in his interest to move toward the end of the range that is more favorable to you, either by paying you more if you are the plaintiff, or asking you to pay less if you are the defendant. Your strategy can be designed to cause opponents to redefine the limits of their settlement range because you are able to show them that your case is either stronger than they initially believed, or that their case is weaker. In a litigated dispute, the benchmark point of reference in the competing strategists' calculations of value and outcome probability will be what they realistically consider is likely to be a jury's decision, minus the transaction costs of obtaining that decision.

What if a plaintiff is asking for $30 million in punitive damages for an alleged tortious interference with contract? We know such a verdict is possible because it happened in California. Assume that figure represents the absolute maximum outcome that could conceivably be recovered in the case under the most ideal terms. It may even be a fairy story put forth in the complaint for its *in terrorem* effect. Or plaintiff might just like the sound of the figure. In civil-rights litigation or cases involving allegations of tortious fraud, lawyers in my office always wanted to sue for huge amounts in an effort to intimidate an opponent and to attract media attention. In 1994, a DES case was filed in my jurisdiction requesting $500 million. It may not go anywhere, but it makes people sit up and pay attention. DES may also turn out to be the next wave of asbestos-type cases, so it is too early in the development of DES litigation to automatically discount such claims.

How does either side calculate a realistic figure when such claims are made? As the plaintiff's lawyer what are you really willing to do? These questions cannot be answered without evaluating the probability of achieving various levels of outcome. First of all, unless the tortious interference with contract case is tried, there is no chance the plaintiff could receive anything close to that outcome through negotiation. If the trial path is followed, the case would be tied up in court for a minimum of five years, and probably more. If, for example, you estimated a 90 percent probability of winning a judgment of $30 million through trial and only $3 million through negotiation, then a five-year wait is a good investment risk. But what do you do if the defendant makes an initial preemptive offer early in the process to pay the plaintiff $1 million? As the plaintiff's lawyer, how should you respond? What does that offer represent and what does it reveal? At a minimum, it could reveal that the case may be settled at a level of at least several million dollars. Or, if the defendant is making a realistic preemptive offer to end the problem before it becomes more serious, the rejection may lead to years of hard-fought litigation and expensive legal representation.

In the case of the tortious interference with a contract, why would the plaintiff's lawyer start out with a demand for $30 million? Even though the lawyer might privately believe it is not even remotely possible to achieve a negotiated settlement anywhere near this figure—or even a trial verdict for that matter—such an aggressive demand can help put the defendant in the frame of mind that a tremendous amount of money might have to be paid. While the corporate defendant probably doesn't believe it could actually happen, the uncertainty of the trial outcome makes anything seem possible at some point in the process. This factor can force the opponent into a defensive mindset. Setting forth this huge amount in damages is an obvious manipulation, but that still doesn't prevent it from having a powerful effect. The high initial demand helps to create the desired emotional climate. It defines the highest conceivable end of the case's damage continuum in which, if the figure for one side is $30 million and the defendant offers only $1 million, the offer and counteroffer just don't seem in balance. The result can be that the final outcome is forced to a higher level because the initial demands set the agenda and the expectations at a much higher level.

The defendant's lawyers may begin to wonder whether their client is hiding evidence of predatory behavior that will be revealed in discovery, and that can be made to appear as a serious violation of antitrust law. The client will inevitably be concerned about the possibility of being found liable for the full amount. After all, the client pays if the case turns out badly, not the lawyers—unless there is serious and provable malpractice. The defense lawyers will also begin to wonder what secret and damning knowledge the plaintiff's lawyer possesses about the defendant that gives him the confidence to make such an assertion in the first place.

Central to all these calculations and estimations of probability of outcome by a jury, is the absolutely basic and overriding issue of whether any judgment you might obtain will be collectable. Unless you are primarily into symbolism, a collectable $100,000 is worth more than a noncollectable $10 million. If you can't obtain the money, then all you have is a piece of official paper that really has no worth. A significant part of a plaintiff's case evaluation must look at the defendant's ability to pay, and your ability to make him or her pay if you obtain a judgment. What are the defendant's resources, earnings, assets, insurance? Where are they located? Are there other claimants who might have a higher legal priority to the assets if you drive your opponent into bankruptcy? Is the defendant solvent? How much will it cost to enforce the judgment? Will the defendant be able to discharge the claim in bankruptcy?

These are the kinds of realistic factors that need to be considered in determining your real versus your hypothetical or ideal settlement range. You could waste months negotiating with a lawyer who knows his client is preparing to go into bankruptcy and who is just collecting fees while stalling you. Just as you think you are nearing a deal, a notice arrives listing your claim on a bankruptcy filing as an unsecured creditor or claimant.

Settlement ranges and case evaluations are not about best-case scenarios that assume everything goes just right. They are about if you "win" a judgment or someone "wins" one against you, is it collectable, in full, part, or not at all? This is why you must understand your opponents—particularly their resources—and build this into your case strategy. It is also why the existence of insurance, some other deep pocket, and the policy limits of any applicable insurance policies become such a vital part of your case evaluation, discovery and investigation, and settlement strategies.

Offers

Let's assume that in our $30 million tortious interference with contract case, the defendant makes the first offer. If $1 million was offered, the plaintiff's response could be, "$1 million. Well, let's break down what our actual damages are. This is what I have already paid, so I cannot even consider accepting a figure as low as $1 million." The defendant's first offer can, however, be useful in triggering response patterns by the plaintiff that provide insight. After all, someone has to start. By making a substantial offer, a more legitimate response is forced from the opponent. Implicit in the plaintiff's response as set out above, for example, is the message that the plaintiff isn't seriously pushing to recover $30 million, but will be willing to settle for a figure that is significantly lower.

A strategist must know the conditions under which he or she is willing to settle a case. Many negotiations fail because one or both sides either have not thought clearly about their settlement terms, or have no intention of actually settling—regardless of representations they might make during settlement discussions. Remember that each strategic path has a different outcome potential. Sometimes the differences between one path and another are so striking that there is no realistic possibility that anything close to the strategist's desired outcome can be achieved through anything but a jury trial. It is as if you are trying to force a square peg into a round hole. The fit between the desired goal and the path being used simply isn't there.

A significant part of negotiation involves trying to determine if you can resolve the dispute short of all-out war, or its legal equivalent, trial. At some point in the process the two sides start making realistic proposals, or discover that there really appears to be no common ground on which to resolve the dispute by mutual agreement. Both sides may decide the dispute will have to be submitted to the judgment of an external decision-maker, whether in the form of arbitration or trial.

Among the most difficult aspects of negotiation are the making of initial offers, evaluating an opponent's offers, weighing their responses to your proposals, adjusting your own case and strategy based on the direction the case is taking, and, finally, responding to your opponent's offers. Effective strategists tend to conceal so much that it is difficult to know when conditions have reached the point at which it becomes possible to close the deal, or be substantially certain one can't be achieved. How do you make offers or proposals that produce beneficial effects or useful responses? How do you actually settle a dispute to your advantage? How do you say what you are willing to do, when you don't know where the other side is drawing the line?

Negotiation Through Mediation

The ability to make people agree—even if they don't want to—and the ability to reach a decision and impose that decision on other people, is the key difference between formal authoritative power, such as trials and binding arbitration, and the strategic paths of negotiation, mediation, and even nonbinding forms of arbitration. Mediation is a kind of triangular negotiation akin to what is called shuttle diplomacy. It has even been described as having a "zen-like" quality, in which the mediator operates on intuitive feel rather than logic as the parties are carefully nudged toward a resolution.

Many aggressive advocates are very good at creating conflict and pressure, but not nearly as good at resolving it. Mediators can show the competing parties how the world at large will react to the way they are presenting their arguments, the issues, and problems that are at the center of the conflict. The mediator can help adversarial lawyers by deflating the posturing that often characterizes negotiations. As was suggested in the section on releasing from deadlock, lawyers need to be given face-saving excuses for why they shift claims and positions and not seem weak. A mediator can legitimize the change in positions.

Mediation is a variation on negotiation. It is advisory in nature, but also creates a communication triangle that encloses all the interests in a field of enhanced reasonableness. The effective mediator can't become personally involved, or be seen as an advocate for one side or set of issues. While mediators lack authoritative power, the participation of an independent third party alters the interaction between the opposing lawyers. A mediator is a reflector and facilitator whose task is to help the opposing parties gain insight as to how people who are not subjectively and competitively immersed in the dispute will perceive, react, and judge the case.

Mediation can help break deadlocks, and the mediator can reflect the nuances of opposing positions back to the parties and help the adversaries see their cases, potential deals, or problems, through more neutral eyes. Think about the facilitative role Jimmy Carter played in helping Israel and Egypt reach the Camp David accords. President Carter provided both a neutral site and a neutral player. This helped the adversaries overcome the relentless tension of high-stakes negotiation. If he had not done so, the negotiations would certainly have broken down many times. In much the same way, Norway played a significant role in the secret dialogue between the PLO and Israel that led to the agreement that gave Palestinians self-rule powers in Gaza. The Norwegians offered a secluded site and secrecy. In doing so, they provided the kind of facilitative environment sought in mediation. Otherwise the negotiations would have fallen apart because hostile interests would have struggled mightily to sabotage the process, and the participants would have thought, felt, and behaved differently if the process were public.

Mediation takes many forms. It can be quite informal, as when a third person provides limited feedback in an effort to get a stalled negotiation moving. Mediation can also be much more formal, such as the services of a federal mediator being requested in serious labor disputes. If the adversaries actually want a settlement, but are having difficulty because of their egos, mistrust, antagonism, or the like, use of a mediator can provide the kind of altered emotional climate and objective feedback needed to move ahead.

Assume the parties in the *Clark v. Mega* dispute aren't getting anywhere and the lawyers agree to bring in a mediator in an effort to break the deadlock. Neutrality is one of the most essential characteristics of a mediator. A mediator obviously can't turn to Mega's lawyer and say, "You know, your sex discrimination claim is stupid," because that will poison the company's attitude about the mediator. They would decide the mediator is too favorably oriented toward Louis Clark or too much against their own position.

Mediation is not a solution for all kinds of disputes. When seeking significant money damages with extensive "soft" elements, for example, the mediation path is unlikely to be productive. On the other hand, situations in which people have problems with each other, don't trust each other, need to continue in a relationship, or which are highly charged emotionally, are more likely to benefit from the intervention of an impartial, skilled, and creative mediator. A mediator's participation is particularly appropriate when the intervention occurs before the growing conflict explodes. For example, the problem between Mega's Jim Miller and Louis Clark might well have benefitted from the involvement of a mediator, even very informally, before lines were drawn and lawyers directly involved. The point is that the mediator is intended to be a defuser, a facilitator, a reflector, and a generator of alternatives, but the mediator's ability to do this requires good-faith participation of all the parties involved.

If the parties decide to use a mediator, it is important to select a person who is impartial—both in training and in personal experience. The mediator needs to understand the difficulty of being a nonjudgmental facilitator. Respect and moral authority are extremely useful, but the mediator cannot force the parties to do anything. In theory, the mediator should be impartial, but there is the inevitable danger of bias. Mediators are human, and there is always a risk they will unconsciously develop greater liking or respect for one side in a conflict, or dislike for another, which can influence their judgment. The mediator may have had personal experiences that have created biases. Even if the mediator is not actually biased, it is important for the parties to perceive him or her as unbiased, or the process will break down. Similarly, a legal strategist may go into a mediated situation, decide it is not going the way he or she had hoped, and can sabotage the mediation process by suggesting the mediator is biased (one way or another), or by refusing to cooperate.

One major function of mediators is to help overcome deadlocked negotiations by altering the emotional climate and facilitating the development of alternative approaches. Individuals engaged in face-to-face negotiations often reach sticking points at which deadlock occurs.

They fight, threaten, back off, and disengage. They say such things as, "Well, that's it then. See you in court." They may or may not mean the threat, but at that time they may feel there is little hope for an agreement. They may wish there were a realistic chance for an agreement, or the competitive bloodlust may take hold as the opponents begin to gear up for all-out conflict. Whether the deadlock is part of a bluff, is a real threat at that moment, or is a ploy intended to buy time or to put pressure on the opponent to make the next move, parties are often afraid of being seen as weak if they change their positions. They can become committed to specific positions, and be unable to envision acceptable alternatives. They become "stuck" even if they don't really want to be. Pride, habit, subjectivity, fear, and being blind to the reality of a situation, all get in the way. This is why Musashi says there are times to *release four hands* and to step back from the situation in which you are entangled. Similarly, his *mountain-sea* change involves a fundamental shift in perspective and strategy, which a mediator can help the parties accomplish.

As a strategic path, mediation is most useful when continuing relationships are at stake, or people don't want to end up hating each other. If the opposing parties are in a continuing relationship with each other or will need to deal with each other in the future, this must be taken into account. Such problems as workplace disagreements, labor contracts, disputes between neighbors, or divorces involving minor children in which the parents will need to have continued contact are examples of situations where mediation can be most useful.

Some situations are not likely to be resolved through mediation. This can be due to the type of case involved, because the claim is almost certainly going to trial or binding arbitration, because the parties really hate each other, or because one of the lawyers or parties refuses to use the process or does not participate in good faith. If there is no need to have a future relationship, a lawyer may decide to push as hard as possible for the largest amount of damages, or fight to keep from paying anything. Mediation is unlikely to be useful in such situations.

Additionally, for lawyers whose strategies depend on either stretching out the case or on taking rigid positions and deliberately creating deadlock, mediation will not be a desired process because a good mediator will expose what they are doing. One way a lawyer might not appear to be entirely unreasonable is to seem to be willing to participate in mediation, but then subtly sabotage its effectiveness. The lawyer pretends to be willing to participate in mediation, but takes forever to negotiate the terms of the mediation process and selection of the mediator. Then the lawyer may claim conditions have shifted and decide against mediation after all.

The Judge as Authoritative Mediator

The judge is an important part of the strategic environment within which a case occurs. Judges are increasingly intervening in litigated disputes in an effort to compel lawyers to settle. Given the increased role judges are now taking in case management and settlement, judges can be thought of as a kind of mediator, but one with much greater influence than the typical mediator. The differences, of course, are that this "judicial" mediator isn't thought of as such, and the judge does have some degree of authority over the case—even if it is to be tried to a jury. If it is a nonjury trial, the judicial authority is obviously very significant.

A trial judge's suggestion that one or both of the parties is being unreasonable carries considerable weight. A suggestion such as this carries with it the authority of the court and the possibility that your refusal (or your opponent's) to accept an offer the judge feels is reasonable can lead to consequences. This is particularly important because you might not recover as much at trial, or perhaps won't win anything, or if you are the defendant and the plaintiff wins far more than you could have agreed to in a settlement. The imposition of substantial "delay damages," as is now being done in Philadelphia, increases the need to ensure that your trial judge considers your behavior reasonable. Similarly, discretionary power in setting the trigger point for the allowance of prejudgment interest also enhances judicial power.

ADR rules are being created that reflect the clear preference that courts want lawyers to settle cases rather than waste the legal system's time and resources in what judges consider needless trials. Proposals for changes in both tort and product-liability cases that are before Congress contain extensive ADR provisions in which parties in product-liability cases would be required to submit written offers to each other. Many states are passing so-called tort-reform laws that put caps on tort damages and severely restrict or even eliminate punitive damages. Consequences can include attorney-fee awards to prevailing parties, or damage limits that include collateral sources of recovery if the case was tried and the verdict suggested refusal to accept an offer was ill-founded. As we have already described, the problem with this is that a jury verdict is inherently uncertain, judges' estimations of what is reasonable are very different from those of jurors, and evaluation of what a jury is going to do is an art form. But most judges across the United States basically don't want to try as many cases—certainly not ones they think should have been settled—and are doing their best to figure out ways to avoid them. This includes imposing sanctions on parties who exercise their constitutional right to have their day in court.

Eleven
The Trial and Arbitration Paths

*"When you appreciate the power of nature, knowing the
rhythm of any situation, you will be able to hit the
enemy naturally and strike naturally."*
Musashi, *The Book of Five Rings.*

Sun Tzu tells us to avoid fighting the ultimate battle whenever
possible, but if it becomes necessary in spite of your efforts, fight
only after positioning yourself in a way that makes your victory inevitable. The same rule applies to legal strategy. It is almost always best
to avoid trial or an all-out legal "war." But there are times when the
battle should not be avoided, and signing a "peace treaty" or settlement agreement would not be in your client's best interest. Legal
strategists should, however, never forget that trial is expensive, labor-intensive, emotionally draining and often destructive for both sides,
and ultimately uncertain in outcome. Just as is done by Sun Tzu's
excellent general, lawyers can position themselves in ways that substantially increase their probability of success at trial. But it is undeniable
that trial outcomes are inherently uncertain, and this cannot be completely overcome because trial outcomes depend on the capabilities,
qualities, perceptiveness and values of other people, and on the skills
and knowledge of lawyers, clients, and witnesses.

Even though the legal strategist seeks to resolve a dispute short
of trial, the ability to resort to trial is the indispensable element in
the ability to resolve disputes. Just as we know that war is often the
result of failed diplomacy that should have succeeded, so is trial often
the consequence of failed negotiations that ought to have resolved the
dispute. It is not always possible to resolve disputes by negotiation,
however, and trial or binding arbitration provide the ability to obtain
a final and enforceable resolution.

Lawyers can't provide a guarantee to their clients as to what a jury will do. With a jury, all we can do is give our best guess or estimate, and quote percentages and probabilities. The ultimate uncertainty in regard to what the jury's decision will be—and the willingness to surrender control to the jury over what happens—provide the force that drives the process of dispute resolution. Large institutions, for example, will do almost anything to avoid a decision by a jury because they know that juries tend to come down against them. This is why such institutions are increasingly writing binding arbitration clauses into employment contracts and consumer agreements. Arbitrators are nearly always legally trained, and they also depend on continuing arbitration assignments, and therefore will try not to offend the most powerful clients. This means that arbitration results are not going to approximate the decisions of jurors.

The Owens Corning litigation and its $54 million punitive damage verdict mentioned earlier is one example of why powerful defendants seek to avoid populist juries. Among the themes that most predictably trigger jury outrage are a defendant's bad faith, abuse of trust, severity or type of injuries, arrogance, greed, or callousness. Consider these examples:

- In a medical malpractice case in New York City, a pregnant mother began bleeding during labor, and it was overlooked and not properly investigated by the delivery-room personnel. The bleeding resulted in severe oxygen deprivation in one of the twins she was in the process of delivering. There were indications of problems with the first-born infant, but the staff still didn't rush the delivery of the second-born twin and that child suffered severe brain damage. A Brooklyn jury returned a verdict of $47.3 million. (Trust in doctors, brain damage.)

- A jury decided that a woman was sexually harassed by PEP-SI® co-workers and was awarded $1.6 million. (PEPSI® was on notice of prior behavior.)

- A Chicago jury gave $6 million to a karate instructor who became disabled after surgery to repair a slipped disc. (Trust in doctors, paralysis.)

- A Los Angeles jury entered a $3.1 million verdict, including $2.5 million in punitive damages, against an insurance company for refusing to pay more than $100,000 in medical bills for an insured's surgery for an intercranial aneurysm. (Trust, contempt for people, greed, bad faith.)

• In a medical malpractice case in which loss of oxygen to a child's brain at birth caused severe shoulder injury, mild retardation, a learning disability, and a paralyzed arm, a New York jury returned a verdict of $8.8 million. (Trust, brain damage, paralysis.)

No lawyer can consistently predict the size of these verdicts prior to trial. Compromises through negotiated settlements are often caused by lawyers being uncertain who will be on the jury. But all lawyers should know that jurors are usually regular people who will view what happened in terms of the "Golden Rule." The jurors will think, for example, about how they would want the defendants to behave if they (i.e., the jurors) were on the operating table, helpless, and forced to trust their well-being to doctors and hospitals. Similarly, most jurors will have dealt with insurance companies and will be aware of the tendency of many of those companies to try to not fulfill their contractual obligations. When they decide someone much the same as themselves has been harmed by such behavior, juries punish. But there is no certainty that a jury will buy into such themes with the totality needed to achieve a high verdict. Certainly, a lawyer's skill and track record provide some sense of the probability, but each jury and each trial is unique.

A critical fact of trial uncertainty for both sides is that no one knows in advance how witnesses will actually be perceived on the stand—regardless of how well they have been prepared. Even the most thorough case preparation and planning is only practice or simulation. As Musashi tells us, *"You must practice constantly,"* but while absolutely necessary, practice is not the "real thing." Trials are real. There are no "outtakes." Unlike a movie or a television series, when mistakes are made at trial you don't get to stop the process, edit the transcript, and then do it over again until you get it right. A trial is a live performance with amateurs playing the key roles of jurors and witnesses. You can't ever be quite certain what is going to happen.

Preparing your clients or key witnesses for trial sometimes reveals they will come across in an unpalatable way that you can't change. You may decide that you can't win if they testify to the jury. But if your opponents don't know this—or at least can't be certain—they may still be open to the belief that you are willing to go to trial and that your witnesses will be believed. You can't allow your opponent to know your trial weaknesses or it will sabotage favorable settlement probabilities, but you must find out your own flaws and take them into account when deciding how to proceed. This is an important part of what Musashi means when he warns us not to think dishonestly. Deceive others, but never yourself.

Flaws in your case don't inevitably mean you must settle before trial. Musashi warned us to not overestimate the opponent and automatically think that you are fighting a skilled master strategist. There aren't that many really good litigators. Always keep in mind that your opponent's case, just as yours, will inevitably have imperfections, uncertainties, and the potential for going either way once the jury begins deliberating. Absolute certainty—as opposed to a high level of confidence—just isn't a relevant concept in predicting what a jury will do.

In the midst of this uncertainty and stress, how should a strategist approach a trial? It helps to equate a lawyer's need to develop the equivalent spirit of Musashi's *resolute acceptance of death* to cope with the stresses generated in the ultimate combat of trial. Many lawyers are so apprehensive of going to court because of inexperience, lack of ability, or insufficient resources or time to prepare, that they lose out in the negotiation process because they settle on mediocre terms to avoid court. Even if they don't settle, their apprehension or lack of preparedness causes them to perform ineptly. Trials are intense, but they can also be great fun. One of the problems is that they are very expensive and time-consuming. Clients often can't afford to pay the full costs of litigation, and in many situations a lawyer's caseload is too heavy to allow full preparation.

The inability to fully prepare cases for trial is a common affliction of lawyers. Simply because 95 out of 100 cases are settled doesn't mean a lawyer should automatically begin by expecting that percentage of his or her cases to be settled. The expectation of settlement creates a self-fulfilling prophecy that results in nearly all cases being settled. Even if this is the reality of what will happen, a useful approach is to go into the initial diagnostic phase of a case with the attitude that it will end up in court. It is a mindset that allows you to better visualize a case's potential and problems. Because so few clients can afford the full cost of case preparation, quick, efficient, and early evaluations that provide both a sense of the worth of a case and a guide to your strategy are even more important.

In most instances, you will be a better negotiator if you are an effective litigator. You will settle more often and on better terms when opponents realize you are highly competent, know what the case is about, enjoy the conflict and competition of trial, and honestly feel, "If there is a deal, fine; if not, so what?" When your opponents understand and accept this about you, your interactions with them will usually begin from a position in which you are accorded more respect. This position can allow you to cut through much of the chaff and deception involved in lawyers' posturings. You will be given the benefit of the doubt by opponents in close situations, and you will be able to back up your threats and promises. It will save you an enormous amount of time, and efficient use of time is vital to lawyers in private practice.

The tradeoffs that full trial preparation and performance demand in the allocation of your time is one reason few lawyers actually want to try a case. They don't have the time to put other work aside and so—no matter what they say during negotiation—are still patching the case together on the eve of trial. This is why many settlements occur at trial (or even a little way into trial) when all bluffs have been called and/or lack of adequate preparation catches up to one or both sides. The lawyers know they aren't prepared for more than an opening statement and perhaps one or two witnesses, and don't want the embarrassment of being exposed.

Trials are extremely uncertain processes in which skill, resources, evidence, and law are very important, but it all comes down to the strange combination of individual and collective judgments made by jurors who are hearing this case for the first time. Losing a case may be as simple as your key witness speaking in a way this specific jury doesn't like. Although another jury might react differently, you have to deal with the values, prejudices, and attitudes of this particular jury. You cannot be sure about a case until actually in the midst of the trial process and members of the jury can be seen smiling or nodding in agreement when one witness is testifying, but not when your client or key witness is on the witness stand. Or your client might be a saint who has the misfortune of looking or sounding like somebody who tortures cuddly little animals. Even then, nothing is certain until it's done and the verdict has been returned.

During the trial of *Clark v. Mega,* the sexual-harassment allegation made against Clark is important to both sides. Depending on the discoverable facts and witnesses, Clark's lawyer can, for example, take the position that the company is deliberately aggravating a baseless allegation in order to damage Clark's reputation. The lawyer can argue that Mega sought a pretext for firing Clark, or wanted to create such a demoralizing work environment that Clark would resign rather than endure the situation. Clark can argue that Mega maliciously turned innocent behavior into a cynical justification for terminating him. He can argue these allegations have ruined his reputation and destroyed or seriously impaired his ability to attract consulting work after leaving Mega. The loss of reasonably anticipated consulting opportunities is another category of potential lost income and damages. Other executives at Mega do consulting work without being threatened or dismissed so it is presumably an accepted practice—at least until now. Mega seems to have singled out Clark and sought to blacken his reputation. Negative information circulates rapidly in the business world. Mega has therefore taken away not only his present job, but his future job opportunities by poisoning the minds of people who otherwise would have wanted to retain him as a skilled consultant on personnel matters. These themes are chosen to resonate with a jury. They are also part of negotiation efforts to demonstrate to Mega that there are reasons the company should be concerned about going to trial.

How much are those lost opportunities worth? It depends on whether we are talking about lost consulting earnings while employed at Mega, or lost consulting income while fully employed in consulting. We should first look at what Clark has made from consulting in the recent past; then assume a reasonable increase. If he retires from Mega at age 62, and as long as he retires with the equivalent of an honorable discharge, everybody will still say Clark is a wonderful guy, respected, and that he has good continuing business connections. Otherwise, he could be blacklisted by the business community. If Mega is allowed to get away with what they have done, they will have effectively cut Clark off from his ability to engage in profitable consulting after he leaves Mega.

If this analysis of deliberate and malicious action by Mega to fabricate a justification for discharging Clark is accepted, there is the possibility of punitive damages. If a jury is convinced this characterization of Mega's behavior is accurate, then in addition to pursuing $3.6 to $4.2 million in actual damages for salary, benefits, pension, and lost consulting opportunities, there is the possibility of awards for mental anguish and other emotional torts, and for malice and punitive damages. If the jury believes Mega has blown the sexual-harassment allegation out of proportion to justify Clark's dismissal simply because Miller doesn't like older workers generally—or Clark specifically—then Louis Clark can expect to receive a great deal of money beyond the hard economic damages. The punitive damages could approach as much as $5 million if the jury becomes righteously indignant. Does either side know for sure how a jury will decide? No. There is the potential for enormous losses for Mega, however, and even if it is only a 25 percent possibility that the company's total losses will go as high as $5 to $6 million in damages and expenses, why should Mega accept that risk if it can get out for $1 million?

If we assume the jury could be convinced of Mega's liability and bad faith, what is the most realistic characterization of what they are likely to award? Many cases include "softer" categories of such damages as pain and suffering, emotional distress, loss of reputation, and sometimes even more speculative or punitive types of damages. These cannot be accurately predicted, but they still must be specifically outlined for juries, and the jurors given convincing and understandable paths to decision. Simply because the damages are soft doesn't mean they don't have significant value. The jury in Bernhard Goetz's civil suit, for example, awarded one of his "victims" $43 million. If you are a defendant, the downside exposure in such situations is enormous. If you are the plaintiff, how can you settle? There is no real room for settlement in such situations. Soft damages have their greatest value primarily in the hands of a jury, and are less often attainable in significant amounts through negotiation, mediation, or arbitration.

The critical questions for the strategist are how do you know when these "soft" damages are worth pursuing and how much are they worth? The "hard" damages can be proved with bills, receipts, earnings records, and so forth. But the "soft" damages involve an almost aesthetic aspect predicated on an understanding of how people think and feel, the kinds of experiences most people have had, their hidden values and biases, and what makes people indignant. In the Goetz case, for example, Goetz's alleged racism certainly had an effect on the jury's decision. Of the six jurors, four were African-American and two Hispanic, and this might have influenced the outcome, whether based on the jurors' personal experiences or generalized resentment.

Jurors' life experiences are critical parts of a legal strategist's analysis. Mega may argue they have a strong case of sexual harassment against Clark. Clark's attorney might respond that the allegation is a pretext, a single, entirely misinterpreted incident, and that there are no similar instances of misbehavior in his long and productive work history. People who have worked with Clark for years might be willing to testify about his innocent actions, or about the completely uncharacteristic mistake, due to intoxication, involving this young woman who had just been hired at Mega. The woman could be viewed as either setting up Clark for Miller, or as having overreacted. Clark could argue it is a very weak case that will blow up in Mega's face if they try to push it. This doesn't really answer the question of what Clark did. His lawyer may believe him or not, and Clark may or may not be telling the truth. This is a constant dilemma for the litigator who must be much more concerned with whether anyone can prove Clark acted improperly.

Questions a Strategist Must Ask Regarding a Trial

The importance of visualizing a case's "endgame" and defining the terms of victory has already been emphasized. This visualization requires you to think about what you want to achieve for your client, and how to achieve it. Knowing this requires you to take into account an enormous range of information. Who is your opponent? What are the relative resources, strengths and weaknesses? Where are the certainties and uncertainties? The questions listed in Figure 5 demonstrate the complexity and uncertainty involved in predicting the outcome of a trial. The range of strategic considerations is extreme, and there are no clear answers to many of the questions until either the judge resolves them by judicial ruling or the jury delivers its verdict. As the lawyer, you are responsible for putting detail, content, and weight into these concerns. As the legal strategist you can use these questions to more accurately reflect on what is known and unknown about a case. They also help illuminate what is involved in high-level trial work, how much time it will take, and why nearly all cases are settled.

Figure 5. Outcome Probability Questions

Victory and Goals

What happens if we win?
What happens if we lose?
How much do I win if I succeed?
How much do I lose if I fail?
How collectable is the opposing client?
How long will it take to collect?
What important positive and negative nonmonetary outcomes or consequences are there?

Financial Costs and Other Resource Expenditures

How much will a trial cost me?
How much will a trial cost my opponent?
How much will it cost me to prepare for trial?
How much will it cost my opponent to prepare for trial?
How much will the appeal cost me?
How much will the appeal cost my opponent?

The Opponent's Evidentiary Strengths and Weaknesses

What are my opponent's legal strengths and weaknesses?
What are my opponent's factual strengths and weaknesses?
What are my opponent's human strengths and weaknesses?

Risk and Probability Factors

What is the probability of winning or losing on liability issues?
What is the probability of damages?
How much do I win if I succeed?
How much do I lose if I fail?
How much more or less will I be able to achieve compared to pretrial negotiations?
How much more or less will my opponent be able to achieve compared to pretrial negotiations?

Knowing Self

Who is the client?
Who are the witnesses?
Who am I?
What are my professional strengths and weaknesses?

Diagnosis and Evaluation

What are the outrage factors?
Does the outrage help or hurt me?
What are the standards and categories of damages?
Are the damages "hard" or "soft?" i.e., what is the scale of contingent exposure?
What are my most compelling trial themes?
What are my opponent's most compelling trial themes?

(Continued)

Figure 5. Outcome Probability Questions (cont'd)

Evidentiary Strengths and Weaknessess

What are my case's legal strengths and weaknesses?
What are my case's factual strengths and weaknesses?
What are my case's human strengths and weaknesses?
How do I prove my factual strengths?
What are the benchmark or anchoring factors around which I should organize my case?
What are the benchmarks around which my opponent's case can best be organized?

Knowing the Opponent

Who is the opposing client?
Who are the opponent's witnesses?
Who is the opposing lawyer?
What are my opponent's professional strengths and weaknesses?

Knowing the Decision-Makers

Who is the judge?
What are this judge's past decision patterns?
What are other judges doing in similar eases?
Who is likely to be the jury?
What are juries' past decision patterns?

Timing Considerations

Are there likely to be serious appellate issues from pretrial rulings?
Are there likely to be serious appellate issues from trial rulings?
How long will the trial take?

The Aesthetic Dimension of the Litigator

Discovery and investigation are about acquiring facts, but the best lawyer is someone who can see deeply into the human significance of the mass of evidence that has been submitted and pull it together in compelling and persuasive ways. Trials are a process, not of truth as is so commonly professed, but of the reconstruction of an advocate's version of a purported reality designed to persuade the jury that you are right and/or your opponent is wrong. In this reconstruction of reality, you can still surprise an opponent with an approach he or she did not recognize, with effective arguments they had not anticipated or are not prepared for, with a different perspective on evidence, or the implications of a witness they had not thought about. This is far more likely in criminal cases because of the considerably more limited discovery rules, but it applies to civil cases as well. It is entirely possible to accomplish this given the relatively low level of preparation most lawyers have been able to put into their cases prior to trial. In so many instances, all the lawyer has been able to do is to prepare thinly and without depth, and when questions are asked for which the preparation isn't adequate the situation can quickly begin to unravel.

Even with the expansive discovery rules in civil cases, an opponent can be surprised at trial with a compelling theme, or an unanticipated variation on evidence or argument. Formal discovery doesn't tell you the subtlety, power, or effectiveness of jury themes. Remember Johnnie Cochran's "if the glove doesn't fit, you must acquit" theme that resonated so well with the Simpson jury? Of course, the irony is that Cochran could never have planned for this prior to trial, because he couldn't take the risk of having Simpson try on the glove, and could never have realistically expected his opponents to risk something even inexperienced trial lawyers knew was stupid. Both Sun Tzu and Musashi tell us of the need to prepare ourselves against surprise and the importance of using it to unbalance our opponents. This highlights the continual possibilities of surprise, and the need to capitalize on them when they go in your favor, or deal with them when then go against you. Musashi recognized this in his admonition that we must train to make quick decisions.

Another factor is that if you estimate your opponent to be functioning at a mediocre level, then you would be unwise to reveal the greatest artistic and aesthetic strengths of your trial case in the pretrial phases, including negotiation. If, on the other hand, you are working against sophisticated, thorough, perceptive, and talented opponents, you can usually be more upfront because they will probably already know most of what you know. Because good lawyers visualize the case through the eyes of their opponents and decision-makers, your themes ought to be known or at least suspected by skilled opponents. In such a situation, there is more likelihood for a reasonable meeting of the minds, either about a settlement or the recognition that the matter will have to be resolved through trial or binding arbitration. Having a skilled opponent allows you to realistically explore the terms of an intelligent settlement before trial. Settlement still isn't guaranteed, because the risks may be those that you or your opponents are willing to take if the potential settlement value of the case and the amount you estimate could be achieved by trial are too far apart. This is probably what happened in the Owens Corning verdict. Each side was too far apart and was forced to roll the dice. But, at least, it is much more enjoyable to go up against a talented opponent.

Knowing the Decision-Maker

Judges with clear track records in specific types of cases can also make the process easier. Judges are less susceptible to a lawyer's tricks, thematic presentations, and other manipulations, because they have done such things in their own practice prior to becoming judges, or have seen them regularly in their courtrooms. Even the best of a lawyer's persuasive tools tend to lose much of their effect when seen regularly.

An important factor is that judges view cases in a much more legalistic way than do juries. Lawyers understand that most judges don't take a case's human issues into account in the same way as jurors. Judges are willing to resolve a case on technical and procedural issues that would be of no importance to a jury. That is the reason that if defense lawyers in a criminal case have a technical defense, they sometimes prefer to waive a jury and submit the case to a judge.

Lawyers want to know during jury selection if any of the prospective jurors have been serving in the jury pool for some time or if they have served in other cases at different times or in other jurisdictions, because experienced jurors begin to pick up on attorneys' techniques and games. Trying a case to jurors with prior knowledge of the trial process and greater awareness of the games lawyers play means you are dealing with a different kind of juror than when a juror is completely new to the trial process. The proliferation of trial-oriented television, books, and media has altered this to some extent, as millions of people are being exposed to trials as both a dramatic and melodramatic phenomenon and have developed expectations about the experience.

The jury's outcome is based on their idea of what is reasonable, just, and fair. It also involves who the jury likes best, whether the plaintiff has overreached, or if the defendant has engaged in outrageous actions or omissions. Large monetary jury verdicts are obtained on the basis of jury emotion, sympathy, and indignation. Obtaining such verdicts requires having "real" people make the decision. Given the inescapable dynamics of their professional experience and training, judges and lawyers are no longer "real" people. The legal strategist understands the seemingly simple fact that the characteristics of the people who make the final decision will have a radical effect on what a case's outcome is likely to be. Nor is it simply the individual characteristics of each decision-maker, but the interactions and contradictions of their personalities, values, experiences, and biases. The collective persona of the jury enhances the likelihood of high damages in appropriate cases.

The individual juror becomes much more important in a criminal case in which the prosecution generally must obtain a unanimous verdict, and the defense needs only to convince a single juror of reasonable doubt. In civil cases, when a plaintiff is seeking substantial damages, the facts and witnesses must be presented in a powerfully thematic way that causes people on the jury to be angry or indignant about what happened to the injured client. Recovery is maximized if the jurors accept and internalize the plaintiff's characterization of the defendant's behavior. If the jury doesn't accept the theme of injustice, callousness, or unfairness, they will give a relatively nominal recovery, even if the plaintiff wins on the issue of liability. This is one way in which jurors negotiate compromises. It is not quite all-or-nothing, because jurors have great latitude to reduce damages, to increase discretionary categories of damages, to find lesser-included offenses in criminal cases, or to even nullify the law when they consider it to be appropriate.

There is a close connection between trial uncertainty and settlement timing. Settlements often occur during trial because only after the jury has been selected can both sides reexamine and reevaluate their case with anything approaching concreteness. Until then, no matter how much you prepare, you are speculating about who will be on the jury and what faceless, hypothetical jurors will do. After jury selection has been completed, you will have a somewhat clearer understanding of the jurors, or you will at least think you do. When you can talk to them, hear them, and see their faces, you may say, "Oh no, the luck of the draw," and decide you should try to settle. Or you may feel you were lucky, and decide to go for broke because you sense it is a good jury for you and your client.

A trial may go on for a certain amount of time because of the uncertainty factor, or a settlement may be reached even while the jurors are deliberating. In the DuPont defense against five Florida farmers who alleged their crops had been ruined by DuPont's fungicide Benlate, the case was tried, the jury retired, and while the jurors deliberated, DuPont reached settlements with four of the five growers. One plaintiff did not agree to settle, and the jury surprised everyone by returning a verdict in DuPont's favor.

Not only are cases settled during jury selection and deliberation, or when the pressure builds and the lawyers begin to second-guess themselves and imagine the worst outcomes, but many settlements are reached even after the jury verdict is in. If the losing party has arguably legitimate issues for appeal, if the plaintiff wants the money now rather than waiting another two or three years for appeals to be exhausted, or if there is a risk the defendant will not be able to pay in the future, a post-verdict settlement can be the most intelligent approach. The Microsoft/STAC patent infringement verdict in STAC's favor was a precondition to Microsoft being willing to negotiate a deal that arguably was in the best interest of both companies. The problem prior to verdict was that if Microsoft honestly felt it was entitled to the disk-compression technology without paying licensing fees or royalties then it had little reason to settle. Only after a jury disagreed with its position could productive negotiation take place.

In *Clark v. Mega Corporation,* the trial could easily be halfway through the defense testimony before Mega puts on evidence of the claimed acts of sexual harassment that allegedly led to Clark's discharge. What if the young woman making the allegations against Clark is perceived as an extremely favorable and believable witness, and the jury is sending signals that they accept her story and like her? The plaintiff's lawyer, sitting beside Clark and looking at the jury, becomes convinced they are thinking, "She is a sweet young thing, and if she said that is what this guy did, then that is what the dirty old man did!" The defense lawyers could have been hoping she would come across effectively, but even they couldn't be certain until her testimony was completed. Each side took the risk, and now has to realistically evaluate her short and long-term impact on the jury.

Clark's lawyer must be able to recognize how the jury is reacting and depending on the read, decide whether to shift to an alternate approach. This might include damage control, a different approach to cross-examination, rebuttal witnesses aimed at showing the woman's motives for fabricating or exaggerating the alleged event, or even exploring the possibility of reopening settlement discussions. Mega's lawyers must also be able to evaluate what is happening. Both plaintiff and defendant may be willing to discuss a settlement based on their perception of how the case is unfolding before the jury, but if either side is too obstinate about the possible settlement figure, the advantage that appeared to be gained for Mega by the critical witness may dissipate. Mega's lawyers may respond with such a low settlement offer that it would be worth it to Clark's lawyers to redouble their efforts and go for broke because they will have nothing to lose.

This brings out another aspect of trial uncertainty. There is a frequent ebb and flow during trials during which each side's estimation of how well they are doing changes character. Lawyers can develop a kind of paranoia concerning what is going on in the mind and hearts of a jury, or an equally problematic false emphasis that a momentary "victory" has won the war. In fact, as Musashi demands, the lawyer must keep a balanced spirit. Juries often shift back and forth during trial, and the plaintiff's lawyer might be able to repair the damage done by the "harassed" woman. If you are Clark's lawyer, you may have evidence to present on cross or rebuttal that she has a relationship with Miller, has been "fast-tracked" in the company, and therefore has a motive to make Clark look bad. The apparent short-term advantage gained by the defense may boomerang with a vengeance when the jurors realize what happened and resent being "conned."

Strategists don't evaluate cases based only upon financial issues. When you first look at *Clark v. Mega* you might ask, for example, "Is Clark active in his church? Is he married? Is he a decent citizen? Does he have a reputation that he wants to protect and that he would hate to have dragged in the mud"? Such factors have weight when you are evaluating a case. Clark may not want to risk contesting Mega's allegation even if he was totally correct in his behavior, because if it comes out in the newspaper or even by rumor, too many people will unfairly conclude he did something wrong. Our reputations are very important to us, and this means they have significant value in negotiation. The converse of this is that if Clark's reputation has weight and value, and if Mega has done something or allowed something to be done that damages his reputation, the harm will have already been done and Clark's attorneys can be expected to go for Mega's—and Miller's—jugular. A conflict that could possibly have been settled in a decent way now becomes a legal bloodbath in which everyone loses in some way.

After a party such as Mega has inflicted serious consequences on your client, they must be made to pay for their actions. It is Newtonian physics applied to law. Once a threat is acted upon it ups the ante and often increases the opponent's motivation. Threats are most useful as inchoate potentialities that generate apprehension and the desire to avoid the consequences. They are seldom useful after being carried out because they have imposed costs or harmful consequences of some kind on the other side. Once an opponent has experienced the worst and withstood it, or has little left to lose, he or she may fight to the end when otherwise the dispute might have been amicably settled.

Plus, there is an adrenalin surge involved in conflict. When the adrenalin takes over, often there is no turning back. We begin operating on a more intense and combative level, and it is hard for many of us to turn off the joy of conflict. Humans are still primitive in many ways, and even usually gentle people can become tigers when challenged. Two fitting cliches are *"it's better to let sleeping dogs lie"* and *"he got more than he bargained for."* A quiet and seemingly placid opponent may be a most savage fighter when roused. So don't play needless games with people, and don't think there won't be consequences when you gratuitously hurt someone.

If Mega fired Clark using sexual harassment as one of the grounds, the allegation will become a key factual issue throughout the trial and negotiation process. Mega will have to actually establish that Clark sexually harassed the woman. Mega would have to put the young woman on the stand and she would say, "He fondled my posterior in front of all these people when we were dancing and tried to kiss my forehead and then leered at me." Even if true, what does it establish? The jury might sit there and think, "OK, go on. What else?" Clark would then testify, "Yes, I did that. Quite a few people, including myself, had some drinks. It was an office party, and this just happened unexpectedly. She is an attractive woman, but she doesn't even work directly with me. I don't have much of anything to do with her job." Even if Clark testifies to that, as opposed to saying she misunderstood what he actually did and said, what are the possibilities for how a jury would perceive the situation?

Think about how you construct your jury and who is on your jury. The jurors' own experiences become quite relevant. Depending on the specific circumstances, people might say, "This man has worked at this company for a long time. They were dancing and they both had something to drink. She was part of it too. He probably should have known better, but you don't fire somebody just for that!"

Many people could conclude that the incident was an excuse on Mega's part to discharge Clark. The words "sexual harassment" sound horrendous when you first hear them, so the company probably decided to use the allegation as an excuse to dump Clark because it was the only thing they had. But what happens when you are Mega and have to give that justification to a jury? How do you control all its implications, and the fact that when it is exposed to the light it could very easily shrivel up and blow away? Even if Clark does not have an explanation for what happened, he could still win the case unless he tries to give some obviously concocted and unbelievable explanation. If the allegation is true, Clark could say, "She pressed really close against me, and I had had too many drinks. My hand slipped and brushed her rear and I did kiss her on the forehead. I shouldn't have done it, and I'll never do it again. I don't blame her for being upset. I'm very shocked it happened and very embarrassed. I've apologized and I'm sorry."

Clark's lawyer could have a chance of winning at trial even if the woman's version is correct. Sexual harassment requires a course of conduct or a particularly egregious act. Clark's lawyer needs to construct and effectively communicate a "Big Deal" theme. The impression sought is that he was wrong but didn't deserve to be fired for it. The message to be sent to the jury through everything the plaintiff does at trial is: "The defendants are using that allegation as a trumped-up excuse. They really fired him because Miller decided that he was too old and getting in the way. Something really bad must be going on with that pension fund."

This same attitude about what Mega did and how a jury will view it should be communicated during negotiation. If Miller understands the significance of the theme, it should help create an effective negotiation for plaintiff. If there is a reasonable chance of a good-faith, high-quality settlement, the lawyer's job involves making sure the opponent properly evaluates the case and understands what will happen if the two sides cannot agree. It is useful to have the defendants understand that if they are basing their case on this specific point, then even if Clark admits she is right, Mega could still lose. Remember this incident happened in a public setting. If, on the other hand, she alleged that he grabbed her behind the filing cabinet or brought her into his office and started chasing her, or kissed her on the lips in private and tried to fondle her, that is entirely different. The context of the incident is fundamental to this specific case strategy. There are other contexts, only subtly different, that could also alter the "feel" of the case radically. Even though they wouldn't seem much different factually, they would create a nastier situation for Clark.

This fact tells Clark's lawyers they had better discover anything that even seems like an implication of such behavior on Clark's part with any other female employees at Mega. Discovery strategy must seek to uncover all the possible bad points about your case, so that you will be able to either eliminate possibilities or adapt your strategy to cope with the newly discovered material. The most important thing is to avoid being surprised, and to be able to evaluate your case realistically. This means taking all its negative factors into account as well as the positives. Clark's lawyers should talk with every employee they can find, and anyone else who has said anything or might conceivably know of problems. Obviously, Mega's lawyers should do so too.

Arbitration as Trial

Arbitration includes both binding and nonbinding arbitration. Binding arbitration moves the dispute-resolution process into the realm of authoritative decision-making in which the outcome is increasingly outside the direct control of the parties. Arbitration can be through the court process, in which certain kinds of cases are referred by the trial court to a panel of arbitrators, or by contract. The court-ordered referral process is not binding, and does not preclude the lawyers from proceeding with the case even if they receive an unfavorable decision from the arbitrators. But it can be useful by providing them with a more neutral—or at least different—view of the value and substance of their case and the validity and persuasiveness of the opponent's position. As already noted, one of the toughest achievements in a dispute is an objective perspective on the issues, people, and probable outcomes. Nonbinding arbitration can help do that, although there are some pitfalls to court-ordered arbitration.

Court-ordered arbitrations are reasonably close in form to a trial, but with less restrictive evidentiary rules in regard to hearsay, objections, and the ability of lawyers to introduce evidence through summary statements, among others. In many court-ordered arbitrations, the lawyers may just state the facts, make a brief opening statement, take limited testimony from several primary witnesses, summarize the testimony of other witnesses, and cross-examine opposing witnesses.

Contractually-binding arbitration is not subject to all the procedures dictated by the rules of trial evidence. Because it tends to be, in effect, a final judgment due to the restricted bases for further review of arbitrators' decisions, the arbitration process can be as intense and demanding as a trial. The stakes of binding arbitration are high because there is such a limited chance to win on appeal, and lawyers cannot drag it out interminably, as is characteristic of other appeals. The specific process used in contractual arbitration depends on the terms of the arbitration agreement, and the rights involved. Most agreements now incorporate the standards and procedures of the American Arbitration Association. One advantage of arbitration, is that because the rules of evidence tend to be considerably looser in arbitration proceedings than in trials, lawyers may have arguments that can be developed effectively with the court-appointed arbitrators, or, in a contractual arbitration situation, they may have arguments that could not be made to a judge and that a jury would not be allowed to hear.

Parties can agree to bind themselves by the decision of an arbitrator, as is common in labor-management relationships. Major-league baseball players and owners have done so as one of the terms of their collective-bargaining agreement. They may define the types of disputes and issues to which the arbitration agreements apply, or require all work-related disputes to be resolved through arbitration. The difference between court-ordered arbitration and contractual arbitration is generally in the finality of contractual arbitration, the scope of the issues dealt with in contractual arbitration, and the experience and professionalism of the arbitrators. Securities dealers sign a comprehensive agreement as a condition of their employment agreeing they will submit all their work-related disputes to binding arbitration. This has been consistently interpreted as binding by courts, even to the extent of requiring such disputes as racial discrimination complaints to be disposed of through arbitration rather than resort to court.

Even if there is not a pre-existing contract, parties can agree to submit a dispute to binding arbitration in lieu of other options. Contractually agreed upon arbitration is binding as long as it is done within the authority and procedures specified by the contract or other agreement. The agreements can and often do specify the procedures to be used, including those to be used for the selection or rejection of arbitrators. They often simply incorporate by reference the rules of procedure of the American Arbitration Association.

In contractually-binding arbitration agreements, all parties generally surrender the right to go to court with the dispute. The appeal rights are extremely limited. The decisions of the arbitrators are final unless the decisions are clearly outside the scope of the issues or authority granted the arbitrators by the contract, or if there is no factual basis for the decision, or if there is a serious abuse of discretion by the arbitrators. This standard is similar to the bases for judicial review of the decisions of federal administrative agencies delineated under the Administrative Procedure Act. In other words, don't ever count on winning an appeal from the decision of an arbitrator unless you can show an extremely serious procedural defect, can demonstrate there was no evidence on a key point, or can prove that the decision is clearly beyond the arbitrator's authority.

The original purpose of binding arbitration was to avoid the delay, conflict, and expense of court. Contractually based arbitration is a form of private litigation that was designed to put a quick, fair, and final end to disputes that would otherwise drag on for years in a court. Or the disputes being arbitrated might be of a kind that would never make it to court, but by not being dealt with and allowed to fester unresolved, would create bad feelings in the work environment. Binding arbitration can keep disputes in-house and provide a reasonably simple way to resolve disputes at lower cost and with much greater speed. A serious problem, however, is that as courts have come to rely on arbitration, and large companies have learned how to control the process, it has created a system that is vulnerable to serious abuse.

An example of an arbitration provision is contained in an excerpt from the following agreement I received from a securities firm:

15. ARBITRATION DISCLOSURES

- Arbitration is final and binding on the parties.
- The parties are waiving their right to seek remedies in court, including the right to jury trial.
- Pre-arbitration discovery is generally more limited than and different from court proceedings.
- The arbitrators' award is not required to include factual findings or legal reasoning and any party's right to appeal or to

seek modification of rulings by the arbitrators is strictly limited.

• The panel of arbitrators will typically include a minority of arbitrators who were or are affiliated with the securities industry.

This kind of adhesion agreement is increasingly common. It completely alters the power balance of the system and removes significant leverage from allegedly wronged plaintiffs. As a strategic path, it is important to be aware that arbitration tends to lead to middle-of-the road resolutions. One reason is that arbitrators often must be acceptable to both sides. The adversaries typically have the right to accept or reject an arbitrator or members of an arbitral panel from a list of experienced arbitrators knowledgeable in the specific field. If an arbitrator becomes known as being too biased in one direction, one or both of the parties may stop using that person. Because binding arbitration reaches a decision, the parties will be stuck with the result. This means they want a decision they can live with as being fair and supportable. On the other hand, given the almost total finality of arbitration decisions, and the federal courts' upholding of mandatory arbitration contracts, the dominant side often does not care about fairness, as opposed to winning on its terms. It is a strategic victory for the large companies and industries that have learned how to twist arbitration to their purposes.

Many agreements allow each side to choose one person, and then provide a neutral process to choose the third arbitrator. This means that two out of the three arbitrators on a typical panel can be expected to lean toward one side or the other, and that the third person is the critical element of the final decision. If an arbitrator is biased, and renders decisions that won't stand up or that keep the dispute going in one form or another, the arbitration process will not have achieved its goal. Regardless of whether we are talking about contractual or court-ordered arbitration, the primary function of the process is to end the dispute. Often this means the outcome will be one in which each side is given something, or each side loses something, but the disputants are not excessively alienated. A rare exception is major-league baseball, where the arbitrator has the power only to choose between the final offers of the owners and players made prior to the arbitration hearing.

Court-ordered arbitration is of a different character than binding contractual arbitration. It is less authoritative and dispositive of a dispute than contractually agreed arbitration. This is because, unlike the contractual situation, the parties have not waived their constitutional right to have a case resolved by a judge or jury. In court-ordered arbitration, local court rules typically allow for or require referral of a specific category of case, (e.g., medical malpractice), or only permit a specific size of case, (e.g., a $25,000 maximum potential value) to go to a panel of arbitrators. The arbitrators are lawyers who are paid a fee for their services. Their decision has the legal effect of being an advisory opinion because it is not binding on a party. The arbitration panel therefore often tries to design a decision and damage award acceptable to both parties. Because one of the panel's primary functions is to lessen the burden on the court's time, nothing has been achieved from the court's perspective if the arbitration award does not lead to final resolution and the case still continues on to trial.

Courts are creating court-ordered arbitration and court-ordered mediation processes in an effort to force lawyers to deal more realistically with their cases at an earlier point in the dispute without going through the expensive and time-consuming process involved in full-scale litigation. It can have the effect of forcing lawyers to focus realistically on the prospects of their cases at an earlier point, or at least help identify sticking points or misperceptions. Of particular significance is that it can shift the timing of preparation and case evaluation in many moderately sized cases from shortly before the trial to the earlier arbitration stage.

Court-ordered arbitration may not be binding, but participating in it has the potential to both help and hurt your case. It provides an independent evaluation of your case, but the arbitrator's evaluation is by lawyers—not jurors—and that will almost inevitably be different. This form of arbitration is a specialized procedure that causes many cases to be settled because it forces lawyers and their clients to look more realistically at their cases. It can also be useful for highly specialized claims, such as medical malpractice, in which there is some benefit to expert decision-makers. It can provide insights into the strengths and weaknesses of the opponent's case and of your own. It does not, however, provide a perspective on how a jury would react to the case, and this is a significant limitation. On the other hand, court-ordered arbitration is generally used for relatively minor claims for which the transaction costs for both sides would often be prohibitive in comparison to the stakes involved if the case were taken to trial. In many ways, court-ordered arbitration can be viewed as a larger scale small claims court.

Court-ordered arbitration also gives your opponent insights into your case. Strategic games should be played in the arbitration process, particularly if you are convinced it will be necessary to go to trial. If you feel you can win a jury award of $40,000 to $50,000, and the court values your case at a maximum of $25,000 and sends it to arbitration where you figure the best you can do is $15,000 to $20,000, you should not present your best case in front of the arbitrators because this will fully educate the opponent. Similarly, because the arbitrators are lawyers, they aren't likely to buy into the best themes of a jury case. Why bother revealing your most compelling jury themes if you are reasonably certain you are going to try the case?

Because court-ordered arbitration is not binding, it can be used for a variety of purposes. This includes playing strategic games, testing out your best theories, and misleading an opponent as to the strength of your trial case by pulling your punches. The arbitration can be used as a sort of mini-trial similar to the private mini-trials increasingly being used by corporations to gain a better sense of what their cases are really about. It can serve as a discovery device in which you gain a sense of how your opponent performs in a context reasonably similar to a trial. You can also determine whether he or she has identified the critical points and themes of the dispute, and how quickly he or she thinks on his/her feet and deals with stress.

Conclusion

*"One who is good aims only at bringing his campaign to a conclusion
and dare not thereby intimidate. Bring it to a conclusion but
do not boast; bring it to a conclusion but do not brag; bring
it to a conclusion but do not be arrogant."*
Lao Tzu, *Tao Te Ching.*

Strategic methodology can be distilled into a specific set of principles. These are set out below to summarize and emphasize the main points made throughout this book. As you look at these ten principles, you will be able to see how they apply to diagnosing problems and opportunities, achieving settlements, valuing cases, creating and applying specific strategies, and knowing when you need to fight rather than negotiate a treaty with an opponent.

The Ten Commandments of Strategy

1. Set high, but achievable, goals. Visualize your opponent's goals and recognize that conflict is not always inevitable and that many goals can be achieved through cooperation.

2. Diagnose, plan, prepare, evaluate, reevaluate, and acquire information continuously.

3. Know yourself, the opponents, all the relevant participants, and the decision-makers.

4. Understand the resources, tools, sources of leverage, and weapons available both to you and to your opponent.

5. Always be aware of the internal and external timing of the specific strategic situation and the overall strategic campaign.

6. Remain balanced, centered, and focused at all times, while projecting the strategic spirit appropriate to the situation.

7. Perceive accurately, trust no one, understand the importance of deception, misdirection, and concealment, and see through the deceptions and illusions created by your opponent.

8. Adapt and be flexible.

9. Don't waste time and energy; practice constantly, strategic understanding requires *doing* strategy.

10. Be willing to take the risks necessary to achieve victory, and accept the chance of losing.

Some Useful Reading

Many books contributed to my understanding of strategy, most having nothing to do with the direct process of strategy, but with Musashi's urging to seek a diverse range of insights from many disciplines. The few books that are listed below are far from a complete reading list, but they do represent the beginning of an intellectual diversity that offers a great deal to a strategist. A complete list of recommended reading would take up far too much space and include a wide variety of works on moral and religious discourse, even more philosophy, the Bible and scriptures from other religions, economics from a variety of perspectives, politics, psychology and sociology, and more. Also included would be an extensive range of fiction or stories from which we derive many of our most fundamental insights.

Abe, Masao, edited by William R. LaFlear, *Zen and Western Thought*, University of Hawaii Press, 1985.

Ames, Roger T. and Dissanayake, Wimal, *Self and Deception: A Cross-cultural Philosophical Enquiry*, State University of New York Press, 1996.

Bellow, Gary and Moulton, Bea, *The Lawyering Process*, Foundation Press, 1978.

Binder, David and Price, Susan, *Interviewing and Counseling: A Client-Centered Approach*, West Publishing Company, 1977.

Braverman, Arthur, ed., *Warrior of Zen: The Diamond-hard Wisdom Mind of Suzuki Shosan*, Kodansha International, 1994.

Brinton, Crane, *Ideas and Men: The Story of Western Thought*, Prentice-Hall, 1950.

Capra, Fritjof, *The Tao of Physics*, Shambhala, 1975.

Ching, Julia, *To Acquire Wisdom: The Way of Wang Yang-ming*, Columbia University Press, 1976.

Chiu, Milton M., *The Tao of Chinese Religion*, University Press of America, 1984.

Cleary, Thomas, *The Japanese Art of War: Understanding the Culture of Strategy,* Shambhala, 1992.

Dallmayr, Fred, *Beyond Orientalism: Essays on Cross-Cultural Encounter,* State University of New York Press, 1996.

Delaney, Kevin J., *Strategic Bankruptcy: How Corporations and Creditors Use Chapter 11 to Their Advantage,* University of California Press, 1992.

Dodge, Theodore A., *The Great Captains: The Art of War in the Campaigns of Alexander, Hannibal, Caesar, Gustavus Adolphus, Frederick the Great, and Napoleon,* Kennikat Press, 1968, c1889.

Ellul, Jacques, *The Technological Society.* Alfred A. Knopf, 1964.

Ellul, Jacques, *Propaganda: The Formation of Men's Attitudes,* Alfred A. Knopf, 1965.

Fisher, Roger and Ury, William, *Getting To Yes: Negotiating Agreement Without Giving In,* 2d ed. Bruce Patton, ed., Houghton Mifflin, 1981.

Goldman, Alvin L., *Settling for More: Mastering Negotiating Strategies and Techniques,* Bureau of National Affairs, 1991.

Harr, Jonathan, *A Civil Action,* New York, Vintage Books, 1995.

Hartshorne, Charles, *Insights & Oversights of Great Thinkers,* Albany, State University of New York Press, 1983.

Hastie, Reid and Penrod, Steven D. and Pennington, Nancy, *Inside the Jury,* Harvard University Press,1983.

Herman, Jonathan R., *I and Tao: Martin Buber's Encounter with Chuang Tzu,* State University Press of New York, 1996.

Hyams, Joe, *Zen in the Martial Arts,* J.P. Tarcher, distributed by St. Martin's Press, 1979.

Iannuzzi, John Nicholas, *Trial: Strategy and Psychology,* Prentice Hall, 1992.

Ilich, John, *The Art and Skill of Successful Negotiations,* Prentice-Hall, Inc., 1973.

Inada, Kenneth K. and Jacobson, Nolan P., *Buddhism and American Thinkers,* State University Press of New York, 1984.

Kagel, Sam and Kelly, Kathy, *The Anatomy of Mediation: What Makes It Work,* The Bureau of National Affairs, Inc., second printing 1992.

Kaplan, Morton A., *Law in a Democratic Society*, Professors World Peace Academy, 1993.

Kearns, John T., *Reconceiving Experience: A Solution to a Problem Inherited from Descartes*, State University of New York Press, 1996.

Keeton, Robert, *The Trial Process*, Little, Brown, 1973.

Kennedy, Gavin and Benson, John and McMillan, John, *Managing Negotiations*, Amacom 1980.

Koller, John M., *Oriental Philosophies*, 2d ed., Scribner, 1970.

Lao Tzu, *Tao Te Ching*, Modern Library, 1948.

Luttwak, Edward N., *Strategy: The Logic of War and Peace*, The Belknap Press of Harvard University Press, 1987.

Machiavelli, Nicolo, *The Prince*, Modern Library, 1940.

Masatsugu, Mitsuyuki, *The Modern Samurai Society: Duty and Dependence in Contemporary Japan*, American Management Association, 1982.

Mauet, Thomas, *Trial Techniques*, Little, Brown, 1980.

Miller, Henry G., *Settlement*, Mathew Bender, 1995.

Mindell, Arnold, *The Leader as Martial Artist: An Introduction in Deep Democracy*, Harper San Francisco, 1992.

Montgomery, Cynthia A. and Porter, Michael E. (editors), *Strategy: Seeking and Securing Competitive Advantage*, Harvard Business Review, 1991.

Moore, Charles A. editor, *The Japanese Mind: Essentials of Japanese Philosophy and Culture*, East-West Center Press, University of Hawaii Press, 1967.

Munger, James P., *What's It Worth? A Guide To Current Personal Injury Awards And Settlements*, 1993 Edition, The Michie Company, 1993.

Murti, T.R.V., *The Central Philosophy of Buddhism*, London, George Allen & Unwin Ltd., 1960.

Musashi, Miyamoto, *The Book of Five Rings (Nihon translation)*, Allison and Busby, 1974.

National Jury Project, Krauss, Elissa; Bonora, Beth (general editors), *Jurywork: Systematic Techniques, Volume 2*, Clark Boardman Callaghan, 1991.

Ohmae, Kenichi, *The Borderless World: Power and Strategy in the Inter-linked Economy,* Harper Business, A Division of HarperCollins Publishers, 1990.

Ohmae, Kenichi, *The Mind of the Strategist,* McGraw-Hill, 1982.

Paret, Peter (editor), *Makers of Modern Strategy: from Machiavelli to the Nuclear Age,* Princeton University Press, 1986.

Phillips, Major Thomas R.(editor), *Roots of Strategy: A Collection of Military Classics,* The Military Service Publishing Company, 1941.

Pirsig, Robert, *Zen and the Art of Motorcycle Maintenance,* Morrow, 1979.

Possony, Stefan T., and Vilfroy, Daniel, *Surprise,* Military Service Publishing Company, 1943.

Ramundo, Bernard A., *Effective Negotiation,* National Law Center, George Washington University, 1984.

Scharfstein, Ben-Ami, *Philosophy East/Philosophy West: A Critical Comparison of Indian, Chinese, Islamic, and European Philosophy,* Oxford University Press, 1978.

Schellenberg, James A., *Conflict Resolution: Theory, Research, and Practice,* State University of New York Press, 1996.

Siu, R.G.H., *The Tao of Science: An Essay on Western Knowledge and Eastern Wisdom,* M.I.T. Press, 1957.

Sun Tzu, *The Art of War,* Delacorte Press, 1983.

Suzuki, Daisetz Teitaro, *Essays in Zen Buddhism,* Peter Pauper Press ed., Doubleday, 1956.

Tigar, Michael E., *Examining Witnesses,* American Bar Association, 1993.

Waldrop, M. Mitchell, *Complexity: The Emerging Science at the Edge of Order and Chaos,* Simon & Schuster, 1992.

Watts, Alan, *Tao: The Watercourse Way,* Pantheon, 1975.

Woolf, Bob, *Friendly Persuasion,* G.P. Putnam's Sons, 1990.

Wu Ching Chi Su, translated by Sawyer, Ralph D., *The Seven Military Classics of Ancient China,* Westview Press, 1993.

Zukav, Gary, *The Dancing Wu Li Masters,* Bantam New Age Books, 1979.